Do Museums Still Need Objects?

The Arts and Intellectual Life in Modern America

Casey Nelson Blake, Series Editor

Volumes in the series explore questions at the intersection of the history of expressive culture and the history of ideas in modern America. The series is meant as a bold intervention in two fields of cultural inquiry. It challenges scholars in American studies and cultural studies to move beyond sociological categories of analysis to consider the ideas that have informed and given form to artistic expression—whether architecture and the visual arts or music, dance, theater, and literature. The series also expands the domain of intellectual history by examining how artistic works, and aesthetic experience more generally, participate in the discussion of truth and value, civic purpose and personal meaning that have engaged scholars since the late nineteenth century.

Advisory Board: Steven Conn, Lynn Garafola, Charles McGovern, Angela L. Miller, Penny M. Von Eschen, David M. Scobey, and Richard Cándida Smith

DO MUSEUMS
STILL NEED
OBJECTS?

STEVEN CONN

PENN

UNIVERSITY OF PENNSYLVANIA PRESS

PHILADELPHIA

Published by
University of Pennsylvania Press
Philadelphia, Pennsylvania 19104–4112

Printed in the United States of America on acid-free paper

10 9 8 7 6 5 4 3 2 1

Library of Congress Cataloging-in-Publication Data

Conn, Steven.
    Do museums still need objects? / Steven Conn.
        p. cm. — (The arts and intellectual life in modern America)
    Includes bibliographical references and index.
    ISBN 978-0-8122-4190-7 (alk. paper)
1. Museums—United States—History—20th century.   2. Museum exhibits—United States—History—20th century.   3. Museums—Collection management—United States—History—20th century.   4. Cultural property—United States—History—20th century.   5. Art objects—United States—History—20th century.
6. Museums—Political aspects—United States—History—20th century.
7. Museums—Social aspects—United States—History—20th century.   I. Title.
AM11.C63   2010
069.0973′0904—dc22

2009012615

For Angela,
Because I am truly a lucky, lucky man.

Contents

Introduction: Thinking about Museums   1

Chapter 1. Do Museums Still Need Objects?   20

Chapter 2. Whose Objects? Whose Culture? The Contexts of Repatriation   58

Chapter 3. Where Is the East?   86

Chapter 4. Where Have All the Grown-Ups Gone?   138

Chapter 5. The Birth and the Death of a Museum   172

Chapter 6. Museums, Public Space, and Civic Identity   197

Notes   233

Index   257

Acknowledgments   261

Figure 1. The birth of the museum. Jan Brueghel the elder; Hieronymus
Francken II, *The Archdukes Albert and Isabella Visiting a Collector's Cabinet*, 1621–23.
Photo © The Walters Art Museum, Baltimore.

Introduction
Thinking about Museums

We live in a museum age.

At the turn of the twenty-first century more people are going to more museums than at any time in the past, and simultaneously more scholars, critics, and others are writing and talking about museums. The two phenomena are almost certainly related, but it does not seem to be a happy relationship. Even as museums enjoy more and more success—measured at the gate, in philanthropic giving, and in the cultural influence they command—many who write about them express varying degrees of foreboding.

I think the *New York Times* was right when it proclaimed in 2002 that all over the world we are enjoying a "Golden Age of Museums."[1] From Berlin to Beijing, from the United States to the Gulf States, the last quarter of the twentieth century saw the creation of whole new museum institutions, some modest and some quite audacious. Major cities have added significant new museums to their already crowded cultural landscapes, while more modest metropolises like Kansas City and Denver have recently opened museums big enough and ambitious enough to have garnered national attention. Indeed, all this new museum building, often showcasing the work of a fashionable architect, or "starchitect," hasn't simply added to the inventory of museums. The openings of many of these new museums have been treated as major cultural, geopolitical, or economic events, an enthusiasm captured by the oft-used phrase the "Bilbao effect."

In fact, we are witnessing a second "golden age" of museum building in the United States (and, really, around the world). The first came one hundred years ago during the last quarter of the nineteenth century and the first quarter of the twentieth, and included the construction of the Metropolitan Museum of Art, the American Museum of Natural History, the Philadelphia Museum of Art, and the Field Museum of Natural History, to name just a few. Many of these older institutions have participated in this second golden age by undergoing transformational additions or renovations, such as the Museum of Modern Art (MoMA), the Morgan Library in New York, and the Tate in London. According to one report, $4 to $5 billion has been spent on construction in American museums over a ten-year period, and that report came out in 1998.[2] Nothing in the first decade of the twenty-first century suggested that the pace of building had slackened.

At the beginning of the new century, according to the American Association of Museums (AAM), there were more than 17,500 accredited museums in the United States, although the association acknowledges that the count is probably incomplete. And while some in the cultural world fret that this number is probably unsustainable, the turnstiles continue to turn: according to a 1999 study by Lake, Snell and Perry, "American museums average approximately 865 million visits per year or 2.3 million visits per day."[3] It is not exaggerating to say that there have never been as many museums doing as many things and attracting as many people as is the case right now. The best of times indeed. But you wouldn't know it by reading much of the writing produced about museums by historians, sociologists, anthropologists, "media critics," and others.

Causally or coincidentally, the building boom in the museum world has corresponded with an equally large boom in the writing about them. Late into the 1980s, the museum remained largely unvisited by scholars, covered, as sociologist Eilean Hooper-Greenhill wrote, in a "blanket of critical silence."[4] Almost all of the writing about museums had been done by and for those professionals who worked there. My own reading suggests that as far back as the 1930s such a literature began to develop about museum education designed for those who were museum educators or schoolteachers who wanted to use museums for schoolchildren and for adult education programs. Individual museums might have their own hagiographies, but those tended to substitute celebration for critical attention.[5]

By the 1990s, however, scholars were silent no more on the subject of museums. By 2006, Sharon Macdonald, a leading figure in the field, could announce, "Museum Studies has come of age. . . . It has moved from being an unusual and minority subject into the mainstream."[6] Certainly over the last two decades, books, articles, anthologies, conference proceedings, and symposia on museums have proliferated to daunting quantities for anyone who would try to keep up with it.

Happily, for our purposes, I don't have to repeat it all here. In 2005, Renaissance historian Randolph Starn, playing the role of an academic Roger Tory Peterson, provided historians with an indispensable field guide to museum studies scholarship.[7] Offering to navigate historians through what he calls the "tidal wave of museum studies," Starn divided his historiographic survey into four broad sections: "the genealogy of museums; the shifting status of the museum object; the politics of museum culture from the ideal of universality to 'museum wars' over cultural difference; the past and future of the 'museum experience.'"

These seem perfectly sensible groupings to me, encompassing virtually all of the important work that has been done in the last two decades. Rather than summarize Starn's essay, however, let me add some additional thoughts about museum scholarship to help clarify the way I have approached the history of museums in the chapters that follow. I will keep my scholarly squabbles to a minimum, but my approach to the history of museums differs in important ways from much of what is now current in museum criticism.

Any casual perusal of the literature reveals that French historian and critic Michel Foucault stands as the patron saint of the new museum studies, and much of what his disciples have produced is pretty bleak, filled with what Ivan Gaskell calls "naïve outrage" and "museophobia." Eilean Hooper-Greenhill and Tony Bennett stand among the first and certainly most influential of those who brought Foucault to the museum.[8] Bennett's work is nuanced, thoughtful, and provocative. Many who have followed in his path have been less so. They have seen museums crudely as part of an apparatus of cultural and political hegemony, to borrow from some of their language, as instruments of the nation-state reifying itself and naturalizing its behavior—insidious places, or, as Douglas Crimp has called the modern art museum, places of "confinement."[9] As far as I am aware Foucault wrote about museums only in the posthumously published essay "Of Other Spaces," but his work on other institutions—prisons, asylums, and hospitals—became the model for analyzing them. No wonder, then, that in some of this literature museums resemble penitentiaries, but with better interior decorating.[10]

There is, of course, an obvious problem with a critical stance that posits museums as places where people go to get disciplined and punished. Treating museums as part of the same institutional constellation as prisons, asylums, and hospitals simply begs the question of why people would ever go, because, of course, only schoolchildren are forced to. We can acknowledge that there may have been social pressures of bourgeois emulation at work in the nineteenth century—and in the twenty-first— that directed people through the doors of museums. But to write, as Timothy Luke does of the entertainment role of museums, that there are "powerful carceral implications that suggest a practice of containment and confinement" is simply absurd.[11] As any resident of the former Soviet Union will happily tell you, a day at the Hermitage is not the same thing as a day in the Gulag. To conflate the two insults the intelligence

of those who come to museums and the dignity of those who have suf-
fered real imprisonment.

In a similar vein, a number of critics, some following the lead of
another French critic, Jean Baudrillard, have seen museums as being
thick in the muck of a postmodern consumer culture, itself a kind of
comfortable, well-appointed prison. So, for example, sociologist Nick
Prior sounds an almost apocalyptic death knell for the museum project:
"In essence, the museum, the theme park, the bank lobby, and the mall
are transferable, all equally appreciated in a state of distraction. By this
transformation, the foundational principles of the museum—the pure
aesthetic, bourgeois contemplation, the disciplinary efforts of the
nation-state—disintegrate. I. M. Pei's glass pyramid becomes a head-
stone on the grave of the project of the museum."[12] Andreas Huyssen
has nicely summarized this shift in the critique of museums. Critics of
museums, he writes, have been "surprisingly homogeneous in their
attack on ossification, reification and cultural hegemony even if the
focus of the attack may be quite different now from what it once was:
then the museum as bastion of high culture, now, very differently, as
the new kingpin of the culture industry."[13] Museum directors might be
forgiven a certain frustration here. They have addressed charges of elitism leveled by an earlier generation and increased their audience by
adding cafés, shops, performance events, and so forth, only to find
themselves accused of turning museums into Disneyland.

As even this quick gloss suggests, and Starn's essay elaborates, much
of the poststructuralist analysis of museums amounts to social critique.
That there is a relationship between culture and politics is a truism, but
much of this scholarship makes the two virtually synonymous. They are
not.

For those on the left, especially the academic left, largely disconnected from the real politics of governing and economic power, the
petit politics of the academy and the museum substitute rhetorically and
practically. Only in such a fundamental confusion could one academic
critic write of museum work, "Representation is a political act. Sponsorship is a political act. Curation is a political act. Working in a museum is
a political act."[14] Pity the poor intern updating the collection database
who is not able to translate her experience into an influential lobbying
job on K Street.

Understanding the intersection of culture and politics is vital for both
the past and the present. Understanding the difference between the two
is equally important. To continue to elide the two therefore cheapens
real culture and avoids real politics. In the chapters that follow I try to
respect the integrity of each.

Two final observations about the state of museum scholarship. The vast bulk of writing about museums focuses on art museums and anthro-pological collections. That too is not surprising, as these museums lend themselves most readily to the kinds of analysis scholars want to impose on them. Perhaps most museum scholars would rather spend time in art and anthropology museums, sneaking off guiltily to the café or to the gift shop; perhaps these humanists suffer like so many of us from a gen-eral scientific illiteracy. But ignoring science museums is curious and regrettable given how central science museums have been in the West since the nineteenth century. As Sally Kohlstedt has observed,

Ironically, insofar as twentieth-century historians of science considered muse-ums in their accounts of the natural sciences, they focused largely on collecting activity and taxonomic results, without much attention to the institutions that sponsored and facilitated such work. Historians of biology have tended to ignore or be dismissive of the work of naturalists done either in the field or in muse-ums, instead documenting the establishment of laboratory science. Historians who were key in formulating the history of natural science in North America, though often attentive to other institutional development—including that of universities and corporate laboratories—virtually ignored museums.[15]

And in the United States, at least, they attract far and away the largest number of visitors.

I will have more to say about science museums in Chapters 1 and 4, but for now suffice it to note that I believe a more thorough examina-tion of the history and practice of science museums will yield a different set of questions about the nature of museums, about the relationship between knowledge and display, and about museums and the public than has been asked thus far.

Finally, my sense is that the lion's share of work in the new museum studies has been written about the European experience. No surprise, perhaps, given the richness of that history and its length. Further, much of this European history has been written by scholars other than historians. In the European context, museum studies includes work by sociologists, anthropologists, and those who have gathered under the somewhat leaky umbrella of "cultural studies."[16] My approach is more prosaically historical, by which I mean simply that I prefer to begin with the messy particularities and work my way up to larger conclusions and observations rather than start with a broad critical position before mov-ing down. More specifically, I treat the development of museums as an episode in the history of ideas. While I am fully aware of the social, eco-nomic, and political roles museums have played, I want to take museums seriously as places of ideas—places where knowledge is given shape through the use of objects and exhibitions. I will describe the themes that run through this book more fully in a moment, but let me say here that I approach museums as places uniquely situated at the intersection

Figure 2. In 2005, the Walters Art Museum re-created a "collector's study" in one of its galleries. Photo © The Walters Art Museum, Baltimore.

of objects, ideas, and public space. As the subsequent chapters will demonstrate, exploring that intersection raises interesting questions not just about museums themselves but about knowledge production, about the changing nature of American cities, and about the American public across time.

This, then, is the state of our museum age: museums proliferating and thriving, attracting record numbers, enjoying a building boom and sitting atop our cultural hierarchy. At the same time, museums are being attacked and challenged in a whole host of ways, walking a perilously fine line between their nonprofit ethos and the world of corporate money, between education and "info-tainment," between opening up and being overrun. With all this in mind, museums have probably never been quite so exciting.

A word about the nature of this book. In the Soviet era, Russian writers used to describe work destined for the *dolgii yashchik*—"the long drawer"—work they knew would never see the light of publication. I can't claim anything quite so heroic for these chapters, but I should acknowledge at the outset that four of them began their lives as public presentations and lectures given over the last few years, and after I delivered them they wound up in that long drawer. Pulling them out one afternoon, I decided that, with substantial revisions and expansions, and with the addition of three more, they fit nicely together and would make a timely and useful book. The chapters assembled here, then, do not constitute a comprehensive history of American museums in the twentieth century. Rather, they explore an interlocking set of themes, grounded in the particularities of history. They refer back to one another and provide, I hope, a sustained and coherent argument.

Tying these chapters together are several themes that interest me particularly. First and perhaps foremost among them is the role objects play in museums of all kinds. In an earlier work, I argued that the organization and display of objects was central to the conception of museums in the late nineteenth century. I suggested that behind those exhibitionary practices lay a faith in the power of objects to convey knowledge, meaning, and understanding—if they were properly collected, classified, and arranged.[17] I refer several times to what I term an "object-based epistemology" in the following chapters. That notion will serve as a benchmark to measure how the function of objects in museums changed over the course of the twentieth century. My contention will be that the place of objects in museums has shrunk as people have lost faith in the ability of objects alone to tell stories and convey knowledge.

In addition, my focus on objects reacts to the drift in museum scholarship toward the literary that I mentioned previously. As I suggested, some scholars have brought to the museum pre-asked questions, formulated originally in other scholarly contexts. This importation risks, among other things, missing some of the particularities in the nature, function, and purpose of museums. Sharon Macdonald is right, I believe, when she reminds us that treating museums simply as another kind of "text" risks denying what makes museums and the objects they display different from other "texts." She writes, "We also need to move towards further elaboration of ways in which museums are *unlike* texts." And in particular we need to consider "the centrality of material culture, the durability and solidity of objects, the non-verbal nature of so many of their messages." So too art historian Alan Wallach has observed that "a successful exhibition is not a book on the wall, a narrative with objects as illustrations, but a carefully orchestrated deployment of objects, images, and texts that gives viewers opportunities to look, to reflect, and to work out meanings."[18] In several of these chapters, directly and indirectly, I have asked questions about how objects have been used to convey meaning, about the differences between scientific and aesthetic objects, and about how the nature of objects in different kinds of museums changed over the twentieth century.

Likewise, I am interested in how museums, and the objects they collect and display, help define particular bodies of knowledge. Or fail to, as we will see in Chapters 4 and 5 when we look at science museums and the ill-fated Philadelphia Commercial Museum. While it is important to recognize the role museums play now in the realms of commerce, tourism, and entertainment, I think it is equally important to examine the role museums have played and continue to play in our intellectual life; to look at the relationship between objects and ideas, museums and education; and to see how those relationships have changed over time and in different kinds of museums.

In the United States, George Brown Goode probably gave this categorical imperative its most thorough articulation. Born in 1851, Goode began his professional life as an ichthyologist. He worked with the United States Fish Commission and eventually as the assistant secretary of the Smithsonian in charge of the United States National Museum. In an 1895 essay Goode outlined six types of museums: "A. museums of art; B. historical museums; C. anthropological museums; D. natural history museums; E. technological museums; F. commercial museums."[19] Goode was something of a visionary. Art museums and natural history museums would have been familiar organizations already in 1895; however, the notion of a historical museum had not yet moved beyond domestic shrines like Mount Vernon, technological museums had been built in Europe but not yet in the United States, and anthropological museums and commercial museums would have struck Americans as wholly novel.

Taken together, Goode suggested, these six types constituted a kind of encyclopedia set of institutions and represented the categories of knowledge that could be given physical form in the museum. In the logic of an object-based epistemology, the objects collected and displayed in each museum stand as synecdoches for the larger body of knowledge, and ideally the correspondence between that body of knowledge and the objects on display would be seamless.

With the exception of "commercial museums," Goode's categories have proved remarkably enduring over the last century, though as I will discuss a great deal later, their boundaries have been stretched. (In the United States, only Philadelphia built a commercial museum, and it lasted as such only until the 1930s. I discuss the rise and fall of the Phila-delphia Commercial Museum in Chapter 5.) The American Association of Museums' *Code of Ethics* lists "museums of anthropology, art history and natural history . . . historic sites . . . science and technology centers, and zoos." (Goode did not include zoos in his original scheme, but in their impulse to collect, organize, and display, zoos certainly did mirror the intellectual architecture of late nineteenth-century museums.) I use Goode's hypothetical encyclopedia set as a way of mapping the changing boundaries between museums and the bodies of knowledge they institu-tionalized over the course of the twentieth century.

Americans by the millions love to visit museums. My research suggests that they always have. Yet this assertion flies in the face of what has come to be a truism about museums: their fundamental elitism. Almost from the moment of their opening—and certainly by the 1920s and 1930s—the grand art museums of the late nineteenth century were accused of being little more than monuments to the taste of wealthy plutocrats. This accusation was brought particularly by artists—the Futurists in Europe, members of the Ash Can group in the United States—whose work did not yet hang in those mausoleums of art.

Those first accusations of elitism had vaguely class overtones. Over the last generation or so, the charge of elitism has taken on a new flavor, growing out of the identity politics of the 1960s. More specifically, cer-tain critics have insisted that in multicultural societies museums have ignored or alienated an increasingly diverse audience and, further, that they have a responsibility to fix the situation. In the United States and increasingly in Europe, these complaints are made largely in terms of ethnicity and race. They arise out of the larger phenomenon of identity politics and identity academics and participate in what the hugely influ-ential critic Edward Said called the "ominous trend" of "the fetishiza-tion and relentless celebration of 'difference' and 'otherness.'"[20] One solution to this problem has been to broaden the museum's appeal, to target new audiences and to shed the museum's traditional goal of time-lessness and universalism, replacing it with a notion of contemporary relevance that responds to the particular concerns of those committed to difference above and beyond commonality.

Indeed, for some the very notion of "difference"—defined at an alti-tude-defying level of abstraction—is at the heart of the entire museum enterprise. Daniel Sherman, in his introduction to a recent anthology, writes that museums should be studied with "an approach based on a phenomenological notion of alterity—one that takes difference as the essence of museums, and museums as the essence of difference—must recognize that difference . . . does not exist in itself, and cannot be analyzed apart from its historical instantiations."[21] Somewhere between the galleries and the gift shop we began to walk in circles.

I investigate the nature of museum audiences in several chapters, but most explicitly in Chapters 4 and 6. In these explorations, I find myself disagreeing with the view that museums are oppressive, repressive, and otherwise controlling. My own sense of what it means to be a "public," informed by the work of sociologist Richard Sennett among others, and my sense of how museums have related to the public leads me to believe that museums have indeed been a vital part of what we call the public sphere and that they have worked hard to make good on their promises of democratic access and have worked just as hard to keep up with the way that idea has changed.

An example, a British one, to illustrate my point: In the 1850s Parliament began to worry that the paintings in the National Gallery might be destroyed by the abundant crowds that came to see them and by the even more abundant air pollution in the center of London. Perhaps, Parliament wondered, the gallery ought to be moved farther out, to Kensington, say, or Highgate. This raised a furor that the paintings would then be too far away from the working people who came to see them. So in 1857 Parliament surveyed the employers in and around Westminster to see how many of their employees had gone to the National Gallery, the Natural History Museum, and the British Museum in the previous year. The results were definitive: Hooper the Coach Makers' 46 employees had made 66 visits to the National Gallery in 1856; the 338 men who worked for Jackson's Builders made 583 visits.

Still, simply demonstrating that the National Gallery was well visited by the workers of central London did not allay the concerns of those who worried for the safety of the paintings. That question was addressed head on by High Court Justice Coleridge, who weighed in on the issue and whose opinion is worth quoting at some length: "But after all, if it were demonstrable that the pictures in their present position must absolutely perish sooner than at Kensington, I conceive that this would conclude nothing. The existence of the pictures is not the end of the collection but a means to give the people ennobling enjoyment. If while so employed a great picture perished in the using, it could not be said that the picture had not fulfilled the best purpose of its purchase or that it had been lost in its results to the nation."[22]

It is a stunning conclusion—better that the paintings be ruined while being enjoyed than be preserved by being removed from their audience. One can hardly imagine even the most populist museum curator today taking a similar position, and Justice Coleridge's opinion ought to challenge our too-easy assumption that these nineteenth-century museums existed only as vaults to preserve the treasures of the wealthy for the wealthy. Needless to say, the pictures stayed exactly where they were, the public having won a victory of access to them.

A related phenomenon with which historians will have to wrestle is the relationship between museums, objects, and changing ideas about architectural space. The museums of the first golden age stand in a magnificent sameness. Almost without exception, these museums speak the language of Beaux-Arts neoclassicism. From the 1890s through the 1940s, that language dominated American museum architecture. Quite by contrast, the museums of the late twentieth century, the major ones at least, each attempted to make a distinctive architectural statement, and museums competed fiercely to outdo each other with their buildings. As architecture critic Martin Filler noted, reviewing Renzo Piano's Broad Museum in Los Angeles, "During the past three decades . . . the museum has superceded the skyscraper as an architect's dream. . . . [Museums have become] the defining architectural category of our time."[23]

In this sense, while most museums—though certainly not all—are built to house and display objects, the museum building itself has increasingly been treated as an object, and, some might snidely argue, a more significant one than the pieces inside. While major architects at the turn of the twentieth century, such as the firms of McKim, Mead and White, and Carrere and Hastings, built museums, libraries, and other cultural edifices, they worked by and large within an architectural consensus about form and style. I think it is fair to say, and I explore this further in Chapter 6, that Frank Lloyd Wright's Guggenheim Museum of 1959 broke this mold. The statement he made with his cylindrical volume on Fifth Avenue was all the more dramatic because he put it in the middle of a Beaux-Arts streetscape, just up the road from the greatest Beaux-Arts bastion of all, the Metropolitan Museum of Art.

Wright's Guggenheim influenced museum building in two mutually reinforcing directions. After the Guggenheim, museum trustees increasingly demanded "signature" buildings—buildings that would attract publicity, visitors, and donors. At the same time, Wright freed other architects to explore any number of architectural possibilities. Museums no longer had to be well-appointed Beaux-Arts boxes.

The post-Guggenheim era, then, has seen an extraordinary flourishing of museum architecture. This is not to say that all the buildings that have resulted have succeeded by any stretch, but the variety has been remarkable. I think it is also fair to say that museums constitute some of the very best work of architects ranging from Louis Kahn to Robert Venturi to Renzo Piano. It is fitting, too, that perhaps the most heralded building of the recent past has been Frank Gehry's Guggenheim in Bilbao, Spain.

One question that historians will have to address, as we evaluate the legacy of this era of museum architecture, is how all these architectural experiments have shaped, or reshaped, what goes on inside museums now. It seems clear that these buildings have altered the way visitors move and pause as they tour the galleries. They have attracted people who come for the experience of the building itself. That experience now routinely includes food, shopping, music, social gatherings, movies, and the like, all made possible by the spaces dedicated to these other-than-exhibition uses. In addition, the galleries in these new buildings have created different relationships between viewers and objects. Museums are now much more concerned about lighting and other atmospherics, traffic flow, and flexible exhibition space than was the case in the late nineteenth century. As a result, I suspect we look differently at objects than our museum-going predecessors did.

At the same time, we should examine how museum commissions have influenced the direction of contemporary architecture as a whole and trace how all this high-profile museum building has affected other kinds of projects as well. If Filler is right, and I think he is, we should explore how libraries, concert halls, university buildings, and even skyscrapers have come to resemble museums, at least at the level of architecture. We might well discover that the museum is the defining architectural form of this cultural moment.

There are surely other facets to the history of the American museum in the twentieth century. The question of money—of funding, philanthropy, and patronage—is one of them; the professionalization of the museum is another. But these three broad themes encompass what I feel to be the most compelling issues that museums have faced and continue to face, and these themes knit the following chapters together. They are, in my view, the concepts that best enable us to examine what museums do and how they do it.

Chapter 1 provides a broad overview of the role of the object in different kinds of museums across the twentieth century. If in the late nineteenth century museums were imagined primarily as houses (some might say warehouses) for collections of objects, that is no longer the case. In this chapter I examine the changing place and use of the object inside the museum. In so doing, I study the way different kinds of objects have functioned in different kinds of museums, the ways in which museums use objects to define areas of knowledge, and how objects participate in the redefinition of those boundaries. I also examine the ways in which objects have receded—or disappeared altogether—from museums.

The second chapter continues this focus on the role of objects by looking at them from a different direction. While we think of museums as places where objects enter, never to leave, in Chapter 2 I look at the small but significant phenomenon of repatriation, the process by which museum objects have been leaving museum collections. A few American art museums have found themselves in the middle of these controversies as foreign governments—the Italians most aggressively— have demanded the return of antiquities. More commonly, however, Native American objects have been returned from anthropological collections housed in natural history museums, art museums, and anthropological and archaeological museums. Specifically, I am interested in putting repatriation into two contexts, one political, the other disciplinary. First, I want to ask why the repatriation movement succeeded in this country when it did, an exploration of the politics behind repatriation. Second, I am interested in how repatriation is connected to the changing role of the "ethnological" object in anthropological theory and practice.

Chapter 3 continues the examination of how non-Western cultures have been represented in American museums by looking at the case of the East. If museums used the frameworks and tropes of "primitivism" to represent Native Americans, Africans, and others, then Eastern cultures have posed a more complicated set of categorical problems to Western museums. Clearly not Western but clearly not savage either, the East confounded those collectors and museum builders who tried to fit it into easy hierarchies and categories. Chapter 3 looks at the presentation and representation of the East in American museums from the nineteenth century through the first third of the twentieth century. More specifically, it explores what I see as the two competing, but not contradictory, strategies used to display Asia. The first has been to create a framework and apparatus of Asian art as art that corresponds roughly to the frameworks used to present Western art. The other is to use objects in a less systematic, taxonomic way to convey some sense of Asian experience—often spiritual or religious experience—that satisfies the yearnings Westerners have had. Broadly speaking, this chapter asks the question "What is the idea of the East, and how has that been defined in the museum setting?"

Chapter 4 tackles the question of museum audience and, specifically, the audience in science museums. By looking at three case studies—the American Museum of Natural History, the Museum of Science and Industry in Chicago, and Philadelphia's Franklin Institute Science Museum—I chart how science museums came to be places catering almost entirely to children. Further, I look at how that decision to focus on children as their primary constituency was connected to how these museums saw their relationship to the changing nature of scientific research. Science as a discipline, more so than art or anthropology, has changed radically since the big science museums were founded in that first golden age of museums, and this chapter examines how three struggled to adapt to those changes.

Chapter 5 examines how one museum died. While we have a good understanding now of the birth of the museum, the Philadelphia Commercial Museum provides a remarkable opportunity to examine how a once-great institution faded away. Founded as the first, and only, museum in the United States devoted to commerce, the Philadelphia Commercial Museum thrived in the early twentieth century and then died a slow death. My contention in this chapter is that the Commercial Museum's failure to survive was rooted in the inability of its objects to embody a coherent body of knowledge about commerce. In the end, the museum could not display "commerce," and unable to do so, the museum lost its role as a place for the "scientific" study and promotion of commerce to other kinds of institutions. In this sense, Chapter 5 brings us full circle to the role of objects in museums.

The final chapter pulls our lens back a bit. It moves from the objects in museums to the space of the museum itself. Chapter 6 explores the role of the museum as public space and as part of the urban public sphere that emerged during the Progressive Era. As I have already indicated, my argument runs counter to the conventional wisdom about the relationship between the museum and the public. Museums are elitist bastions, so the wisdom goes; they are alienating or off-putting to the public and designed to be so. Temples or mausoleums, take your pick, but not intended for ordinary folks. (This line of thinking refers to art museums, of course. Science museums, as I have already mentioned, have been largely ignored by most writers.) Two things about this perception strike me as worth interrogating further. First, to what extent is this charge of elitism fair, and to what extent have museums—even art museums—made an honest attempt to fulfill their democratic purpose? As I have already suggested, my research indicates that the elitist museum may have been less forbidding than we have assumed.

Further, in claiming that the museum has intimidated or excluded the "public," we have assumed that the very idea of the public—its definition and constitution, its demands and expectations—remained the same over the course of the twentieth century, waiting for museum practice to catch up with it. My own sense is that this isn't quite true either. My belief is that the nature of the "public" has changed significantly since the late nineteenth century, and in this final chapter I argue that museums have responded to those changes. Indeed, I believe that periods of perceived crisis in museums—and there have been at least three since that first golden age: in the late 1920s and early 1930s, in the late 1960s and early 1970s, and at the turn of the twenty-first century—

correspond to those moments when the nature of the American public shifted in significant ways and museums faced the challenge of responding to those changes.[24] They did so, as I will discuss, in several ways: by reshaping the space inside museums, by paying more attention to the demands made by visitors, and by changing the experience visitors had with objects on display.

As this brief gloss indicates, I have ranged across several different kinds of museums, trading a certain depth of treatment for a greater breadth. Part of this choice results simply from my own interests in all these places. Part of it, however, is driven by a sense that most museum scholarship remains tightly focused on specific kinds of museums without exploring the interesting comparisons that might come from moving from art museums, say, to science museums, and then to historic house museums. Some while ago Sally Kohlstedt challenged historians of museums to take up comparative studies of museums that would highlight "both the curious parallels that existed among museums and those characteristics that mark out individual institutions."[25] This collection makes at least some of those comparisons and invites readers to draw even more.

As I have probably made clear already, I am not interested in indicting museums for their alleged crimes against culture. I am not a museophobic historian; in fact, I quite like museums and visit them as often as I can. I especially enjoy bringing my two children. But there are some things about the role museums play in this cultural moment that do trouble me. Call them the perils of the museum age.

On the one hand, museums are being asked to substitute for politics. Over the last two decades we have watched museums used as the stage sets for badly conceived morality plays where right-wing culture warriors fume and fulminate—against Robert Mapplethorpe in Cincinnati, against "The West as America," and against the *Enola Gay* exhibit in Washington to name three. Simultaneously, and we have touched on this already, museum studies critics demand political penance from museums for the sins of colonialism and capitalism and redress for the complaints that arise out of identity politics. Too left-wing for some, not nearly left-wing enough for others, but at the end of the day, the real facts of politics remain unaltered. I worry that forcing museums into this realm of faux politics detracts from the real cultural, scientific, and educational work of museums that is precious and important on its own terms.

On the other hand, museums are also being asked to serve as economic engines in postindustrial cities hoping to replace manufacturing with culture. It is more than a little ironic that while critics and curators

Figure 3. A museum age. The Taubman Museum of Art opened in 2008 with the promise of revitalizing downtown Roanoke, Virginia. Courtesy of Randall Stout Architects, Inc.

develop their critique of the museum, politicians, business leaders, and others view museums more and more as central to the postindustrial economy. In 2008, for example, the new 81,000-square-foot addition to the Taubman Museum of Art opened in downtown Roanoke, Virginia, to great expectations and not a little controversy. At a cost of roughly $66 million, the museum is certainly a high-stakes gamble for a small city with tight financial resources. Proponents have touted the museum's economic potential for the city and the region. As Nicholas Taubman, a major contributor to the project, put it, "I think the museum will be a hinge on which the economic future of downtown Roanoke will swing, as well as the region."[26]

Roanoke, of course, could be any number of cities banking on high-profile cultural projects—especially museums and performing arts centers—to reinvigorate their local economies. And there is no question that "culture" has become a major part of any urban revitalization strategy, not just in this country but in Europe as well. In a postindustrial society, so the rationale goes, culture becomes the product cities have to sell.

It clearly works in some places and under some circumstances. Bilbao has been transformed by its museum; North Adams, Massachusetts, is now a cultural destination thanks to MassMOCA. But in other places and under different circumstances it isn't nearly so clear that museums can ride to the rescue of local economies. Several years ago, for example, the Milwaukee Art Museum added a stunning wing designed by Santiago Calatrava. Attendance increased initially but has subsequently fallen back to earlier levels. Either way, perhaps it is too early to pronounce a verdict on this strategy of using museums for urban redevelopment. Still, expecting museums to save cities, especially those smaller places that have experienced years of job losses and disinvestment, seems to me to expect too much. My concern is that to ask museums to solve our political and economic problems is to set them up for inevitable failure and to set us up for inevitable disappointment.

My final unease about our current museum moment is this: Regardless of what fills their galleries, regardless of what bodies of knowledge museums were or are built to represent, they stand, finally, as historical projects: the history of art, the history of the natural world, the history of technology, and the history of cultures now changed. This is certainly true today, and it was true during that first great age of museum building, despite the confidence with which those museums displayed the unity of knowledge and the continuity between past and present. Museums are places where we can measure the distance between then and now. In other words, whether they mean to or not, all museums race against "the acceleration of history."

The phrase is Pierre Nora's, taken from his enormously provocative and influential chapter "Between Memory and History." Nora included museums among his litany of "*lieux de memoire*," places of memory that substitute for what he saw as the whole, integrated memory of preindustrial, premodern societies. As he put it, with a certain Gallic overstatement: "Museums, archives, cemeteries, festivals, anniversaries, treaties, depositions, monuments, sanctuaries, fraternal orders—these are the boundary stones of another age, illusions of eternity. It is the nostalgic dimension of these devotional institutions that make them seem beleaguered and cold—they mark the rituals of a society without ritual; integral particularities in a society that levels particularity; signs of distinction and of group membership in a society that tends to recognize individuals only as identical and equal." Nora sees history as the archenemy of memory, writing, "At the heart of history is a critical discourse that is antithetical to spontaneous memory. History is perpetually suspicious of memory, and its true mission is to suppress and destroy it."[27]

Of course, we don't need Nora to point out the effects of the acceleration of history. It is what Henry Adams struggled with through the entirety of his autobiography, *The Education of Henry Adams*. After searching for "a dynamic theory of history," he settled on and titled his penultimate chapter, dated 1904, "A Law of Acceleration." There, surveying a world governed by power without purpose, force without direction, he predicted: "At the rate of progress since 1800, every American who lived into the year 2000 would know how to control unlimited power. He would think in complexities unimaginable to an earlier mind. He would deal with problems altogether beyond the range of earlier society. To him the nineteenth century would stand on the same plane with the fourth." Adams, who in the book's most famous chapter, "found himself lying in the Gallery of Machines at the Great Exposition of 1900 his historical neck broken by the sudden irruption of forces totally new," fully understood the rupture between unity and fragmentation, between memory and history that Nora observed nearly one hundred years later.[28]

It is too easy a dichotomy but useful nonetheless for thinking about what drives much of this new golden age of museum building. Whatever their economic hopes or political goals, many of these new museums promise to function as places of our collective memory. They attempt to straddle that line between memory and history, whether the exhibits deal with the traumatic or the comparatively trivial: the Holocaust or rock and roll, slavery or *Star Wars*. They use the frameworks of history to ensure that we never forget, even as the anxiety that we will forget increases the urgency to build museums in the first place.

Indeed, the urgency may come from the fact that more and more of us know less and less of our collective past. As Tony Judt has nicely put it, talking about the European context: "Whereas until recently . . . the point of a museum, a memorial plaque, or a monument was to remind people of what they already knew or thought that they knew, today these things serve a different end. They are there to tell people about things they may not know, things they have forgotten or never learned."[29] In this sense, museums are not being asked simply to stand in for memory but to stand in between memory and oblivion.

"The struggle of man against power," Milan Kundera wrote, "is the struggle of memory against forgetting." And yet, perhaps in our mad race against the acceleration of history, we have forgotten the importance of forgetting. As Paul Ricoeur has wisely noted, "We shun the specter of a memory that would never forget anything. We even consider it to be monstrous." He wonders whether and how we might achieve some sort of balance between remembering and forgetting: "Could there then be a measure in the use of human memory, a 'never in excess' in accordance with the dictum of ancient wisdom? Could forgetting then no longer be in every respect an enemy of memory, and could memory have to negotiate with forgetting, groping to find the right measure in its balance with forgetting?"[30] We certainly recognize the need for individuals to forget, to forgive, to let go, to move on. At a collective level, the risk in our attempt to "never forget" is that our landscape, metaphorically and literally, becomes so cluttered with our attempts to remember the past that they crowd out our capacity to imagine the future.

Museums certainly can't solve all these dilemmas. But I do think they can be places where these questions and others can be asked. Places where people can come to explore the extent of our differences and of the things we all share; to measure the distance, short or long, between past and present; and to contemplate the meanings of continuity and change.

These are the challenges and the possibilities of living in a museum age.

Chapter 1
Do Museums Still Need Objects?

In the introduction I visited briefly the politics of museums, or more properly the political lenses through which scholars have viewed museums. Here, I want to move from that abstract level to the most specific and basic component of the museum: the object. The purpose of this chapter is to sketch what happened to objects in different kinds of museums throughout the twentieth century.

Though the definition of what a museum can be has grown elastic over the last generation, according to the AAM objects are what they all have in common. The organization's *Code of Ethics for Museums* notes that all museums make a "unique contribution to the public by collecting, preserving, and interpreting the things of this world." What I suggest is that while museums as institutions continue to enjoy considerable civic and cultural authority, and while they are lauded more and more for their economic prowess, the use of objects inside them has changed significantly. In some cases, objects continue to play a central role in the function of the museum; in others, their role is clearly a reduced one; in still others, objects have virtually disappeared from galleries, replaced by other didactic devices—audio-visual, interactive technologies, and so on.

If the museum, etymologically speaking, is a place of the muses, then the connection between objects and muses goes back at least to the Renaissance. The potted history of the Western museum goes like this: The museums of today trace their origins back to the princely collections and cabinets of curiosities assembled in early modern Europe. Starting in the eighteenth century, the institutional settings for those collections began to change. Private collections became public—most spectacularly at the Louvre—and what was perceived as the irrationality of the cabinet became rationalized. In the United States, Peale's museum in Philadelphia represents a critical development, organizing as it did the natural and human world and putting it in the service of a nascent nationalism.

These twin drives toward increased public access and increased rationality culminated, certainly in the United States, in the creation of the great civic museums of the late nineteenth and early twentieth centuries. This amounted to more than mere institutional rearrangements, of course, but represented important intellectual shifts as well. As Stephen Bann has observed, "Paradigms of knowledge themselves shifted, over the period between the Renaissance and the late nineteenth century, in such a way as to ensure that collections of objects acquired a new epistemological status, while being simultaneously adapted to new forms of institutional display."[1]

That epistemological shift was driven by what I might call a categorical imperative. Museums in this era prided themselves on their rational organization into categories and departments. They beautifully reflected Durkheim's observation that a society orders the world of things to reflect the way it orders everything else.[2] This was true at both the intramuseum and intermuseum levels. No individual museum could fulfill its mission to educate and uplift unless its collections were organized in "scientific" ways. Likewise, museums could not make rational sense out of the world unless they devoted themselves to collecting, organizing, and displaying particular categories of knowledge.

This is the intellectual context in which the Smithsonian's George Brown Goode outlined his six-part museum plan discussed in the introduction.[3] Taken together, Goode suggested, these six constituted a kind of encyclopedia set of institutions and represented the categories of knowledge that could be given museum form. In this logic, the objects collected and displayed in each museum stood as synecdoches for the larger body of knowledge, and ideally the correspondence between that body of knowledge and the objects on display would be seamless. And as I mentioned earlier, with the exception of commercial museums, these categories have proved remarkably enduring over the last century. (In the United States, only Philadelphia built a Commercial Museum, and it lasted as such only until the 1930s. I discuss the rise and fall of the Philadelphia Commercial Museum in Chapter 5.) (In its most recent guide, the AAM has added zoos to Goode's list, and it has modified history museums into historic sites. Curiously, zoos have not yet been studied much by scholars, though zoos and natural history museums did share specimens, in a slightly macabre way.)

In this chapter, I follow Goode's conception as a guide to see what happened in the twentieth century to the objects that were used by museums to constitute those categories. I start with some preliminary

observations and generalizations and then visit art museums, anthropological collections, history museums, and science museums of two kinds,
natural and technological.

This means that, although the very notion of the categorical museum
has expanded remarkably, I won't consider places like the Mustard
Museum in Mount Horeb, Wisconsin, or any of the nation's museums of
barbed wire—there are at least three—save to say that they too aspire
exactly to encyclopedic collection, organization, and display of their particular category of "knowledge." Yet while we continue to categorize
museums in a way that reflects their late nineteenth-century origins, the
relationship between categories of knowledge and the objects that were
once thought to constitute them has certainly changed a great deal. At
the same time, objects have lost pride of place in many museums
because they aren't necessary to fulfill some of the functions we now
expect museums to perform. If in the late nineteenth century museums
were conceived of as primarily places to display objects, by the turn of
the twenty-first century it had become possible to imagine museums
without any objects at all.

Vanishing Acts?

The first way to answer the question of whether museums need objects
anymore is, naturally, to qualify it. While all museums at the turn of the
twentieth century conceived of themselves as places to display objects,
over the course of that century it became clear not only that different
kinds of museums require different kinds of objects but also that they
make use of objects in very different ways. Thus some museums, such as
those exhibiting art, continue to need objects to do what they do; others,
such as science and technology museums, don't exhibit objects as much
as they invite visitors to interact with them; still others, such as those
devoted to history in some sense, may or may not require objects at all
to convey the messages they want visitors to absorb.

Still, with that said, the first observation we ought to make is that over
the course of the last one hundred years, the place of objects in museums of all kinds has shrunk dramatically. Museum exhibits of whatever
sort make use of far fewer objects than was the case at the turn of the
twentieth century. While I can't quantify this in any rigorous way, even
the casual observation of old photographs and the reading of old
museum guidebooks reveal that the galleries have simply become less
crowded with stuff. Art museum walls that once hung floor to ceiling, in
what is often referred to as "salon" style display, now only exhibit in a
single horizontal line, known as the "modernist" approach; natural history specimens displayed in an endless collection of glass cases have

been replaced first with dioramas and more recently with interactive technology.

As Stephen Weil, formerly of the Smithsonian, has written, over the last fifty years or so the American museum has changed from "an establishment-like institution focused primarily inward on the growth, care, and study of its collections" to one with "its focus outward to concentrate on providing primarily education services to the public."[4] Museums in the nineteenth century, of course, provided education to the public as well, and museums today continue to care for their collections, but Weil is largely right in noting a shift in emphasis. The museums of the late nineteenth century used a strategy of visual abundance to underscore whatever story they set out to tell. Now visitors are asked to look at fewer objects altogether.

This raises at least three sets of related questions. First, if they are no longer on display, where did all those objects that we can see in the photos from the late nineteenth and early twentieth centuries go? Some reside in study collections, which art museums began to put together by the mid-twentieth century and which are often accessible to visitors. Presumably, however, much more has been sent to the basement or exiled to an off-site storage facility. In a sense, museums have created alternative museums with the bulk of material they don't exhibit, a parallel museum universe, access to which is generally quite restricted. And yet we know very little about that world not on display, at least not as much as we know about the famous collections that are. What can these other "museums" tell us about changing tastes, about notions of value and authenticity? What ethical questions do they raise about acquisition, preservation, de-accessioning, and public trust? These museum basements may represent for museum scholars a vast undiscovered country.

Second, the reliance on fewer objects in museum galleries and exhibit spaces poses questions about the work those objects are being asked to do. Museum exhibits still use objects to tell stories, but with fewer objects to tell those stories, each object must do more of the telling. What's more, fewer objects mean fewer opportunities for alternative stories to compete. When museum galleries were stuffed to the rafters with objects, they certainly conveyed a narrative, but with so many objects filling our visual field there well may have been more space for the accidental or unintentional for visitors. Even as museums have worked hard to promote differing points of view in their exhibits, serendipity has been replaced with carefully chosen curation. The smaller number of objects in museums now raises questions about the rise of the curatorial profession, about the relationship between museum curators and other professionals within the same disciplinary fields, and about the expecta-

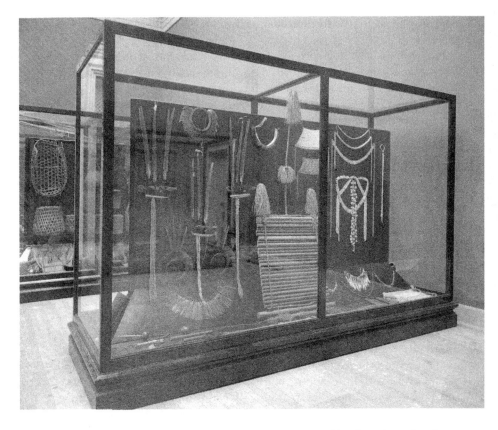

Figure 4. Natural history exhibits old. Cases of objects, like these from South America, characterized natural history museums at the turn of the twentieth century. © The Field Museum, #CSA11897.

tions that museums now have about the effectiveness of objects to tell stories.

Finally, we should ask what is filling up museums nowadays if objects are not. As I pointed out earlier, museums new and old went on a building binge at the end of the twentieth century, and while I have not pulled out a tape measure, it is probably correct to say that object displays occupy less space, as a percentage, than they did at the turn of the last century. As has been well noted, museums now include gift shops, casual cafés, high-end dining, and a host of other spaces devoted to functions other than the display of objects. Museums, so the argument goes, need these spaces to keep up with the demands of a commercial culture, and to take advantage of a consumer economy, but between

Figure 5. Natural history exhibits new. A century later, those cases had largely been replaced. An example is this entrance to the Central American exhibit that opened in 2008 at the Field Museum. © The Field Museum, #GN90960_002Cd.

lunch in the café, holiday shopping in the store, and a jazz performance in the atrium, it isn't clear how much time visitors have to engage with the objects on exhibit.

My sense, however, is that objects began to lose their centrality inside museums much earlier than the arrival of gift shops and film series. Museums at the turn of the twentieth century were built on the assumption that visitors would receive an education by visually engaging with objects—lots of objects, with little else to distract visitors from looking at them. That was the ideal, at any rate. Almost immediately, some museums began adding more explanatory labels, charts, and graphs to help visitors reckon with the objects on display.[5] Thus did the eternal debate within the museum world—about how much text is the right amount of text—begin. Certainly by the second quarter of the twentieth century at least, that faith in the ability of objects to communicate meaning easily and transparently had eroded further. By the 1920s and 1930s increasing numbers of museums were adding educational programming to their activities and hiring educational specialists to provide it to the public. The objects needed help.

As educational programming grew in institutional importance, objects receded. Dorothy Canfield Fisher, for one, saw this as a positive development. As museums learned more and more to cater to their visitors, they put less and less on display. "The old method," she observed in 1927, "of putting on view everything the museum contained was seen to be not only a sin against the very essence of art, but wholly unadapted to the limited powers of human attention." More recently, she believed, "the hideous ideal of mere size, mere numbers, began to disappear. The conception began to take shape that it might be better to thin out the hundreds and thousands of slightly varying specimens to a few, suitable for a general view of any given subject or period, and to put the rest away in archive-storage-rooms, where they could be consulted by students, the only people who really needed to see them."[6]

The disappearance of objects, then, corresponds with the rise of other kinds of activities inside the museum and might prompt some questions about the relationship between those activities—educational, recreational, commercial—and the objects themselves, and how those relationships have changed over time.

These are just a few generalizations and observations with which to start. What I propose now is a quick jog through specific kinds museums—almost exclusively American—to see what has happened to the objects inside them.

Art Still Triumphant

On the face of it, the relationship between art objects and art museums would seem to be the most stable over the last century. Even if there are fewer of them on the walls, art objects continue to function largely as they did when American art museums began filling up with collections one hundred years ago. They remain, by and large, invested with the "aura" that Walter Benjamin described in 1937; their power continues to trade on what Igor Kopytoff has called "singularity." As he defines that idea, "Singularity, in brief, is confirmed not by the object's structural position in an exchange system, but by the intermittent forays into the commodity sphere, quickly followed by reentries into the closed sphere of singular 'art.'"[7] Singularity and authenticity remain at the core of what "art" means, just as they did a century or more ago.

It is certainly the case that the relationship between art objects in museums and the market for art objects as commodity remains mutually reinforcing, and art museums generate fierce controversy when they propose to put objects back into the art market. One has only to remember the events of 2007 at Randolph College and Fisk University when each tried to sell off substantial portions of their art collections to raise cash, or the decision made by the Albright-Knox Museum to sell certain collections in order to strengthen others. Put in Kopytoff's terms, deaccessioning upsets many because, by selling off a singular work of art, the museum allows the piece to make one of those "intermittent forays into the commodity sphere" for the financial gain of the institution.

This is so despite numerous predictions and attempts over the twentieth century to undermine, challenge, or reject how art objects function and how they are defined. After all, Benjamin's essay was itself a prophecy of sorts that the "age of mechanical reproduction" would eliminate the aura that clung to art objects. Mechanical reproduction, Benjamin believed, challenged the very idea of an object's authenticity, and because, Benjamin wrote, that authenticity contributed to the authority of an art object, that too would dissolve in a coming age. As he put it somewhat opaquely:

The authenticity of a thing is the essence of all that is transmissible from its beginning, ranging from its substantive duration to its testimony to the history which it has experienced. Since the historical testimony rests on the authenticity, the former, too, is jeopardized by reproduction when substantive duration ceases to matter. And what is really jeopardized when the historical testimony is affected is the authority of the object. One might subsume the eliminated element in the term "aura" and go on to say: that which withers in the age of mechanical reproduction is the aura of the work of art.[8]

Made at roughly the same time, Paul Valéry's breathless assertion about the impending transformation of the category of art is worth quoting at length:

Our fine arts were developed, their types and uses were established, in times very different from the present, by men whose power of action upon things was insignificant in comparison with ours. But the amazing growth of our techniques, the adaptability and precision they have attained, the ideas and habits they are creating, make it a certainty that profound changes are impending in the ancient craft of the Beautiful. In all the arts there is a physical component which can no longer be considered or treated as it used to be, which cannot remain unaffected by our modern knowledge and power. For the last twenty years neither matter nor space nor time has been what it was from time immemorial. We must expect great innovations to transform the entire technique of the arts, thereby affecting artistic invention itself and perhaps even bringing about an amazing change in our very notion of art.[9]

In art museums themselves, however, the way objects function and are presented betrays scant evidence of any "amazing change in our very notion of art." While the critical fates of individual artists have waxed and waned, with the result that their work goes up and comes down from the walls with shifting curatorial moods, categorically speaking, almost nothing that was considered "art" one hundred years ago has been demoted since.

Nor has the use to which these objects have been put in the museum changed that much either. The master narrative on view is still largely what it was one hundred years ago: an evolutionary, historicizing tale of Western art moving, in more or less agreed upon units, through time. The art objects displayed there are still used to construct that narrative. We begin at the beginning—either in the classical world or in the early Christian world—and march through a series of technical developments, historical eras, and geographic traditions. An Italian Renaissance and a Northern Renaissance, the baroque followed by the neoclassical, and on we go.

Both this narrative and the way art objects are used to articulate it have proved remarkably resilient, even in the face of all the ruptures brought on by modernism. Ironically, nowhere has that resilience been more evident than at the Museum of Modern Art. Born out of the iconoclastic impulses of modernism in the 1920s, MoMA set about to construct an evolutionary narrative of modern art, using its own collections to illustrate it. In this way, MoMA has done all the things of which the stuffier, Beaux-Arts palaces have been accused: it presents its own objects and the narrative they tell as the normative history of modern art, it reifies that narrative, and in so doing it is just as exclusionary as it is inclusionary. Early in the twentieth century, the Italian futurists joyfully talked about blowing up the grand art museums; one hundred years later, there they are, hanging just beyond the cubists and just before the surrealists.

Perhaps the most astonishing development here has been the enormous expansion of the category of art to include all sorts of things that its guardians a century ago would never have dreamed of including in their temples. The category of objects we call "decorative arts" has probably been the most thoroughly absorbed into the framework of the art museum. Whether as part of larger museum collections, or as the sole focus of an institution—as at Winterthur and the De Witt Wallace Museum at Williamsburg—decorative arts now have thoroughly developed standards of connoisseurship, hierarchies of achievement, and genealogies of style. Photography too has quite happily found a home in museum collections and has been joined there more recently by film and video, and even by computer-generated images. "Outsider" artists have been warmly welcomed into the museum for at least a generation. Marcel Duchamp famously stuck a urinal on the wall and called it "art" as a way of tweaking that "very notion of art" in an age of mechanical reproduction. Now successor urinals hang on the museum wall, radiating their own porcelain aura.

Art museums have incorporated the cultural category of "Asia" as well, though as we will explore further in Chapter 3, cultural objects from China and Japan proved vexing to museum builders at the turn of the twentieth century. Asian objects still reside somewhat uneasily in art museums, usually set off in some separate space from the Western narrative. Few art museums attempt an integrated display of art from a global perspective, the Ming porcelain exhibited next to the Renaissance Old Masters, for example. Even so, American art museums are now replete with Asian objects fully understood and displayed as "art."

So, put oversimply, the category of art and the objects that constitute it within the art museum have remained largely the same, only more so. Several reasons suggest themselves. First, as I pointed out earlier, the art objects inside museums are reinforced by a market outside the museum. More than that, I think, is that art museum objects are still allied tightly to the academic discipline of art history, and thus just as the market contributes to an object's singularity, the discipline helps reiterate the story told by the objects; that historicizing narrative has proved remarkably effective and compelling and has been resistant to much revision. The nexus that connects art objects, inside museums and elsewhere, with the production of art historical knowledge remains intact. Finally, the production of that knowledge is still predicated on the act of seeing, and seeing is still what visitors to art museums do. This is quite unlike the production of other bodies of knowledge, especially in the sciences, where what was once visual has become something else. As a result, the art museum idea, and the way art objects are used to construe it, has flourished over the last century.

Art versus Artifact: Anthropological Objects

As many scholars have documented, anthropology had its first real institutional home inside museums.[10] Franz Boas began his American career working first at the 1893 World's Columbian Exposition and, briefly, at the Field Museum that resulted from that event. He left Chicago and moved to New York's American Museum before moving uptown to Columbia. His most famous student, Margaret Mead, occupied a position at the American Museum until the end of her life.[11] Yet despite this long connection between the museum and the birth of the discipline, anthropology as a field of knowledge has had the most troublesome residence in the galleries of museums, and anthropological objects in museums have proved the most vexing, both for anthropology and for the museum.

In his 1895 conception, Goode envisioned anthropology as one of his six museum categories. In fact, very few museums built during that first golden age were dedicated entirely and exclusively to the new and exciting field of anthropology, and all of those, as far as I know, were attached to universities and colleges that saw them as an integral part of their new academic departments. Harvard, Berkeley, and the University of Pennsylvania most famously created anthropology museums, but even small places like Beloit College felt that an anthropology collection was necessary for the research and teaching of anthropology.

Goode imagined an innovative kind of institution, occupying a new intellectual space: "As a matter of convenience, museums are commonly classed in two groups—those of science and those of art. . . . On the one side stand the natural history collections. . . . On the other side are the fine-art collections. . . . Between is a territory which no English word can adequately describe—which the Germans call Kulturgeschichte—the natural history of civilization, of man and his ideas and achievements." And, he concluded, "the museums of science and art have not yet learned how to partition this territory." As I have written elsewhere, more than any other the University of Pennsylvania's museum tried to occupy this space between science and art.[12] It opened, in 1899, as the Free Museum of Science and Art.

The University of Pennsylvania's experiment in filling the space in between, however, proved unusual. More often, anthropology collections found their home as a department within larger natural history museums. There anthropology followed the museum practices of the other natural sciences. Objects were collected, organized, and displayed to illustrate a largely progressive, evolutionary narrative, only this time the evolution was social and cultural rather than biological. The displays of anthropological material from the turn of the twentieth century, to judge from archival photographs, look remarkably like exhibits of stuffed birds or fossil fish.

We can deduce from this that initially, at least, anthropologists believed that anthropological objects could function epistemologically for their discipline in roughly the same way natural history specimens functioned for the natural scientists. Provided they were collected, organized, and arranged properly, anthropological objects could convey knowledge about the people who produced them, standing in for the cultures they represented in museum exhibits—a natural history of civilization, illustrated through objects gathered from all the world's "primitive" peoples.

The fact that the new wine of anthropological material was poured into the old bottle of natural history museum practice underscores both the definitional problem with which the discipline itself has always struggled and the uneasy relationship the discipline has had with the museums out of which it grew. Boas left the American Museum in 1905, so the story goes, after a squabble with museum president Morris Jesup over the anthropological exhibits. Boas, after all, wanted to use these exhibits to present his opposition to the easy and simple notions of cultural progress and hierarchy that had dominated the understanding of "primitive" cultures. He wanted to demonstrate, through objects on display, that each culture had its own internal logic, and he wanted to "illustrate . . . the relation of man to nature." Jesup didn't see it or didn't get it. After touring the anthropology halls, Jesup reported, "I am not satisfied," and he was sure that if he got nothing out of the exhibits, neither would other visitors. Jesup believed that the anthropology exhibits should show "the advance of mankind from the most primitive form to the most complex forms of life."[13] There was a clash between treating human cultures as part of the new anthropology and continuing to treat them as part of the older natural history.

In 1954, roughly a half-century after the foundation of museum-based anthropology, Alfred Kroeber wrestled with the definitional question in a way that verged on the tautological. Kroeber had built the anthropology department at the University of California, Berkeley, and had been a central figure at the university's Phoebe Hearst Museum. Toward the end of his life he wondered why anthropology now found itself lumped together with the social sciences in the contemporary university. After all, he wrote, "anthropology is in part natural science, in part humanity, only secondarily social science." What made anthropology "part natural science," according to Kroeber? "The natural sciences utilize museums as research apparatus in their natural history aspects . . . and the humanities have art museums." And completing the syllogism: "Anthropology grew out of expeditions and museums . . . there have never been any museums of sociology."[14] Anthropology started with museum collections; hence museum collections define anthropology.

Even as he wrote this, however, many others in the field recognized that the discipline had moved a considerable distance from museum concerns and thus away from the centrality of objects in their work. In the very same issue of *American Anthropologist*, Donald Collier and Harry Tschopik Jr. acknowledged that "during the past thirty-odd years the balance of influence has shifted from museum, or museum-oriented anthropologists . . . to non-museum anthropologists." Archaeologists and physical anthropologists, they wrote, "continued to utilize museum collections," but "most social and cultural anthropologists have become less and less concerned with historical problems . . . and have, generally speaking, lost interest in material culture." Further, in their estimation, museum exhibits did not wrestle with any of the "many problems of current theoretical interest," and they believed that "the majority of these exhibits are out of date in terms of the present theoretical position of anthropology." The divorce, as Collier and Tschopik saw it, took place on institutional grounds: the university department now had irreconcilable differences with the museum collection. "How far this development has gone is evidenced by the number of graduate students and recent Ph.D.'s who think of museums as intellectually low grade, if they think of them at all."[15]

According to Collier and Tschopik, writing in 1954, the problem was already about thirty years old. I'll be more specific and say thirty-two years: 1922, the year, as it happens, that novelist Willa Cather wrote that "the world broke in two." Whatever she meant by that quip, 1922 might well be the year that the union of academic anthropology and museums broke in two. That year saw the appearance of A. R. Radcliffe-Brown's *Andaman Islanders* and Bronislaw Malinowski's *Argonauts of the Western Pacific*, both hugely influential books that helped reorient the practice of anthropology.

In his book, Radcliffe-Brown developed ideas about social structure and social relations. He believed that social patterns and practices were the fundamental basis for the study of anthropology, and while his theories, sometimes called "structural functionalism," have been hotly debated, there is no doubt that they formed a crucial foundation of twentieth-century social anthropology. Insofar as Radcliffe-Brown treated art and material culture in his book, he did so from a functionalist point of view. He put his consideration of the material culture of the Andaman Islanders in an appendix at the back. As Anthony Alan Shelton describes it, *Andaman Islanders* ushered in a new era in which "museums were abandoned to material culture studies, most of which amounted to little more than descriptive accounts of technical processes or compendia of material systems."[16] Likewise, Malinowski was also interested in the immaterial aspects of culture rather than its material manifestations, and he is credited with moving anthropologists out of their armchairs and into the ethnographic field. As they went, academic anthropologists walked away from museum exhibits, and as a result, those exhibits reflected increasingly outdated anthropological thinking.

Collier and Tschopik did not present an entirely bleak picture of museum anthropology. They concluded their essay with a set of questions designed to help redefine the relationship between museums and the discipline of anthropology, covering research, theory, and teaching. In their reformulation, Collier and Tschopik revealed that the epistemological relationship between objects and anthropological knowledge had changed. In contrasting the mode of the exhibit with the mode of the book, they asserted "that exhibits, through their visual appeal, excite interest and imagination, and offer experiences not found in books. Even if exhibits can never tell the whole story—and this has not been demonstrated because it has never been attempted—they reach many persons who will not read the kinds of books we are talking about."[17] In searching for a revived role for museums in anthropology, Collier and Tschopik acknowledged that the book, not the object, was the primary medium through which to convey anthropological knowledge and that the real importance of exhibits was to reach the public, not the professional. So it went, and by 1987, most anthropologists, I suspect, agreed with Kenneth Hudson when he observed that "it is quite possible that the day of the ethnographic museum has already gone."[18] William Sturtevant had put the question bluntly in a 1969 essay that appeared in the *Proceedings of the Biological Society of Washington*: "Does anthropology need museums?"[19] For most postwar academic anthropologists, at any rate, the answer was no.

At just about this moment, anthropology's subjects decided they had had enough, and in a variety of ways and at a variety of levels they called into question the fundamental assumptions of cultural and social anthropology. These might be crudely summarized under three related headings: the challenge to ethnographic authority, the rejection of the "otherness" implicit in notions of the "primitive," and the exploration of the relationship between anthropology and colonialism. This wide-ranging critique has generated a tremendous amount of scholarship and inquiry, much of it penetrating and profound, some of it merely hand-wringing, and it is not my intention to review this literature here.[20]

For our purposes, this challenge to the very legitimacy of the anthropological discipline by the subjects of its research meant that whatever epistemological authority still remained with anthropological objects—not to mention their public role in museum exhibits—was undermined still further. The postcolonial, subaltern challenge to the practice of anthropology, and to its presentation in museums, has left a set of questions that remain contentious. In short, having collected all those objects, what should museums do with them? What can be done with them that is both intellectually honest and politically acceptable? As nicely summarized by Saloni Mathur: "How should an anthropology museum present itself and construct its knowledge? How should it conceive of its relation to its own past? What kinds of narratives—personal, scientific, political, art historical—function to produce meaning in ethnographic objects? And how do we assign value to objects across the social hierarchies of different cultural worlds?"[21] That Mathur posed these questions in 2000 only underscores how difficult and thorough the

critique of the anthropology museum has been. The period of confusion over what to do with anthropological objects has now lasted about
as long as the period during which museums felt confident about how
to display them.

The fate of anthropological objects in museums in the last quarter of
the twentieth century was varied. In some natural history museums—
and remember that this is where a vast amount of this material resides—
anthropology has become something of an embarrassment, the relative
no one wants to have at Thanksgiving dinner. At the American Museum
of Natural History, where public programming remained vibrant
through those decades, anthropology was regarded intellectually
as a second-class citizen. After all, the very notion that varieties of non-
Western people should be classed as "natural history" is a central part
of the complaint against anthropological collections in the first place.
So in many ways and in many places these collections and exhibits have
languished as the staff at natural history museums have been unsure
exactly what to do with all this material, and cultural anthropologists
have offered little by way of advice. John Terrell, a curator of anthropology at the Field Museum, wrote bitterly in 1991 that anthropology was
simply being ignored at the third largest natural history museum in the
country. Sardonically he complained, "Not long ago, in fact, it looked
like anthropology as a scientific department at the Field Museum might
be phased out, possibly even thrown out. Rumor had it that curators in
other departments had actually started to carve up our office space."[22]

Thorny political and intellectual questions about how to present
anthropology using objects may contribute to another dilemma facing
natural history museums, and the Field is exemplary of it. Museums have
always fretted about the number of visitors they get each year, but never
more so than now, when corporate sponsorships and grant money are
often tied to gate receipts and while public money for museums has
dwindled. The Field scored a coup some years ago when it purchased
"Sue," the largest, most complete *Tyrannosaurus rex* fossil yet uncovered,
and made her the center of a new exhibit and an aggressive marketing
campaign. Dinosaurs pack the crowds in, and it is hard to imagine the
anthropological analogue to Sue. For the staff in accounting and marketing, the question is whether anyone could design an anthropological
"blockbuster." For the curatorial staff, the question is what such a blockbuster would look like. And for the public relations staff, the question is
what kind of angry response would that blockbuster create? In the
absence of answers to these questions, or to the more basic question of
what can and should be done to exhibit anthropological objects, some
natural history museums find themselves tending collections many probably wish they did not own. Indeed, as I discuss in the next chapter, the

repatriation of anthropological objects out of museums has given some museums a new sense of purpose.

While the discipline of anthropology moved away from objects in the middle years of the twentieth century and toward concerns about kinship and structuralism, not all anthropological objects have languished. Some have jumped categories, ceasing to be artifacts and becoming art instead. In his energetic 1972 novel *Mumbo Jumbo,* Ishmael Reed imagined a shadowy organization called the Mu'tafikah dedicated to rescuing non-Western art objects from big Western art museums, which they called "centers of art detention." This conspiratorial assault on the temples of Western culture in the name of third-world liberation makes for a terrific novel and was entirely of its political moment when it came out in 1972. But as a piece of cultural analysis, it got the situation backward. Anthropological artifacts are not fleeing the art museum; instead those objects have moved decisively into the category of "art."

As early as 1956, the Philadelphia Commercial Museum opened an exhibit of African "art" featuring objects it had collected from ethnographic exhibits at various world's fairs, just at the moment when Collier and Tschopik and Kroeber were considering the fate of the anthropological museum. Still, it is probably fair to say that the installation of the Rockefeller collection in the Metropolitan in 1982 exemplifies this transformation as dramatically as any single museum event.[23] The collection, after all, began its museum life as the Museum of Primitive Art, founded in 1954. The Met had no collection of objects from Africa, Oceania, or the Americas, or any interest in them, until 1969. At that charged moment, Nelson Rockefeller offered the museum his entire collection, and a new forty-thousand-square-foot wing, named for his son Michael, was built to house it.

The creation of the Rockefeller Wing was not the first time an American museum treated "primitive" objects like pieces of Western art, but that hardly matters. Where the Met goes, other museums will follow—and many have. The result has been a two-part transformation of the way these objects are treated in the museum context. First, and most obviously, the objects are selected for aesthetic, rather than cultural or scientific, reasons. They are displayed—often with dramatic lighting—in ways that stress the formal aspects of each piece. As art, the objects are presented to us as beautiful, and so they unarguably are. The second transformation is more subtle, more complicated, and more equivocal. If "art" objects draw their power, to return to Kopytoff, from their singularity, as anthropology objects they functioned as synecdoches for cultures that were understood to be "organic" and unified. In the museum setting, anthropological objects drew their epistemological power from being the opposite of singular, from their ability to mirror, more or less

Figure 6. Anthropology as art. The Metropolitan Museum of Art's Michael Rockefeller Wing, Oceanic Art Gallery opened in 1982. Courtesy of The Metropolitan Museum of Art. Image © The Metropolitan Museum of Art.

effectively, the whole of the culture that produced them. Treating them as art attempts to imbue them with some of Benjamin's aura, though the "historical testimony" often remains incomplete or is lacking altogether. Yet at the same time, the objects are still asked to stand in for the peoples from which they came. A heavy burden for any object to bear.

The blurring boundary between art and artifact has also been much discussed in recent years and was even the title of an influential show of African objects mounted by curator Susan Vogel. Called "ART/artifact," the show opened in 1988 and received a great deal of attention. The critical response, both to that show and to the wider phenomenon of treating anthropological objects as art, has been decidedly mixed—one particularly aggressive review of "ART/artifact" began with an epigraph from Georges Bataille: "The origin of the modern museum is thus linked to the origin of the guillotine," which certainly didn't bode well for anyone going to the show or, for that matter, reading the review. Arthur Danto derisively described the Rockefeller Wing as "failed" and accused it of looking like a "detached segment of Bloomingdale's" in its display strategy. Others have complained that treating non-Western objects this way amounts to yet one more cultural appropriation, this time by art culture "consumers" rather than by anthropologists.[24] Analyzing and admiring objects for their formal qualities is historically a Western art practice, after all, that dates back at least as far as Heinrich Wöfflin.

These reactions to one side, however, "art" would seem to be the category where more and more anthropological objects are headed, regardless of the problems inherent in designating them as such. That category represents if not a solution then at least a truce in the political fights over non-Western objects in the museum. In reclassifying objects from anthropology to art, the assumption is that we, as Westerners, will appreciate both the objects and the makers of those objects in the way that we value our own history and traditions. Indeed, accompanying this shift in categories has been, especially over the last generation, the emergence of an art historical apparatus analogous to that which developed for Western art in the nineteenth century. Anthropologist Ira Jacknis has noted the "growing interrelation between anthropology and art history. While anthropology has continued to supply the data and much of the basic approach for the study of these artifacts, as they have been considered more and more as art, the categories and approaches of art history have come to influence scholarly discourse."[25] These objects may get their historical testimony yet.

Thus, when the Smithsonian inherited a private collection of African objects in 1979, it built a new museum for them. When that museum opened in 1987 it was called the National Museum of African Art, and pointedly not the National Museum of African Anthropology. Brooklyn now boasts a Museum of Contemporary African Diasporan Art, and so it goes, whether in older art museums or in new institutions. "Art" is what this material is now called. It is certainly the case that at these places, and in installations and special exhibits in older, more established art museums, attempts have been made to put objects in their anthropological context, as, for example, at the Met's show of African masks, which connected them to religious practice and spirituality. Even so, art, in the absence of any more satisfactory space, is the categorical apotheosis that any object could hope to achieve, and this shift from anthropology to art demonstrates just how expansive the notion of art has become and just how firmly art objects and thus art museums roost atop our cultural hierarchy.

Another solution to the problems embodied by and in anthropological objects that has emerged since the 1980s has been to let non-Western groups have more control over those objects, either inside the museum as curators or curatorial consultants, or more dramatically by repatriating museum objects back to their "original owners." I will have more to say about repatriation in the next chapter, but for now suffice it to note that these two developments are related, not only because of the political context out of which they grew but because they share the same intellectual assumptions being made about "ownership" and "authority," assumptions that connect, in some unsettling ways, culture and biology.

The practice of collaboration between museums and indigenous communities began to percolate, as far as I can tell, in the 1980s and has become increasingly common. In the United States, "A Time of Gathering: Native Heritage in Washington State," the 1989 exhibition at the Thomas Burke Museum at the University of Washington, stands among the earliest examples of a museum show put together with the extensive involvement of a Native advisory board, and the show was widely praised both for the effort and for the results. Coincidentally, 1989 was the same year that Congress chartered the National Museum of the American Indian (NMAI) and authorized its new museum on one of the last pieces of prime real estate on the National Mall.

NMAI opened in 2004 to decidedly mixed reviews (full disclosure: I wrote a particularly sharp review of the museum).[26] I won't repeat all those responses here. Rather, for our purposes, NMAI embodies all the confusions over what to do with anthropological objects in the twenty-first-century museum. It also demonstrates that filling the space that George Brown Goode called *Kulturgeschichte* remains problematic.

The genealogy of NMAI traces back to the Heye Collection, the largest private collection of Native American material ever assembled. That collection has its own tortured history of efforts to find a museum home, and NMAI would seem to be its final and best resting place. NMAI also garnered considerable attention for its decision to use "community curators" to help shape the exhibits. That decision responded to the widespread feeling among Native groups that they have always been "portrayed from the outside," as one of the video talking heads at the museum puts it, and provided instead "our way of looking at Native American history."

Except that it doesn't. That there is a Native historical consciousness, cosmology, or epistemology different from the Western version of those things is simply asserted at NMAI; it is never demonstrated or even argued. In this sense, NMAI stands as a monument to what the historical geographer David Lowenthal, writing mostly about the English situation, has dubbed "the heritage industry." In his description, heritage is not simply "history-lite," though it certainly is that. More than that, however, heritage recasts the past as something always warm and fuzzy, something to be celebrated, and most of all something never to be questioned or challenged by anyone outside the group whose heritage we are celebrating. The heritage on display at NMAI translates approximately as "It's an Indian thing; you wouldn't understand." But at an institution trading on all the authority and legitimacy that comes with the Smithsonian, perhaps NMAI has an obligation to make us understand, or at least to try.

The funniest thing that happened on the way from history to heritage at NMAI, however, was that the Heye Collection, and objects altogether, were left by the side of the road. Whatever the efficacy or effectiveness of using Native people to tell "insider" stories, there is no serious attempt to tell those stories with objects. Technology and effects are at the center of NMAI, and where objects are on display they are either aestheticized, as with a wall of projectile points arranged almost as an abstract mosaic, or on view without any explanatory effort, as with a display of gold pieces that makes no distinction between the several cultures that produced them, or are so cluttered as to make it virtually impossible to view them, as with the "Window on the Collection" display that features three thousand artifacts in a corridor outside the main exhibition area. Ironically, the theme around which NMAI organized itself is that Indians are still here—summarized by the museum's gruesome neologism "survivance"—but the objects that might be used to demonstrate the connection between past and present, to give it a three-dimensional, tactile reality, in the exhibits at NMAI have not survived.

Whether through repatriation or in museum strategies that rely on curators from inside a particular group, Kroeber's definitional dilemmas remain for anthropological objects. Classed now as a social science, anthropology finds itself sandwiched between a collision of the social and the scientific. Science demands that these objects be collected, preserved, and studied so that they yield information, regardless of whose feelings did or might get hurt in the process. The "social" part of anthropology's imperative means taking seriously the complicated political questions that underlie those acts. The objects have been caught in the middle.

History, Heritage, Memory, and Objects

History museums abound in the United States. As a group, they may be the most numerous. Most, however, are small, local, and particular: historic house museums or exhibits associated with county historical societies, for example. By my reckoning, only three museum institutions have attempted to give American history the synoptic, encyclopedic treatment that more typically characterized art, natural history, and anthropology museums. In order of their creation, those three are the Mercer Museum in Doylestown, Pennsylvania; Henry Ford's Greenfield Village outside Detroit; and the National Museum of American History on the Mall in Washington, D.C. (The latter began its life as the Museum of History and Technology and changed its name in 1980.)

That should give us pause, given how encyclopedic the goals of art, anthropology, and natural history museums have been. Why could museum builders in New York or Chicago or Denver confidently contemplate building institutions designed to put the whole of the natural world on display, while only Henry Mercer and Henry Ford attempted to build analogous institutions to present the sum of American history?

The answer, at least in part, reflects a problem of historical narrative: What—or whose—story to tell? Nowhere has a so-called master narrative been more thoroughly critiqued, revised, and rewritten than in the field of American history. It is worth noting that most historic house museums—and certainly this is so of the Williamsburg project when it began in 1928—tended to celebrate the lives of great men living in great houses, even if the "greatness" was only local, and the story of great white men doing great military or political deeds no longer passes as the through-line of American history. New actors and new actions have found their way into our historical tales, and as a result of this expansion, virtually no area of the human experience is beyond historicizing.

In fact, as Ellen Fitzpatrick has ably demonstrated, that old-fashioned narrative was never as hegemonic as historians, especially those trained in the 1960s and 1970s, insisted it was. Her research reminds us that historians as far back as the 1880s, when the discipline coalesced into a profession, were interested in questions of labor and economics, in immigrants and slaves, in ordinary rather than extraordinary people, in regional rather than national stories.[27] That said, it is probably also fair to say that more historical voices compete for our attention today than ever before, and, as a consequence, for museum space as well.

Henry Mercer, for his part, thought he had an answer to the narrative dilemma when he established his museum in the years before the First World War. The story of America, he believed, was the story of work, the story of the ordinary people—of European descent, mostly, though Native Americans did interest Mercer—who settled, tamed, and culti-vated the land. His collection, assembled at the turn of the twentieth century, arranged—as it still is—in precise categories, amounts to a nat-ural history of American preindustrial work, a taxonomy of manual labor. So too with Henry Ford, who built a monument to the virtues and verities of the simple life of ordinary working Americans, oblivious to the howling ironies of it all.

Andrew McClellan, in surveying trends in art museums, believes that there have been salutary results from the critique of the museum: "One positive development in recent years has been the emergence of new museums for different publics. As social activism and critical theory have discredited the aesthetic philosophy of the universal survey museum and the rhetorical oneness of the public for art, we now see that no one museum can please, or serve, all of the people all of the time."[28] I see less of this at art museums than McClellan does, but his assertion seems to describe the development of historical museums exactly. While the vast bulk of places that call themselves history museums are local—such as the boyhood home of Ulysses S. Grant, for instance—or military, two other recent developments interest me more. First has been the growth of museums designed to represent specific ethnic/racial groups (some-times in specific locales). Second has been the appearance of museums designed to present specific historical events or phenomena, often asso-ciated with specific constituencies. At the former, oftentimes at least, we can measure the distance between history and heritage; at the latter, we can measure the distance between history and memory. In both reckon-ings we can see the trouble museums have presenting history through objects.

Most major American cities have some version of an African American history museum; Jewish history museums are probably equally common now as well. A growing number of Native tribes have opened their own history museums, the most elaborate and interesting being that built by the Pequot tribe with money from and attached to its Foxwoods Casino in Connecticut. But the ethnically specific museum dates back at least to 1926 when the American Swedish Museum opened in Philadelphia as part of the Sesquicentennial Exposition. A quick and entirely cursory survey reveals since then a Japanese American museum in Los Angeles; a Hellenic Museum in Chicago; the National Czech and Slovak Museum in Cedar Rapids, Iowa; a Ukrainian Museum in Stamford, Connecticut; and a Norwegian American Museum in Decorah, Iowa. These have been joined more recently by the Arab American National Museum that opened in Dearborn, Michigan, in 2006.

This development is not confined to the United States. As exhibit designer and museum consultant Ralph Appelbaum points out, "We can look on every continent and see an upsurge of interest in creating new museums of cultural identity."[29] This upsurge of cultural specificity undoubtedly reacts to the quickening pace of cultural leveling taking place as a result of "globalization." In a loose sense, these museums stand as the institutional analogs to the micronationalisms that have sprung up around the world even as economic and political forces work to bind together nations and whole regions more uniformly. These places surely race against the acceleration of history.

Without being categorical about it, or as sharp as Lowenthal, it is probably fair to say that many of these places elide the distinctions he makes between heritage and history. These museums are intended to endow specific groups "with prestige and common purpose. . . . [They are] created to generate and protect group interests."[30] So, for example, this is the way the American Swedish Museum describes its mission: "The Museum has been dedicated to preserving and promoting Swedish and Swedish-American cultural heritage and traditions for nearly 80 years. The Museum is a place where Swedes, Swedish-Americans, and people of all nationalities who appreciate Swedish contributions to history, art, architecture, music, science and technology can come together." This sounds a great deal like the mission statement of the Arab American National Museum: "The Arab American National Museum's mission is to document, preserve, celebrate, and educate the public on the history, life, culture and contributions of Arab Americans. We serve as a resource to enhance knowledge and understanding about Arab Americans and their presence in the United States."[31]

The similarity of mission is remarkable, and not just because putting Arab American-ness on display is clearly more charged at this cultural and political moment than exhibiting Swedish American-ness. Rather, these statements reveal that for Arabs or Swedes (or Ukrainians or the Japanese) there is a "story of America" to which each group has contributed. Each museum begins, revisionism notwithstanding, from the assumption that there is a master narrative of American history and asks simply that Arabs or Swedes be acknowledged as part of it. These museums, then, are built around the idea of inclusion, even, one hesitates to say, assimilation. They illustrate *e pluribus unum*. They are not built, I think it is fair to say, around collections of objects.

The objects assembled to illustrate the successful "Americanness" of various ethnic groups are eclectic, if predictable. They usually include items associated with the first arrival, objects that demonstrate some cultural influence of the "old country," photographs documenting the early communities of the particular group in the United States, and sometimes perfectly quotidian things that happened to have been owned by an exemplary member of that group. The Arab American National Museum, for example, owns a portable, manual typewriter that was used by the famous journalist Helen Thomas. One wonders whether children viewing this machine in the future will be more astonished by the fact that Helen Thomas once banged on its keys or by the very notion of a manual typewriter.

In this sense, the proliferation of ethnically specific history museums presents us with an irony. While each asserts the presence of a single, particular group, and does so as a strategy of political and cultural empowerment, the message each museum wants to deliver, and the way it deploys objects to deliver that message, turns out to be remarkably the same. It is generally an uncomplicated story of adversity, struggle, and triumph, and because most of these institutions present an insider's version of the story, they tend to be celebratory rather than reflective or analytic. These institutions tend to present the notion of a group "heritage" rather than a group's history. So, for example, while Joseph Scelsa, the founder of the new Italian American Museum in New York's Little Italy, insists that "the museum's mission is to present the whole story, the true story, whatever that story is," he also believes that "there's so little of [the negative] that it shouldn't overshadow everything else."[32] At one level, of course, it is absurd to substitute Swedish objects for Arabic objects, and yet at another level, one could. The story would, by and large, remain unaltered.

In shifting from the fairly stable ground of history to the slipperier ground of heritage and culture, the "pluribus" runs the risk of subdividing into finer and finer parsings. For all its subjectivity and ambiguity, history gives us something shared to know and to debate. It is, or can be, an intellectual common ground. "Culture," as the notion has been used popularly, offers much less such space. Indeed, Emily Dennis Harvey put her finger accidentally on this dilemma as far back as 1971 when she participated in a symposium to discuss how to open up and decentralize museum institutions so they would be more relevant to inner-city residents. Harvey explained the fiery anger the discussions generated: "Culture is, after all, an intensely personal matter."[33] The statement is wonderfully if inadvertently contradictory: culture, if it is to have any meaning at all, cannot be purely personal. It is, whatever its further definition, a social concept. But Harvey's contradiction betrays a central problem with museums devoted to notions of group culture and heritage. If, in the end, I have my culture and you have yours, and if knowledge of that culture resides inside some biological construct of ethnicity or race, it is hard to imagine an institution that could engage us both.

The second and related development in the building of history museums has been the construction of institutions devoted to particular events or to specific ideas. These have been among the most visible museum projects of the last decade or two, and their growth is certainly not limited to the United States. In this country we have seen the Holocaust Museum in Washington, D.C.; the National Underground Railroad Freedom Center in Cincinnati; and the Civil Rights Museum in Memphis. Several other museums of this sort here and abroad are in the works as I write this.

At one level, I think, these museums function more as memorial projects than as museums in the traditional sense. We no longer pay much attention to the more or less static shrines and statues with which we used to commemorate important historical events, and the solemn promises made that in our midst those memorials would serve as a constant reminder to us have largely been broken. As objects themselves, these memorials have lost much of their original power. Memorials work best when they are connected to the living memory of people for whom the event has meaning, and their effectiveness wanes as those memories fade and the number of people with an actual connection to the event declines. Think here of the difference between the way the Vietnam Veterans Memorial in Washington functions today as compared to any number of memorials to the First World War.

Indeed, late in 2006 the National World War I Museum opened in Kansas City. The museum sits next to the city's World War I memorial, a behemoth obelisk 250 feet high. Yet the opening of the museum suggests that even at that size, the memorial was failing to keep the event alive in our memories. As the epochal events of the twentieth century, whether the Great War or the Holocaust, move from the realm of memory into the realm of history, museums replace memorials as the way to ensure—or at least to try to ensure—that we never forget.

As often as not, however, specific historical understanding is not on offer at these museums. In Kansas City, for example, the goal of the museum's organizers is to use World War I as a way of reminding people of the fragility of peace and the cost of war—a perfectly noble and worthwhile objective—but not necessarily the fragility of peace in 1913 or the costs paid at Verdun. The disconnect between what we know about the history of events and what we experience at a museum is even greater in Cincinnati at the National Underground Railroad Freedom Center. There, the antebellum phenomenon we call the Underground Railroad is used as the platform upon which the museum engages a much bigger set of issues related to slavery and freedom, rather than simply an exploration of American slavery and the escape from it to freedom. In its own words, the Center wants "to promote an understanding of the horrors of slavery, the active resistance movements, and the achievement of freedom against the odds." And it certainly succeeds in providing visitors with a sense of the horrors of slavery.

At the same time, however, the Center doesn't make much of an effort to incorporate recent, and even not so recent, scholarship about the phenomenon into its exhibits. In this way, as Edward Rothstein has put it, "the center regularly taps . . . into melodrama and myth": the Underground Railroad as we want to know it rather than as we really do understand it.

Instead, the Center works very hard to make the experience ultimately uplifting. According to its mission statement, the stories here illustrate "courage, cooperation and perseverance in the pursuit of freedom." More than that, by bending the experience toward the "feel good," its mission seems to veer toward self-help. As Director Spencer Crew writes, the Center wants to "encourage every individual to take a journey that advances freedom and personal growth."[34] In the space of a few galleries we have moved from Harriet Tubman to Dr. Phil.

The Freedom Center, the NMAI, and others might best be described as therapeutic museums, places designed to make us better people by moving from the political to the personal. Having grown out of the political impulses of the late 1960s, they address psychic rather than political grievances and promise emotional resolution rather than critical engagement. Toward the end of the Freedom Center's exhibits, visitors enter the "Dialogue Zone," where they can react to the troubling displays they have just seen. They are greeted there, however, not by an educator or interpreter but by a social worker, and they are instructed on the wall: "Avoid terms and phrases which define, demean or devalue others, and use words that are affirmative and reflect a positive attitude." Lois Silverman, who founded the "Museums as Therapeutic Agents" project in Indiana in 1997, has suggested that the "therapeutic potential" of museums be pushed even further and that museums be made more useful to people with a variety of mental health and self-esteem problems. After all, she reminds us, and probably correctly, "museums assume a healthy visitor population."[35]

As C. Vann Woodward noted over a half-century ago, Americans make heavy demands of our history.[36] Writing during the Cold War and in the aftermath of World War II, he had in mind the political uses to which history was being put, and he worried that by constantly appealing to the past as a way of justifying actions in the present Americans evaded having real political debates. In these new history museums we place an additional burden on the past and ask it to make us feel better about ourselves. In describing this goal, Ralph Appelbaum writes: "By including self-questioning and self-criticism in our definition of history—and by including the voices of people who have been wronged or neglected by the dominant forces in history—the museum itself becomes a marvelous, humbling and inspiring artifact of our moral evolution as human beings."[37] In moving as he does from intellectual understanding to the realm of "moral evolution," Appelbaum underscores that these new museums aim for the heart and the spirit more than the mind, and he brings us, inadvertently I suspect, full circle. The old museums too—cathedrals of art and science as they were often called—promised their visitors uplift, bringing them closer to God through great art or through the wonders of the natural world. Now the uplift comes from seeing just how far along we humans have evolved on the moral ladder—from a temple of the muses to a palace of the therapists.

Nor is there necessarily anything wrong with refashioning museums so they become places to confront difficult contemporary dilemmas, though whether or not these new museums will do a more effective job in helping us collectively remember historical events or in making us more virtuous individuals remains to be seen. Either way, the success of these museums does not depend on objects on display, because objects are largely secondary to the museums' strategies. As Noah Shoval and Elizabeth Strom have pointed out, these new museums have themes rather than collections.[38] They want to convey values rather than knowledge, and they use language and images—in various old-fashioned and newer electronic forms—rather than objects to do that.

This impulse to therapy began as a result of the struggle we have already discussed over how to display anthropology. The 1972 *Guide* to the American Museum of Natural History (AMNH) acknowledged that "the Man in Africa hall deals largely with the past." The museum believed that those galleries would "help to give a better understanding of the present by showing the heritage that remains and influences the character of new nations and that, in the New World, gives Afro-Americans an individuality of their own." Somewhat later, describing how natural history museums might deal with their problematic ethnographic collections, the AMNH's Robert Sullivan suggested that displays ought to emphasize "concepts of cultural equity, respect, empathy, empowerment, tolerance and comprehension, and pride," and by 1992 the anthropology halls had been renamed "culture halls."[39] Those might all be worthy goals, but note that neither description of the function of the

AMNH's galleries mentions scientific—that is, anthropological—understanding of other cultures or their connection to the larger world of natural history.

Nor is the unease about the use of objects to do this kind of therapeutic work limited to these heritage centers. In 1969, Stephan F. de Borhegyi thought that the whole problem with anthropology in museums lay with the objects themselves. In trying to imagine a "new role" for anthropology in natural history museums, de Borhegyi complained "that the full potential of the museum in this respect has yet to be realized, largely because museum anthropologists persist in designing displays that are object-oriented rather than concept- or problem-oriented." As the objects themselves—"organized clutter"—receded in importance and were reduced in number, the public who did not "read the kinds of books we are talking about" took center stage.

De Borhegyi described developments then happening at the Milwaukee Public Museum, which proved to be very influential around the museum world. The Milwaukee Public had undertaken an extensive set of visitor surveys to discover exactly how visitors responded to different kinds of exhibits with the goal of designing things people wanted to see. De Borhegyi enthused about the results: "Here, the museum anthropologist and artist might be well advised to take their cue from modern industrial management, which studies the saleability and effectiveness of each new concept or product before putting it on the mass market. . . . These and similar studies made by other museums could become the backbone of future anthropology exhibit planning and programming."[40]

De Borhegyi's report from Milwaukee, coming as it did in 1969, also argued the case for "relevance." "Exhibits should be primarily of topical interest," de Borhegyi insisted, and he provided two pressing examples: "With Vietnam so much in the headlines, special exhibits showing the geography of the country, its native population, its history and ethnology are certainly in order. Similarly, in connection with the social unrest in our country, good exhibits emphasizing the cultural and historical background of our Negro citizens are sorely needed."[41]

Driven as they are by a shared politics, the Freedom Center, the NMAI, and several other such institutions share a similar unease about objects. Perhaps they simply do not have the faith museum builders once did that objects can tell stories in a unique way, and these museums stand as the acknowledgment that objects no longer carry the same explanatory power they once did. Perhaps, conversely, by not making greater use of objects, these museums reveal a certain suspicion that objects might get in the way of telling the stories they want to tell just the way they want to tell them. It is possible that the disappearance of objects from these history museums testifies to the subversive and less controllable epistemological power of objects. Perhaps objects aren't presented in these museums because they can't be trusted.

Which suggests a final irony about the recent development of historical museums. Having grown out of the demands that the hegemony of the conventional historical narrative be broken, these museums have substituted other narratives, equally rigid and unbending, and there is little room for the argument, debate, and polyphony that is the very essence of history itself. As one writer complained after touring the new African American Museum in Detroit, the museum still tells you what to think.[42]

The Objects of Natural Science

In terms of sheer quantity and bulk, more objects reside in natural science museums than in any other kind. I suspect no one knows—or could know—exactly how many specimens have finally come to rest in natural history museums, but that number runs easily into the many millions. According to a 1903 survey, thirty-one American natural science museums had collections greater than seventy-five thousand specimens;[43] by 1981 the AMNH housed an estimated 35 million objects, fewer than 1 percent of which were on display. By 2005, the National Museum of Natural History alone held nearly 125 million objects.

Those remarkable numbers remind us that, just as anthropology began its disciplinary life in the museums, science in the nineteenth century grew up there too. Historians of science have largely ignored this history, according to John Pickstone, because of "their fondness for 'laboratories.'" As Pickstone points out, when Oxford and Cambridge first made institutional investments in science, in the mid-nineteenth century, they did so by building museums. That pattern was true to some extent, at least in the United States. Harvard, under the leadership and prodding of Louis Agassiz, built a museum, and several other colleges and universities amassed scientific collections even if they did not house them in a formal museum. If we add to this the even larger institutions built by nations—in England, France, and the United States, for example—and by philanthropists in American cities like New York and Chicago, it becomes clear that Pickstone is right when he declares the nineteenth century "the great age of 'scientific' museums."[44]

Even if art, anthropology, and natural science objects were all exhibited in approximately the same way in late nineteenth-century museums, by the first quarter of the twentieth century it had become clear that the relationship between museum displays and the biological sciences was changing. In a review written for *Progressive Architecture,* Albert Parr, director of the AMNH, took the opportunity to make a distinction: "A confusion of issues results from the unrestrained partiality for the object-orientation of art museums with total disregard for the message-orientation of other institutions." He went on to point out that in science museums "mutable concepts must take precedence over immutable objects."[45] In his testy way, Parr reminded his readers that while both art museums and science museums collected and displayed objects, they did so in fundamentally different ways.

In thinking about the nature of objects in both kinds of science museums, Kopytoff's notion of singularity doesn't quite suffice, as Parr reminds us. The objects that constituted natural history were collected, organized, and displayed precisely because they were representative rather than singular. Their value came not because they were removed from the dynamic commodity sphere and put into the static sphere of museum but because of their typicality, because one such specimen, for the purposes of the museum, was largely indistinguishable from another. The goal of the natural history museum was to hold up a mirror to creation and radiate a perfect reflection of it. As William Henry Flowers observed a century ago, "It is not the objects placed in a museum that constitute its value, so much as the method in which they are displayed and the use made of them for the purpose of instruction."[46]

Indeed, natural history museums in the late nineteenth century worked very hard to distinguish themselves from the Barnumesque displays of oddities and "monstrosities" common before the Civil War. Writing in 1904, David Murray asserted that the older museum had been "a collection of curiosities . . . there was generally implied in it the idea of strangeness or rarity." When he went on to claim confidently that the museum of 1897, "is far in advance of the museum of 1847," he meant in part the substitution of representativeness for "strangeness or rarity."[47] In other words, visitors were supposed to come to the natural history museum not to see a specific butterfly or fossil trilobite, one that could only be seen in New York or Denver, but rather to see the story of nature made sensible and illustrated with specimens that were more or less interchangeable.

There are a few notable examples of "singular" natural history specimens, specific objects exhibited to draw visitors—the aforementioned T. Rex Sue, the African elephant in the rotunda of the National Museum of Natural History in Washington, D.C., which is billed as the largest such creature ever recorded—whose fame and notoriety are attached to specific biographies, but these would seem to be the exceptions that prove the rule. Scientists continue to use "type specimens," the specimen with which any new species is first identified and described, to categorize new specimens, but there is no particularly compelling visual or educational reason to exhibit type specimens above other examples of the same thing. The point, after all, is that, within species, individuals are all roughly the same, and one mounted bald eagle is as good as any other mounted bald eagle. If, after all, "it is not the objects" that matter but the ideas they illustrate, then perhaps there are better ways to convey those ideas, and natural history museums seem to rely less and less on natural historical objects to do that.

That very goal, in turn, may have contributed to the disappearance of natural history objects from the galleries of these museums across the twentieth century. And disappear they have. Though the holdings of these museums increased almost beyond counting in the twentieth century, far fewer objects were on display in any given gallery at the end of the century than at the beginning. AMNH director Albert Parr, whose own exhibition strategies stressed ideas over objects, lamented the move toward culling objects from the galleries in a 1959 essay: "Elimination, selection, and rigorous prefocusing of attention could ultimately banish from all our halls the excitement of personal discovery. Let us therefore not forget to preserve . . . some wilderness areas among our exhibits."[48]

Likewise, the relationship between objects in natural history museums and the disciplines of the natural sciences is almost exactly the opposite of the relationship between art objects and art history that we discussed earlier. Over the course of the twentieth century, cladistics and systematics moved from the center stage of the life sciences to the wings, and laboratory experiments have replaced collecting expeditions. What Henry Fairfield Osborn of the AMNH called "naked-eye science" became over the twentieth century less important to the production of knowledge in biology and related fields.

As the twentieth century progressed, therefore, the permanent exhibits at natural history museums had greater and greater difficulty keeping up with advancing ideas about science—those "mutable concepts" to which Parr referred. The dioramas that began to appear early in the twentieth century gave visitors a more visually exciting experience than the glass cases that they replaced, but the information those dioramas conveyed went out of date quite quickly. In an ironic twist, the dioramas at the AMNH, to take one example, survive in part because of their aesthetic appeal rather than their scientific presentation.

We should be clear here: many natural history museums continue to engage in active research agendas, though only the very biggest are able to employ large numbers of scientists or sponsor expeditions. And university researchers in several fields continue to rely on the specimens in the storerooms of natural history museums for their work. In the field of paleontology, which has enjoyed a real renaissance over the past generation, university researchers make regular use of museum collections, especially as several universities have divested themselves of their own paleontology specimens. Museums are thus central to this work. But I think it is fair to say that natural history museums simply have not had the resources to keep up with the growth of science in the way that universities have. To claim, as many historians of biology have, that lab science simply replaced museum science in the twentieth century is surely an exaggeration, as John Pickstone points out.[49] Still, it is also fair to say that natural history museums and their collections have had their scientific role greatly reduced as life sciences have moved into the laboratory.

Having said that, however, more recently natural history museums have reemerged as actors in the scientific discussions of what we might broadly call "ecology"—biodiversity, the effects of climate change on species and the global distribution of species, and the interconnected way ecosystems work. As more people become concerned with ecological sciences, and more specifically with the implications of a changing climate, natural history museums are poised to play a central role in the debates, putting them at the very center of some of the most urgent questions of our time.

Or rather their collections—their objects—are poised to play that role.

As several writers have pointed out, measuring and mapping the changes to our biodiversity or the effects of global warming on the planet's flora and fauna requires exactly the information embodied in and by the millions of specimens housed in natural history museums. Indeed, this specimen information exists only in these museums. Leonard Krishtalka and Philip Humphrey of the Natural History Museum at the University of Kansas believe that "museums must immediately harness their vast, authoritative, collection-based information" to better understand what they call "the biodiversity crisis" and to take the "evolutionary and ecological pulse of the earth's . . . 15 million or more species." In this way, Krishtalka and Humphrey write, "natural history museums should be poised to inform the environment management of the planet."[50] Put like that, those dusty specimen drawers and that faint smell of formaldehyde never seemed so important.

Many natural history museums do indeed seem to be moving in these directions. Yet even as they do so, I am struck by two difficulties. First, as I have already mentioned, it is the objects themselves—those specimens stuffed or pickled—that interest ecological and evolutionary scientists. The relationship between those specimens and that work to the public function of the museum has not yet emerged. In this sense, the importance of the museum comes back to its warehouse and storage function rather than its function as a public display of objects. Krishtalka and Humphrey might welcome the development of natural history museums as centers of "biodiversity informatics," but it isn't clear how to make that into a meaningful exhibit.

Second, and more poignantly, the objects preserved in these museums were collected, as we have discussed, because of their "representativeness." As we preside over the destruction of so many environments around the globe, the value of those very same objects comes precisely because of their increasing rarity. In a growing number of cases, those birds and beetles carefully classified and preserved now represent the last best information we have about individual species and about their larger ecological relationships. In the era of global warming, these objects have achieved a grim singularity.

Objects of Technology and Industry

George Brown Goode made a distinction in his conception of science museums between those of natural sciences and those of science and technology. Conceptually, he thought that science and technology could be collected, classed, and displayed in much the same way that art and natural history could. Certainly, such exhibits could illustrate the evolutionary progress of all sorts of things that were reshaping the nineteenth-century world: electricity, steam power, and metallurgy to name just three.

As I examine more fully in Chapter 4, Americans did not build museums of science and technology until the 1920s, long after they had built comprehensive art and natural history museums. Chicago's Museum of Science and Industry and Philadelphia's Franklin Institute Science Museum stand as the first two significant institutions of their kind.

They began their existence at almost exactly the same moment in the 1920s. The former was the brainchild of Chicago industrialist Julius Rosenwald. The latter traced its origins back to the nineteenth century as a mechanic's institute. The connection between those institutes and libraries, working-class educational culture, and the development of technology and engineering in that century remains to be fully written. By the early twentieth century, however, such museums modeled themselves, to a greater or lesser extent, on the Deutsches Museum in Munich. There curators organized exhibits to illustrate the development of different kinds of technology: transportation, mining, metalworking, and so on. "The German museum in Munich," museum director Oskar von Miller described in 1926, "shows the development of the various branches of natural science and technology by means of original apparatus and machines."[51] Following the path laid out at the Deutsches Museum—and by one reckoning, the full tour went for eleven miles!—visitors saw the progressive evolution of technology.[52]

In this way, the museums of science and technology resembled museums of art and natural history, and the objects collected, organized, and displayed in them were to function epistemologically in the same way. As Henry Ford put it, describing the museum at his Edison Institute in Dearborn, "A piece of machinery or any other thing that is made is like a book, if you can read it."[53]

The Munich model did not last long, at least in the United States. As early as the 1930s, the Franklin Institute transformed itself from an institute that used objects to teach into a museum where the line between education and entertainment was often difficult to determine. When the new museum opened on January 1, 1934, visitors were promised no "Do Not Touch" signs and were encouraged to push buttons, pull levers, and in a variety of ways to "interact." When the "Bakelite Travelcade" came through the Franklin Institute, touting the miracles of modern plastics, the ad might well have summed up the new museum ethos: "a year's education in an hour's entertainment."

In the postwar era, museum exhibits in science and technology museums have followed this course almost entirely. While there may still be a handful of the older exhibits, using historical artifacts to illustrate the growth and development of a certain technology, most of the floor space is devoted to interaction and demonstration with the goal of presenting more or less "modern" science. Bernard Finn, a curator at the Smithsonian, noticed this trend in 1965. The science and technology museum, he wrote, "is in effect a large public demonstration laboratory, at about the high school level."[54]

Finn's observations sum up several factors at work in the mid-twentieth-century science and technology museum, all of which are connected to the function of objects in the museum setting. First, the museums have felt a fundamental tension between the history of science and its present and future. The historical approach can be easily illustrated through artifacts, and professional historians of science have been making use of museum collections for some time.[55] Presenting the public with a picture of the current state of various sciences does not necessarily require, and in fact might not be done effectively by, exhibiting "original apparatus and machines." More often than not, the education offered at these museums replaces the history of science with the principles of science, and doing that does not inherently require artifacts.

In fact, several of the most beloved "objects" in these museums were created, rather than collected, for particular displays: the coal mine exhibit at Chicago's Museum of Science and Industry and the giant heart at the Franklin Institute to name two.

Further, conveying knowledge through objects is a visual exercise, and many of these objects simply have no visual appeal. Finn complained

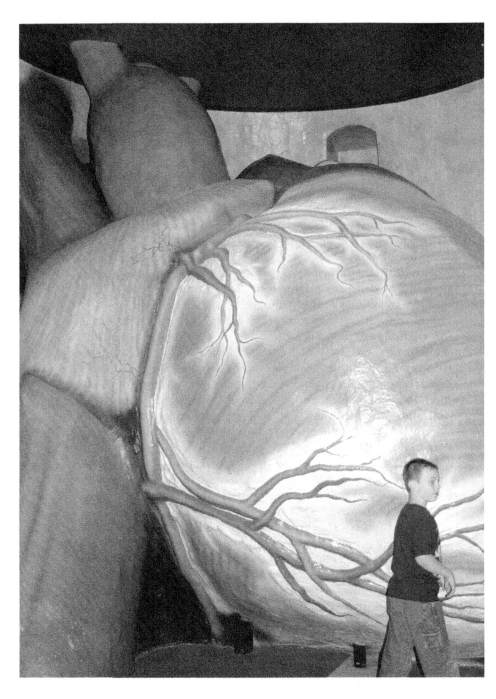

Figure 7. The giant walk-through heart at the Franklin Institute Science Museum. A favorite of generations of museum visitors, can the heart be considered a museum "object"? Photo: Steven Conn.

about what he called "a much greater emphasis on the aesthetics of exhibits" in the science museum and noted that "many important machines and instruments simply are not aesthetically pleasing." He expressed a certain suspicion about this drive to aestheticism and thought that trying to make these exhibits "pretty" would "falsify the record."[56] One suspects that exhibit designers and museum administrators, worried about attracting visitors, weren't entirely moved by this argument.

Besides, if we return one more time to Kopytoff's notion of singularity, the kinds of "original apparatus and machines" that were once displayed more commonly at science and technology museums raise analogous questions to those raised by the butterflies and clamshells over at the natural history museums. If art objects achieve their singularity in a museum because they are removed from a highly specific—and rarified—commodity sphere, and if natural history specimens served because they did not function at all in a commodity sphere, much of what is displayed at science and technology museums comes from a much wider and more familiar world of commodities. Exhibits of communication, transportation, or computer technology are apt to feature consumer objects, and I am not convinced that putting them on display in a technology museum successfully invests them with much aura.

In fact, the timing of the establishment of these museums may also explain the role of objects in them. As I mentioned earlier, museums of science and technology arrived on the cultural landscape fully a generation after other types of museums. By that time, the faith in objects to function educationally and epistemologically was on the wane. These museums were founded just at the moment when museums were no longer conceived of entirely as houses for collections. They represent, then, the first of the museums for which objects have not been entirely necessary.

While the Franklin Institute remained committed to both a public museum and a research institute, most of the other technology museums never had links to disciplines of science and applied science. By the time they arrived on the cultural landscape, American technology museums were not central to the work of physicists or chemists or even engineers.

Finally, we should pause over Finn's quip that the scientific principles being demonstrated at these museums are pitched "at about a high school level." I shall talk a great deal more about the audience for science and technology museums in Chapter 4, but for now suffice it to say that of all the shifts to have taken place at science museums over the last half-century none has been more dramatic than the shift in audience from adults to children. By anyone's best guess, children under the age of sixteen now make up two-thirds to three-fourths of those who come to science museums each year, as a result of the changing notion of the museum's educational mission, the demands made on museums by funders and other agencies, and the perceived inadequacies of science education in our schools.

For our purposes, this influx of children into museums forces us to ask a set of very basic questions about museum objects: Does their power, whatever that may be, affect children differently than adults? Do children interact with objects in fundamentally different ways, and how? At the end of the day, do kids care much about an object's singularity or its aura, and do they derive different meanings from it for different reasons?

So, Do Museums Still Need Objects?

If the first golden age of museums took the centrality of objects and collections for granted, our second golden age does not. Further, the connection between museums and their objects, and the production of knowledge using those objects, has grown more tenuous. Certainly some museums have added more space to give their existing galleries room to breathe, but on the whole visitors see far fewer objects now than they did a century ago. For some museums, collections are only secondary to their institutional mission. At others, objects are almost irrelevant to what the museum wants to do and how it does it.

In fact, as museums—and other cultural infrastructure as well—are linked more and more to civic identity and economic development—and more about this in Chapter 6—museums have become objects in and of themselves, studied, admired, and used in a variety of ways that may or may not involve the objects inside them.

This would suggest that collections of objects have lost some of the visual and epistemological power they seemed to have during that first generation of museum building. At the same time, however, more and more people are collecting more and more objects, creating typologies and taxonomies of everything from beer cans to Star Wars figurines. Writing in 1890, one Mrs. Montiesor told her readers, "Every house ought to possess a 'museum,'" and that seems to be more and more the case.[57] A century or so later, one has only to visit the flea markets, "collectibles" conventions, and eBay to see that people are still drawn to the collection of objects, even while the relationship between objects and categorical knowledge may have changed.

It is easy enough to conclude that the changing demands made on museums, the reevaluation of their mission and purpose, has meant shifts in the way objects are deployed inside them. Museums perform important civic and social functions as well as exhibitionary ones. And as those social roles expand, in many cases, objects have been crowded out.

Taking on these roles is one way museums hope to remain "relevant" in a media-saturated, hyperconsumer society. Providing jazz concerts, movie screenings, and happy hours, museums attempt to compete for entertainment dollars. By building whole museums around issues or "themes," institutions hope to tap into some sense of contemporary political relevance. In either case, objects can be seen as stodgy and inert. There are risks here, surely, for museums. The line that separates relevant from irrelevant, urgent from out-of-date, often gets crossed pretty quickly, and museums that invest too much in an easy sort of relevance may find it hard to keep up.

Whatever else can be said of them, objects endure. And in that endurance they offer people the simple pleasure of looking at and the thrill of being in the presence of real things, made by human hands through time and across space or fashioned by nature in all its astonishing variety. Museums filled with objects may provide an education or lessons in moral uplift, but perhaps more than anything they offer the opportunity to see things in three dimensions—things that are beautiful or odd or horrifying or consoling. Museums—some of them anyway—may not need objects anymore, but without objects we all may miss the delights and surprises that come with looking.[58]

Chapter 2
Whose Objects? Whose Culture? The Contexts of Repatriation

In the previous chapter I charted the changing—that is, diminishing—role of objects in different museums across the twentieth century. In this chapter I extend that discussion and observe that the museums built in the late nineteenth and early twentieth centuries were conceived of as great encyclopedias of knowledge and great storehouses of objects. They were built for and around great collections: art pieces, anthropological artifacts, natural history specimens. Museums were the end result and logical extension of a process of collecting, classifying, and cataloguing that defined much of the scientific outlook of the nineteenth century. A century later, as I have previously remarked, objects are no longer as central to the conception and function of the museum.

In addition, the diminished role of objects in museums comes at a moment when museum objects, albeit in small numbers, have started to leave museums. Broadly speaking, they are exiting by two doors. Through one, some museum objects—art primarily—now find themselves for sale on the open market. They are put there in some cases by institutions in genuine financial crises, such as Fisk University and Randolph Macon Women's College, and in others by institutions that see these objects simply as liquidatable assets. In an example of the latter situation, Thomas Eakins's masterpiece *The Gross Clinic* was sold in 2007 by Thomas Jefferson University for a record sum, about which I will say more in Chapter 6.

The other door is marked "repatriation." Some of the examples of this phenomenon, such as certain antiquities at the Metropolitan and the J. Paul Getty Museum and the artifacts from Machu Picchu now on their way back to Peru from Yale University's Peabody Museum, have made international headlines (and police reports). Most repatriations in the United States, however, have happened quietly and without incident, under the process established by the Native American Graves Protection and Repatriation Act (NAGPRA). Thus objects once assumed to have found their final resting place in the collections of museums now find themselves uprooted and relocated.

Either method of exit raises its own set of tricky questions that deserves to be taken seriously. No one would deny, for example, that Fisk University needed the cash. As one of the oldest and most distinguished of America's "traditionally black colleges," where does its institutional responsibility lie: in raising operating money or in preserving the collection of art entrusted to it by artist Georgia O'Keeffe in 1949? I, for one, do not envy Fisk's trustees in sorting that out. In cases like these, however, art objects are seen to have a monetary value. There is a market into which the object can go—out of which it perhaps once came—and thus, like any commodity, its monetary value is fixed by the workings of that market.

Repatriation cases raise a different though equally vexing set of issues. At one level, objects in repatriation cases are treated like children in custody battles between parents. At another level, those objects serve as proxies for fights over larger issues involving imperialism and the legacy of conquest, the nature of how native and non-Western people can be represented by Western institutions, and the very question of whether or not "culture" can be owned, and by whom and under what circumstances. Repatriation demands that ethical issues be translated into workable legal frameworks. Objects sit at the uncomfortable intersection of law and justice.

That intersection has been well examined and debated by scholars of various stripes, and while I will review some of those debates in the pages that follow, it will not be my primary focus here. Instead, I want first to examine the political context out of which NAGPRA emerged and the political claims made for it by its supporters and then, second, to explore repatriation within the intellectual context of anthropology, to trace the relationship between anthropological ideas of "culture" and cultural objects, and to see how repatriation makes objects valuable, not in a monetary sense, but rather in a cultural sense.

Return of the Natives, Return to the Natives? The Politics behind Repatriation

Until the 1980s, the term *repatriation* referred almost exclusively to the return of people to their homelands. Though the word itself can be traced back to the seventeenth century, the twentieth-century experiences of imperialism and particularly war put the word into more common usage. In the aftermath of the Second World War, when millions of people found themselves in the wrong place, repatriation became a subject of international deliberation among diplomats, generals, and humanitarians.

Insofar as anthropologists concerned themselves with repatriation, their attention also centered on the movement and dislocations of people. So, for example, anthropologist Barbara Gallatin Anderson described the experience of "culture shock" in a 1971 article: "Culture shock is a phenomenon associated generally with a culture change cycle that terminates not with a successful rooting in a new culture but with a final re-transplantation back to the mother culture. Except in cases of emigration the cycle terminates in repatriation."[1] Repatriation was of particular interest to anthropologists who studied migratory labor patterns or the problems facing refugee populations. In 1982, to take another example, David Howell sketched out a role for anthropology in shaping the policies of refugee resettlement for readers of *Anthropological Quarterly*.

By the 1980s, however, that which could be repatriated was growing to include objects as well as people. My own sense of this expansion is that the usage of the term began with archaeologists, fittingly enough, because they deal with objects as a matter of course. In an essay pointing us "Toward a Critical Archaeology," Mark Leone, Parker Potter, and Paul Shackel thought that this new notion of repatriation might help archaeologists rethink how they went about their business. "A further encouragement to explore a reflexive epistemology," they wrote, "is the growing controversy in archaeology over ownership and control of remains and interpretations of the past. The reburial of human remains and the 'repatriation' of some artifacts to native groups may be a political issue as well as a scientific one."[2] Notice, tellingly, that the scholars put *repatriation* in quotes, signaling the novelty and awkwardness of using the term in this altered way.

In 1988 James Faris, in an angry review of the controversial exhibit of African objects "ART/Artifact" I mentioned in the previous chapter, blasted the exhibit organizers for treating "imperialist plunder and anthropological rationalism rather as historical matter of fact." He further complained that the exhibit was "silent" on the question of repatriation.[3] Whether or not Faris's critique was fair or simply hyperbolic, it signaled that after 1988, or thereabouts, no exhibit of non-Western objects—nor any museum that housed them—could remain silent on that question of repatriation.

In 1990 the World Archaeological Congress adopted a resolution calling for "mutual respect for the beliefs of indigenous people as well as the importance of science and education" as a foundation for the negotiations over repatriation that were likely to occur in the future. Thus, by the end of the twentieth century, while the population of displaced people around the globe remained staggeringly high, repatriation, at least in certain circles, had come to mean the return of objects to their original locales. At the same time, in 1990, the United States Congress passed NAGPRA, and repatriation claims on objects and human remains now had a legal framework and process, at least under certain circumstances and conditions.

Even before the act was passed, several museums had already adopted voluntary repatriation practices, notably the Field Museum and the Smithsonian, but NAGPRA certainly put repatriation foursquare on the museum agenda. NAGPRA has created an extraordinary access to museum collections and in that sense has opened up the museums—especially museum basements—in unprecedented ways. At the same time, museum staff and Native groups have complained about the process of pursuing repatriation claims established by NAGPRA, which many on both sides find burdensome and slow.

The much deeper questions raised by NAGPRA and repatriation play out in the bureaucracy. The law requires a petitioning group to establish a cultural affiliation with the material being requested for return. That affiliation can be established on the basis of geography, oral history tradition, or ethnographic records. This begs the following questions: How is oral history to be evaluated? How are ethnographies to be used? Haven't the boundaries of cultural geography changed over time? And why should the use a cultural group makes of its objects trump the other uses a museum might make of them?

Without debating the merits of NAGPRA—whole books have been devoted to that topic—let me turn to the political context out of which it came and the political claims that have been made for it.[4] NAGPRA, and repatriation more generally, has often been cast as a political victory on the cultural front, both for tribal sovereignty against the nation-state and as a Native American example of, in the word now most in vogue among American academics, *resistance.*[5] When the *New York Times Magazine* ran a cover story on the Yale/Machu Picchu controversy, it cleverly titled the piece "The Reconquest," suggesting an analogy between the repatriation of Incan artifacts and the history of imperial conquest in Peru.[6]

Jack F. Trope and Walter R. Echo-Hawk described NAGPRA as the culmination of "decades of struggle by Native American tribal governments and people to protect against grave desecration, to repatriate thousands of dead relatives or ancestors, and to retrieve stolen or improperly acquired religious and cultural property for Native owners." They believe, and the view is widely shared, that NAGPRA "represents fundamental changes in basic social attitudes toward Native people by the museum and scientific communities and the public at large."[7]

That is undoubtedly correct at one level. Repatriation has been on the Native American agenda for at least several decades. NAGPRA represents a culmination of sorts of those efforts, conditioned by a resurgent Native American presence in the majoritarian culture. Since the late 1960s, activists, academics, and even Hollywood producers have successfully repositioned Native America in the larger American imagination. Groups such as the American Indian Movement (AIM), effective lobbying by the National Congress of American Indians, books such as *Bury My Heart at Wounded Knee*, and movies such as *Little Big Man* have all contributed to this reorientation of public attitude. That moment also corresponds to a shift in federal policy toward Native groups. After a set of mid-twentieth-century policies, sometimes dubbed "Termination and Relocation," the 1970s brought a somewhat greater degree of tribal autonomy and self-determination, at least in areas such as education and social services.[8] The successful passage of NAGPRA surely resulted from those activities and from those changes in opinion and policy.

But at another level, NAGPRA emerged in and as part of trends in the mainstream of American life, some of which I see as, if not quite conservative, surely ironic. Instead of seeing NAGPRA only as a triumph of resistance by tribal governments and Native activists, we also need to examine other contexts out of which NAGPRA grew if we are to understand it fully. I want to look at four in an effort to answer the question, why did the NAGPRA legislation finally succeed when it did?

The first of these contexts is legal. There is an international legal genealogy to NAGPRA, and it has been well charted by the legal scholar John Henry Merryman, among others. As he points out, the protection of cultural objects, like the repatriation of people, also grew from the experience of the Second World War. The 1954 Hague Convention gathered to assess the physical damage caused by the war and to draft guidelines about what constituted acceptable and unacceptable destruction during wartime. The preamble to the Hague Convention began with a conclusion: "[We are] convinced that damage to cultural property belonging to any people whatsoever means cultural damage to the heritage of all mankind, since each people makes its contribution to the culture of the world." As Merryman points out, this is a notion of collective rather than individual "ownership," and as such it was entirely of a piece with the universalizing impulses that ran high in the mid-twentieth century. Interestingly, the United States never ratified the 1954 convention.[9]

In 1970, the United Nations Educational, Scientific, and Cultural Organization (UNESCO) revisited the question of cultural property, driven this time not by the fear of wartime destruction but by the fear of an equally rapacious international art market. The preamble to UNES-

CO's 1970 convention, in Merryman's words, "emphasizes the interests of states in the 'national cultural heritage.'" Gone now was the notion, fuzzy to be sure, that "all mankind" owns a shared cultural heritage, replaced with the more definite, though no less problematic, idea that ownership resides in the nation where a particular object was located when its very ownership became contentious in the first place. To quote Merryman again, "The premises of the repatriation movement are a logical extension of those that underlie UNESCO 1970: cultural property belongs in the source country; works that now resided abroad in museums are wrongfully there . . . and should be 'repatriated.'" UNESCO replaced a notion of "cultural internationalism" with a notion of "cultural nationalism."[10] And while the United States did not ratify the 1954 Hague Convention, it did help draft UNESCO's 1970 document.

As Merryman's observations suggest, NAGPRA fits squarely within the view the American government has always held regarding the question of cultural property since the end of the Second World War. The United States has placed a greater emphasis on national sovereignty than on international cooperation, and in this sense NAGPRA extends the notion of the nation-state to federally recognized Native tribes. Yet, at the same time, rather than seeing NAGPRA only as a triumph of resistance by tribal governments against the federal government, we could see it as the extension of long-held federal principles over those institutions within the United States that receive federal money. In the international arena, the United States has always supported— again in Merryman's words—"retentive cultural nationalism." NAGPRA is descended exactly from the impulses behind UNESCO's 1970 document; NAGPRA made that support intranational as well. This does not make NAGPRA any less significant—indeed, by recognizing repatriation claims, NAGPRA does recognize a degree of tribal sovereignty, at least in this cultural realm—but it ought to make us skeptical that as a piece of legislation it represents a dramatic political reorientation.

Trope and Echo-Hawk also point to a second irony behind the politics of resistance allegedly represented by NAGPRA. This one revolves around the very notion of how to define "ownership." To announce, through UNESCO or NAGPRA, that cultural property belongs to a group that can demonstrate geographic or lineal descent to the group that "owned" the material originally only raises an additional set of difficult questions about how to determine those relationships. To put the matter simply, ownership claims under NAGPRA rest on a combination of geographic and/or genealogical connections.

The first of these connections relies on the assumption of historical stasis—we have always been here, thus material on this site belongs to us—which would seem to deny the processes of historical and cultural movement and change. The latter connections, in which ownership of "culture" is found in genetics, strike me as particularly troubling, as they risk leading us back to nineteenth-century notions of racial essentialism.

Those notions saw categories of race as fixed and determined entirely by "blood" and held that race, defined through this pseudobiology, determined culture. Whites had intellect because they were white, blacks had rhythm because that was their "race" characteristic, and so on through any number of preposterous examples. These ideas, of course, have been thoroughly discredited as far back as Franz Boas. The anthropologist Edward Sapir, writing in 1924, already sounded impatient with this racialized essentialism: "The current assumption that the so-called 'genius' of a people is ultimately reducible to certain inherent hereditary traits of a biological or psychological nature does not, for the most part, bear very serious examination. Frequently what is assumed to be an innate racial characteristic turns out on closer study to be the resultant of purely historical causes."[11] Few, I suspect, would argue with that, and yet the premise underlying repatriation does motion back in the direction of those discredited ideas that link cultural traits with biological heredity.

Laws in southern states that defined blackness through some percentage of "blood" have now been repealed, though only recently in certain places. The situation for Native Americans is more complicated, because the federal government still relies on blood quantum to determine membership in federally recognized tribes. Many Native Americans can pull their CDIB (certificate of degree of Indian blood) card out of their wallets even today.[12] NAGPRA, therefore, simply codifies this racial essentialism still further by continuing to rely on the malodorous equation between blood and culture. Even more dispiriting, however, some Native American supporters of NAGPRA seem to have embraced this equation enthusiastically.

That embrace has occasionally led to perfectly predictable if still intellectually indefensible assertions about who can be an Indian and who can't. So, for example, James Riding In, a self-identified Pawnee, insisted that all "real" Indians ipso facto support repatriation policies, and he denounced any Indian who might oppose them:

Imperial archaeologists have had substantial levels of support from real and pretend Indians. The phenomena of co-optation and self-interest reverberates [*sic*] loudly here. Usually found working in museums, universities, and government agencies, some of these individuals claim a heritage complete with a Cherokee princess, but they embrace the secular views and values of Western science. Others belonging to this camp clearly have significant amounts of Indian blood, but they rely heavily on the goodwill of their non-Indian colleagues to promote and maintain their careers. . . . Whatever their motive, degree of Indian blood, or cultural orientation, their willingness to endorse oppressive archaeological practices marks a radical departure from traditional Indian philosophy.[13]

A statement like this raises a further set of questions: How can we tell who "clearly" has "significant amounts of Indian blood" and who does not? Who gets to be the arbiter of "real" and "pretend" Indians? And if you happen to disagree with Riding In, does that mean you can't be a "real" Indian? What happens if one "traditional Indian philosophy" contradicts another over the question of repatriation? We are far too close, certainly for my comfort, to returning to the discourse of quadroons and octoroons.

And these problems only grow stickier with the age of the contested material. How far back into the historical past, or even the prehistoric past, can NAGPRA claims reach? Is it simply enough to demonstrate some genetic connection to human remains that are five hundred, one thousand, or five thousand years old in order to assert ownership? Is there a statute of limitations for the ownership of cultural material, and if so, where on the historical time line does it expire? After all, Native Americans are originally descended from Asiatic groups: Does that provide enough genetic connection to allow Siberian tribes to make repatriation claims?

The reaffirmation of blood quantum and the recourse to the discourse of "blood" by some Native Americans is, it seems to me, part and parcel of the new biological essentialism in mainstream American culture built around advances in genetic testing. Henry Louis Gates Jr. invites famous African Americans to have themselves genetically tested to determine where they come from in a biological sense; talk show hosts stage teary-eyed reunions between adopted children and their "real," that is genetic, parents; many of us are convinced that our medical problems are genetically based rather than the result of behavioral or environmental factors. Genetics is now destiny in the minds of many Americans, and if it determines our future, why not allow it to make claims on the past? NAGPRA thus participates in a larger cultural drift which moves science into the realm of culture.

Riding In also points to a third issue at the heart of NAGPRA that resonates with rather than resists the mainstream of American culture at the turn of the millennium. Sneering at those pretend Indians who hold "secular values," Riding In reminds us that NAGPRA gives "sacred" and "religious" material a high priority in repatriation claims. Archaeologist Rick Hill, for example, believes that "the integrity of American Indian religious practices must be taken into account. Museums must examine their legal and moral responsibilities to ensure the preservation of American Indian culture where it still exists." He continues: "Museums know that there is a spiritual relationship between Native Americans and the objects they created or they would not be interested in collecting the objects in the first place. Their own research describes the emotional, spiritual, and cultural importance of ritual objects to Native American identity."[14]

The demands for the return of skeletal remains and cultural objects associated with religious practice stem from the long and grim experience Native Americans have had of religious intolerance, suppression, and oppression from the federal government and from any number of Christian churches and missionary groups. Yet it strikes me as more than coincidental that the repatriation movement—with religious material at its center—gained traction in the 1980s precisely when a newly virulent right-wing fundamentalism, with Ronald Reagan at its head, began to force religion into public life at a host of levels. The litany of these intrusions is familiar and disturbing: the restrictions on abortion, contraception, and gay marriage; the use of public facilities for private religious practice; and the neocreationist movement that has played havoc with school curricula in a number of states. We now live in a society where clothing political demands in religious robes has become a remarkably effective strategy. I don't mean to suggest for a moment that Native American repatriation matters much at all to right-wing religious fundamentalists, but I do think NAGPRA needs to be seen as having emerged in this context of renewed religiosity.

Vine Deloria Jr., perhaps our most distinguished Native American scholar-activist, hinted at this dilemma in a somewhat tortured essay titled "Secularism, Civil Religion, and Religious Freedom." Deloria's major point is that the free practice of Indian religion has still not been entirely recognized by the courts; further, he argues that this lack of recognition is a threat to all religious faiths should such practices find themselves in conflict with secular law. Pointing particularly to the 1990 Supreme Court case *Oregon v. Smith*, which permitted the state of Oregon to outlaw the use of peyote for "religious ritual purposes," Deloria writes, "The chief victims of *Smith* are mainline churches and their members, insofar as those members take their religious duties seriously." He continues, "Americans crave some form of religious experience. . . . For the first time in American history, then, Indians have common cause with other Americans."

Deloria recognized, I think, that his defense of religious values over secular ones sounds suspiciously like that made by any number of right-wing evangelicals. When he writes that "the attack today on traditional religion is the secular attack on any group that advocates and practices devotion to a value higher than the state," he sounds like no one so much as Republican presidential candidate Mitt Romney in the speech he gave about his Mormonism on the campaign trail in 2007.[15] So in order to distance himself from these people, Deloria draws a distinction between "serious Americans" and those who have been suckered by "a talk show phenomenon" ginned up by "reactionary politicians and huckster preachers." Real religious seekers versus pretend ones—perhaps Deloria can tell the difference; I wouldn't presume. In any event, what forces Deloria into this intellectually untenable position is the uncomfortable fact that all religious assertions are, strictly speaking, conservative: they have recourse to traditions and allegedly timeless truths, to authority beyond human agency, to obedience above inquiry.

In all fairness, Deloria published this essay in 2000, and he died five years later. As I survey the wreckage wrought by eight calamitous years of the Bush administration, caused, on one level, by its insertion of religion into any number of policy matters, I wonder whether Deloria would still want to offer such a ringing endorsement of a faith-based nation. Yet while it is far too simplistic to cast NAGPRA and repatriation as a conflict between rationality and religion, Deloria does certainly glance in that direction, noting dismissively that "the scientific community [. . .] understands birds, plants, animals, and all living things, including human beings, as merely phenomena that can be subjected to scientific inquiry." In his 1999 book *Red Earth, White Lies* Deloria announces that geologists are simply wrong about the age of the earth, allies himself with Christian fundamentalists who believe that human beings and dinosaurs shared the planet, and argues that Native Americans did not enter the Western Hemisphere via the Bering Straits but that they originated sui generis on the continent. He thus resurrects the idea of "polygenesis," another piece of nineteenth-century pseudoscience which posited that each race had its own separate creation. We might laugh this all off as nuts, except that having watched the disastrous effects of policy makers who have repeatedly trumped secular science with their own religious beliefs, I find such statements and sentiments more than a little chilling.[16] In *Red Earth, White Lies* he identifies himself, essentially, as a "young earth" creationist, the position adopted by many in the neocreationist movement. The Creation Museum in Kentucky, for example, features dioramas of cave men cavorting with dinosaurs.

Finally, I am struck by how much of the discourse about repatriation is couched in the language of therapeutic identity. Rick Hill believes that "repatriation must heal old wounds," and he writes, "The loss of these objects from native communities, ritual sites, the classrooms, and homes has caused great deprivation within American Indian society. The museums' possession of our dead and our religious objects has become the main wound that exists between our peoples. The time for healing has come—as mandated by Congress." Likewise, Russell Thornton sees "repatriation as healing the wounds of the trauma of history." Thornton's conclusions about this question are worth quoting at length because they give a full rationale for the kind of therapeutic work repatriation has been asked to do:

> There is a trauma of history whereby groups must be healed from the wounds of traumatic events, much as individuals must be healed from the traumatic events during their lives, if they are to achieve psychological well-being. That human remains and important cultural objects from traumatic events in their history in the United States have been kept in museums and other institutions has hindered if not actually prevented Native Americans from coming to terms with the atrocities of their histories. It is only now, through repatriation of ancestors and objects associated with these events that many Native American peoples may reconcile themselves as peoples with these histories. They will undoubtedly never forget them (nor probably should they), and scars surely will remain, but perhaps there will be no more open wounds and their collective mental health will improve.[17]

There are any number of difficulties here, not the least of which is the collision between the world of the personal and psychological and the world of policy and legislation. After all, can "healing" be mandated, even by so powerful a body as Congress? Will repatriation be judged a failure if "collective mental health" among Indians does not improve? At what point will the process of repatriation, and all that hinges on it, be deemed a success?

The dilemma in the therapeutic use of repatriation is one described astutely by historian John Higham, writing more broadly about the phenomenon of multiculturalism. Therapy speaks to individual needs, not to collective, achievable goals—as Higham puts it, "the needs of victims for greater self-esteem, more ethnic recognition, compensatory assistance . . . needs [that] are subjective and difficult to measure." Precisely because of the subjectivity and the personal nature of "needs," they also work, much like religious claims, to remove certain things from discussion or debate; they are "a present hunger, not a direction." Goals, in a more strictly political sense, as Higham points out, "are public and therefore more open to challenge and to critical assessment. . . . Goals imply change over time and the importance of purpose in shaping growth."[18]

Higham's observations underscore that NAGPRA and repatriation can be seen as part of a shift from politics to "culture" in our public discourse. The ascendance of diversity and multiculturalism as central to our discussions of identity came, to borrow from Adam Kuper, in the late 1970s and 1980s when "intellectual debate concerned itself less with a global politics of clashing empires than with a more personal politics, a politics of identity, gender and representation. The ground contested in this new politics was often defined as 'culture.'"[19] As I suggested in my discussion of the proliferation of ethnically specific museums in Chapter 1, the increasing centrality of a personal ethno-racial identity in the United States has its parallel internationally in the efflorescence of micronationalisms from Indonesia to Chechnya and from Kurdistan to Kosovo, though thankfully the fighting that has resulted from America's identitarian politics has largely been confined to museums and college campuses. But I believe they spring from the same source. They react to the much larger and more powerful forces of globalization and homogenization, and they race, to invoke the phrase again, against the acceleration of history.

Rick Hill, in his advocacy of repatriation, recognized as much when he wrote, "Time is taking its toll on tribal elders who still remember when many of the contested objects were in native hands. If we wait much longer, much of the remaining oral traditions surrounding these objects could be lost. . . . [Museums] retain objects that American Indians believe are essential for their survival. If museums fail to respond, they will have to bear responsibility for the demise of American Indian cultures that they profess they want to preserve."[20] Ignoring for a moment that Hill has inadvertently reiterated the trope of the "vanishing Indian," blaming museums for "the demise of American Indian cultures" is patently absurd. Museums aren't really the enemy here. The repatriation fight is thus a proxy battle where museums are substituted for corporate media, McDonalds, the Internet, and a dozen other acids of postmodernity that people like Hill feel are irreparably corroding Indian identity.[21]

Repatriation thus participates in the whole culture of therapy and "self-help" that has become such a major preoccupation of many Americans. The language Thornton uses to discuss repatriation is exactly the language of Oprah Winfrey. Thornton's own view about collective trauma and the need for group healing borrows, as he acknowledges, from the relatively recent work of just a few psychologists who have extended the notion of trauma, which individuals experience in their own lives, to groups who have experienced it historically. Whether or not there is anything useful or even valid in this notion—and it does seem easy enough to caricature: Are the French still "traumatized" by the Franco-Prussian war? By Agincourt? The English by the Viking invasions? and so on—it certainly does reflect a culture in which traumas and dysfunctions are dissected and celebrated every afternoon on television. In this sense, Native Americans have borrowed a language that is quite current in the popular culture of mainstream America.

My point here is not really to take sides in the repatriation debate. Indeed, my own sense is that the debate has cooled as NAGPRA has become more and more part of the standard operating procedure of American museums, and largely without incident. Museums have not been emptied of their collections, as some feared initially, though the number of repatriated objects is significant. As of November 2006, 32,000 human remains, 670,000 associated burial objects, 118,000 unassociated funerary objects, 3,600 objects deemed sacred, 281 objects of cultural patrimony, and 764 objects that fall into both categories had been returned to Native groups.[22]

My own sympathies, I confess, lie with philosopher Kwame Anthony Appiah's notion of a "rooted cosmopolitanism" and with anthropologist Michael Brown's search for a cultural commons.[23] At its root, repatriation is a debate over ownership and private property. Objects that are repatriated are moved from the public realm—and I would absolutely defend the notion that museums constitute public institutions, about which I will have more to say in the final chapter—to a private space, that is, to groups where membership is necessarily exclusive. This represents, in my view, yet another victory of private interest over the public good, which has been a defining drift in American society since the 1970s and a centerpiece of the New Right agenda. As Appiah and Brown both point out, one extension of the logic of repatriation is for Native groups to copyright their own culture, and several have attempted to do so. In this, Native groups begin to behave a great deal like large corporations. To quote Appiah, "The vision is of a cultural landscape consisting of Disney Inc. and the Coca-Cola Company for sure; but also of Ashanti Inc., Navajo Inc., Maori Inc., Norway Inc.: All rights reserved."[24] That strikes me as a bleak cultural landscape, and one in which the thrilling and completely unpredictable consequences of cultural interaction become increasingly constrained.

We ought to be skeptical of the political claims made by those who celebrate repatriation as political defiance. Far from being an act of "resistance," NAGPRA strikes me as having been formed well within the bounds of the larger, majoritarian American culture, and from some of the conservative elements of that culture to boot. In all kinds of demonstrable ways, Native America continues to suffer through a collusion of policy choices and political neglect. Native America continues to endure unacceptable levels of poverty, to have access only to substandard education, and to lack control of natural resources. All of these conditions and more demand our national political attention. If we are going to address these issues we will do so, ultimately, politically. Writing about the dilemmas faced in Mali about the export of Malian art out of the country, Appiah writes tartly, "The problem for Mali is not that it doesn't have enough Malian art. The problem is that it doesn't have enough money."[25]

Absolutely right, and if we want to confront issues of money and power, and we should, then we should confront them directly. As Michael Brown points out, "Advocates of indigenous sovereignty find it threatening to acknowledge that native peoples, at least in economically developed settler societies, are deeply embedded in the broader civil society. Such an admission seems to undermine the separateness upon which the cultural-rights claims are based." Those who have made a false fetish out of cultural sovereignty, Brown warns, risk ignoring that real solutions to genuine problems must be fashioned in the civic realm.[26] As I insisted in the introduction, culture and politics are not the same thing.

NAGPRA only covers Native American material in American institutions, but the prevailing winds at the moment suggest that repatriation issues will spread much more widely. The Getty, of course, has had highly publicized fights with the Italian and Greek governments over antiquities of dodgy provenance that landed one of its now former curators in a courtroom. So has the Met. And while the charges of imperialism and appropriation that form the basis for repatriation claims must be acknowledged, we should also acknowledge that requests for repatriation, made in the name of "cultural patrimony," proceed from the essentialist assumption that accidents of biology and geography give people unique claims on culture. In demanding the return of the Euphronios Krater from the Metropolitan, Rocco Buttiglione of the Italian Cultural Ministry claimed he wanted the Met "to give back to the Italian people what belongs to our culture, to our tradition, and what stands within the rights of the Italian people." The Krater in question, of course, is Greek originally, and as Appiah nicely put it, "Patrimony, here, equals imperialism plus time."[27]

Appiah points out that these claims ultimately reflect a parochial rather than a cosmopolitan outlook because they transfer ownership of culture from the people of the world to specific peoples instead. He argues that rather than thinking about these questions nationally we should think about them transnationally. While he acknowledges that "the connection to art through identity is powerful," he also asks us to consider other connections: "One connection—the one neglected in talk of cultural patrimony—is the connection not through identity but *despite* difference. We can respond to art that is not ours; indeed, we can only fully respond to 'our' art if we move beyond thinking of it as ours and start to respond to it as art." After all, he points out, do we feel any better about the fate of the Bamiyan Buddhas because their wanton destruction was carried out by Afghanis?[28]

David Steigerwald has shrewdly traced how the Left in the United States has substituted "culture" for politics since the 1960s, and I think he is largely correct when he sums up, "Culture, in fact, is not power."[29] Asking cultural debates to stand in for political ones, which is the way repatriation has been cast by some, is asking culture to perform a function I am not convinced it can or should be asked to perform.

An "Objective" View of Repatriation

Cast primarily as a struggle over ownership, repatriation debates wind up resembling divorce proceedings where, amicably or angrily, custody arrangements are negotiated. Both sides in the divorce agree, however, on a fundamental assumption about the "children." Museums and Native groups insist that the objects in question have "cultural" value (and under NAGPRA, the question of monetary value has not really been an issue), that they contribute to a cultural identity, and that they are integral to Indian culture. The only question at issue is whether it is the museum or a tribal group that is best positioned to preserve that cultural value.

The ways in which repatriation gives objects cultural value are worth examining because they represent a shift in the way objects/artifacts have been viewed by anthropologists over the last century and in the way objects are seen to contribute to the definition of "culture." In other words, it is worth looking at repatriation from the objects' point of view.

It is helpful first to identify some disciplinary distinctions. As it coalesced professionally at the turn of the twentieth century, American anthropology brought together four different intellectual pursuits—four legs of a chair in the well-worn if clumsy metaphor: linguistics; archaeology; the study of human remains, which has become known as physical/medical anthropology; and ethnology, which transformed into cultural anthropology. Each of these pursuits had its own development in the nineteenth century; what brought them together as one discipline was a shared subject: Native America.[30]

It has proved a wobbly chair to be sure. As anthropologist Dell Hymes damningly asked of his discipline in 1974, "If anthropology did not exist, would it have to be invented? If it were invented, would it be the anthropology we have now?" In fact, amid the postcolonial crisis of anthropology, these questions were rhetorical, and Hymes continued, "The answer to both questions, I think, is no."[31] For our purposes here, however, we should note that of the four subdisciplines, three—archaeology, physical anthropology, and cultural anthropology—deal to a greater or lesser degree with material that has become contested or might in the future. Linguists largely do not, although there have been a few examples of Native groups trying to control scholarly use of their language. For physical anthropologists and archaeologists, material, whether biological or cultural, remains important to their work. My sense is that the most controversial repatriation requests primarily involve human remains used by physical anthropologists in their research, and perhaps secondarily archaeological material that was excavated under suspect circumstances.[32]

In these cases, it is easy enough to portray repatriation as a struggle between science and humanism. On the one hand, Native Americans quite rightly resent being treated as the subjects of anthropological poking and prodding, and they want to protect their archaeological sites from what they see as the predations of archaeologists. On the other hand, both archaeologists and physical anthropologists have made stunning discoveries about Native American origins, movements, social practices, and so forth, providing details about the past few thought we could ever know just a generation ago. Indeed, some of the conflicts here arise precisely because that new scientific knowledge clashes with closely held "traditional" conceptions about Native American history.

At least in terms of institutional position and departmental organization, however, the cultural anthropologists have usually been at the heart of the discipline. Archaeologists can often be found in other disciplinary units—many report feeling out of place in departments of anthropology—and physical anthropologists nowadays have a great deal of interaction with geneticists and other medical scientists. Much of what museums have exhibited, however, can be classed as "ethnographic" objects. This returns to some of the tensions we examined in the previous chapter about using objects to represent non-Western cultures. And while we looked earlier at how some of those objects had shifted definitional categories from anthropology to art, what I want to elaborate on here is what became of the object in anthropological theory and how those intellectual developments in turn helped create a context for NAGPRA and repatriation.

I begin with two observations. First, to recap: Anthropology as a professional discipline began its life in museums, though the work of early anthropologists associated with the Smithsonian was certainly important, as was the linguistic work done by missionaries in the nineteenth century. But it is fair to say that the growth of anthropology went hand in hand with the growth of museums, especially natural history museums, in the late nineteenth and early twentieth centuries, and as I noted earlier, Harvard, Berkeley, and the University of Pennsylvania built museums dedicated specifically to anthropology and connected to their emerging academic departments. In this way, anthropology grew up as an object-based discipline, and anthropologists worked to amass and study collections of ethnographic artifacts.

Second, as critic Raymond Williams has most famously documented, the word *culture* has one of the most complicated, protean histories of any word in the English language. Without doing too much injustice to that history, I think it is fair to say that by the early twentieth century two definitions were in use: one, a meaning descended from Matthew Arnold's definition as the best that has been thought and said, the other an anthropological, scientific notion, which most date back to British anthropologist Edward Tylor's 1871 book *Primitive Culture*. Fittingly enough, in 1883 Tylor was appointed keeper of the University Museum at Oxford.

By the first quarter of the twentieth century, professional anthropology had coalesced around the concept of culture, and the discipline had largely relocated from the museum to the university department. We can use anthropologist Ruth Benedict's remarkable 1934 book *Patterns of Culture* as a touchstone of sorts. Translated into at least fourteen languages and issued in dozens of printings, *Patterns of Culture* stands as perhaps the most popular book about anthropology ever published. It surely helped fix the anthropological notion of culture in the public imagination. It also affirmed that the anthropological definition of culture had little to do with objects and artifacts anymore. Benedict's teacher Franz Boas provided an introduction to the book in 1934, and he took pains to note, "During the present century many new approaches to the problems of social anthropology have developed. The old method of constructing a history of human culture based on bits of evidence, torn out of their natural contacts, and collected from all times and all parts of the world, has lost much of its hold."[33] For Boas, dean of American anthropologists, anthropology had moved beyond those "bits" which filled up the galleries and storerooms of museums.

While Robert Redfield could still write as late as 1940 that culture is "an organized body of conventional understandings manifest in art and artifacts which, persisting through tradition, characterizes a human group," by midcentury, objects were clearly not central to the idea of culture.[34] Writing just after the war, Alfred Kroeber and Walter Taylor both asserted that objects were not culture; rather, in Patty Jo Watson's paraphrase, "The locus of culture is mental. Artifacts are not culture, they are only the *objectifications* of culture at several removes from the real thing." As Kroeber saw it in 1948, "What counts is not the physical ax or coat . . . but the idea of them, their place in life. It is this knowledge, concept, and function that get themselves handed down through the generations, or diffused into other cultures, while the objects themselves are quickly worn out or consumed."[35]

In 1952, Kroeber and Clyde Kluckhohn surveyed the field of anthropology to assemble—in a great collection, really—definitions of culture. They began by reminding their readers, decidedly not the general public, just how central "culture" was to their work. They quoted Stuart Chase, agreeing with his assessment that the "culture concept of the anthropologists and sociologists is coming to be regarded as the foundation stone of the social sciences" and going on to insist that "few intellectuals will challenge the statement that the idea of culture, in the technical anthropological sense, is one of the key notions of contemporary American thought. In explanatory importance and in generality of application it is comparable to such categories as gravity in physics, disease in medicine, evolution in biology."[36]

The problem in viewing culture as an explanatory idea in this way, however, turned out to be the astonishing range of definitions Kroeber and Kluckhohn discovered. Physicists generally agree on the principles of gravity; anthropologists in the mid-twentieth century did not share an equally workable consensus on culture. By the end of their study, 370 tedious pages later, Kroeber and Kluckhohn had come up with a stunning 164 definitions of culture, subdivided into seven categories: descriptive, historical, normative, psychological, structural, genetic, and the grab bag "incomplete definitions." There was some common ground in this variety. Many anthropologists thought ideas such as "patterns" or "symbols" or "values" or "behavior" defined anthropological culture. By the end of the book, Kroeber and Kluckhohn still clung to the idea that culture could be made "scientific," that "culture is a general category of nature, and expressly of human nature. As such it is comparable to categories like energy, mass, evolution," but even they had to concede that at least in 1952, "as yet we have no full theory of culture. . . . In anthropology at present we have plenty of definitions but too little theory."[37]

Kroeber and Kluckhohn did, however, reveal something of an agreement among the anthropologists they cited that whatever culture might be, artifacts and objects were not integral to it. In a brief section deep in the book titled "Culture and Artifacts," Kroeber and Kluckhohn quoted two Yale anthropologists, Clellan Ford and Irving Rouse, who agreed "that artifacts are not culture. . . . Ford's position is that culture is concerned with how people act. How people make and use artifacts is part of culture; the artifacts themselves are cultural data but not culture. . . . It is the relationship between artifact and user, the pattern of significance of artifacts that is cultural, not the artifacts as such."[38] By midcentury, culture itself, singular in concept, had become the object to be collected, as when Margaret Mead wrote in a letter in 1932 describing her work, "We are just completing a culture of a mountain group here in the lower Torres Chelles." Thus James Clifford concludes that the entire practice of ethnography should be seen as a form of "culture collecting."[39] For cultural anthropologists at any rate, objects had become of secondary interest.

This resulted in the institutional drifting apart we have already examined, as the world of academic anthropology moved farther and farther away from the museum, and museum anthropologists felt more and more like stepchildren of the field. Many anthropology exhibits in museums looked increasingly dusty and out-of-date, but perhaps few anthropologists noticed, because few of them bothered to visit anymore. While Ira Jacknis maintains that, "after decades of neglect, the field of museum anthropology was revitalized in the mid-1960s," I have found few who sound as sanguine. More museum anthropologists echo Anna Laura Jones, who saw in the mid-twentieth century that "academic anthropology ignored or derided museum anthropology, and [that] museums were considered the most conservative of research institutions."[40]

There has been an intellectual drifting apart to match. If anthropologists concerned themselves with "culture," and if objects have little to do with the culture concept (however it might finally be defined), then how exactly are we to think about and understand cultural objects? What intellectual tools could we use with which to fashion meaning out of things? As far back as 1986 cultural anthropologist Arjun Appadurai thought the time was ripe for "a revitalized anthropology of things," though it isn't clear to me that this revitalization ever took place or, if it did, whether it did so in the museum. Likewise, if modernist anthropology had little use for objects in the study of culture, then a postmodernist anthropology, as archaeologist Ian Hodder has noted, might not fare much better in this regard. Pointing out that two concerns of postmodern thinking have been the instability of language and textuality, he writes that objects pose four particular interpretive difficulties for fans of postmodern thought:

First, it can be argued that material culture meanings are less logical and more immediate, use-bound and contextual than meanings in language. . . . Secondly, perhaps because material culture is often more practical and less immediately concerned with abstract meaning, the meanings it does have are often non-discursive and subconscious. . . . Thirdly, if material culture meanings are often practical and subconscious, then it is hardly surprising that it becomes difficult to be unambiguous in assigning meaning to material symbols. . . . Speech and writing are linear. The reader knows where to begin, and follows the words through one by one in an ordered sequence. Faced with a room of objects, on the other hand, there is no set order or pattern to the way in which reading takes place. . . . The complexity of the message has a much greater potential for ambiguity than in language. . . . Fourthly, once produced, a material symbol often has considerable durability, unlike the spoken word. . . . The meanings of objects may change as they move into new contexts of use. The ambiguity has a greater potential for increase in regard to material culture, simply because the object is more durable than the spoken word.[41]

Repatriation thus arose at a moment of real institutional and intellectual confusion over the use and meaning of anthropological objects within the museum and within the discipline of anthropology itself. By the time Native groups began to ask for the return of objects under NAGPRA, many American cultural anthropologists were themselves already unsure what to do with those objects.

Some museum curators, such as the Field Museum's Jonathan Haas, have wondered whether museums ought to focus on objects so much in the first place. For Haas, the museum should reconceive itself as a forum rather than a temple, where Native and non-Native voices could be heard on equal terms. As Haas sees it, "There is today a dialectical tension between the commitment of anthropology to synthesize and articulate cross-cultural similarities and differences and the post-modern rejection of the authoritative voice of anthropology to speak for or about the 'other.' . . . The dialectic in the case of museums is between their role as a voice for anthropology in public learning and the movement to cede decision-making power to Native peoples represented in collections, exhibits and programs. Voice and power are inextricably intertwined in museums." Replacing exhibits with conversation, Haas believes, could make museums public advocates for anthropological topics and more effective advocates for the peoples represented in the collections.[42]

In this sense, while objects no longer stood in easily for cultures, the indecision about what to do with them represented a larger confusion among anthropologists by the 1970s about the very notion of culture itself. As Eric Wolf put it in 1980, "An earlier anthropology had achieved unity under the aegis of the culture concept. . . . The past quarter century has undermined this intellectual sense of security. . . . Culture, once extended to all acts and ideas employed in social life, was now relegated to the margins as 'world views' or 'values.'"[43] The center did not hold, and cultural anthropology found itself in a profound intellectual crisis that, in some ways, it still struggles to resolve.

Ironically, NAGPRA seems to have remedied the institutional dilemma. While museums initially expressed hesitancy or downright hostility toward repatriation, many now find that it has given their collections a new kind of relevance. Museums are increasingly working in collaboration with Native groups in mounting exhibitions, in conserving cultural material, and in giving some of that material back. If nothing else, repatriation requests by Native groups demonstrate that, even if academic anthropologists don't care much about museum collections, there is another constituency that does.

NAGPRA has also, at least at one level, settled the intellectual dilemma over how objects are understood to have cultural meaning as well. Crudely put, cultural objects now mean whatever the tribal group that can establish legal ownership over them says they mean. Through the NAGPRA frameworks Native groups must demonstrate both a lineal connection to an object and that the object has an "ongoing historical, traditional, or cultural importance central to the Native American group."[44] Theoretically, this stakes out the terms of whatever negotiation might take place between Native groups and the museum. Interestingly, however, as of this writing the NAGPRA frameworks have yet to be litigated. On the face of it, that would seem a terrific victory for NAGPRA and for the collaboration between institutions and tribes. But since NAGPRA has not yet been put to any legal test, it isn't clear how disputes over the definition of an "ongoing historical, traditional, or cultural importance central to the Native American group" would be resolved. In effect, Native groups have been able to assert this cultural importance, and museum and cultural anthropologists have largely agreed.[45]

This represents, at least for some, a happy ending to the crisis of cultural anthropology, and particularly the problematic notion of "ethnographic authority." The project of cultural anthropology came under attack first as part of the apparatus of colonial power. These critiques were given their most influential and sophisticated articulation by Edward Said and Johannes Fabian. When Said asked in the context of his analysis of European interactions with western Asia, "How does one *represent* other cultures? What is *another* culture? Is the notion of a distinct culture (or race, or religion, or civilization) a useful one, or does it always get involved either in self-congratulation (when one discusses one's own) or hostility and aggression (when one discusses the 'other')," anthropologists working anywhere in the world were forced to ask the same sorts of questions.[46]

Almost simultaneously, cultural anthropology came under attack next by those who had taken the literary turn and who insisted that all ethnographic writing is first and foremost an act of writing. As such, ethnographic writing is simply a text constructed by the writer, not an authoritative, "objective" account of the culture in question. As a text, any ethnography is really about the ethnographer, hopelessly trapped as he or she is within the bounds of his or her own culture. As British anthropologist Adam Kuper has impatiently described postmodern ethnography, "Some early post-modernist ethnographies seemed to herald a retreat to a world of privacy, to the examination of the self. The true purpose of ethnographic research in other cultures was really to gain self-knowledge. . . . The first wave of post-modernist ethnographies was largely about the ethnographer's own experience of cultural dislocation, inspiring the joke in which the native pleads with the ethnographer, 'Can't we talk about *me* for a change!' "[47]

There has been an institutional analog to this self-reflective impulse inside the museum. While we have already discussed the way the museum and the academic discipline of anthropology drifted apart in the first half of the twentieth century, there has been more recently a small revival of interest in museums and their collections by anthropologists. But much of that interest has been, in essence, in the anthropological study *of* the museum rather than the study of anthropology that happens *in* the museum. Collections have been recast, often with fascinating results, to tell stories about the collectors, about the museum institution itself, and about the processes of expansion and colonialism of which these collections were a part rather than about the indigenous "cultures" they were originally thought to represent.[48] It is as if biologists went to the lab in order to investigate the lab itself rather than the things growing in the Petri dishes.

I want to be clear about the result of the postmodern critique for this discussion. Certainly, repatriation claims rest on a resounding "no" to Said's challenging questions. For some postmodernists the idea of a distinct culture is a useful one despite whatever problems Said and others have identified with it. In addition, ethnographic authority has not been dethroned and replaced with the complex and contradictory polyphony that some anthropological theorists had hoped for. Instead, the authoritative voice has been shifted from one group—academic anthropologists—to another—Native groups. This is true of objects repatriated from museums under the NAGPRA frameworks and also of the related practice of inviting Native groups into the museum to curate exhibitions about themselves. The premise here, as Kuper points out, is that the only authoritative knowledge is self-knowledge and that the only valid point of view is an insider's point of view.

Such a view, quite obviously, sidesteps the problems that come with insider knowledge and self-reflection. Historians and others have for many years cast a suspicious critical eye on autobiographies, diaries, and oral testimonies for the truths they tell and the truths they hide. In the context of a postmodern anthropology, apparently, we are asked to suspend that disbelief. Kuper calls this notion that only natives can understand natives "the *reductio ad absurdum* of a whole movement in academic anthropology."[49] More than that, it represents a retreat from the cosmopolitan to the provincial, denying the notion that any of us can understand anyone different from ourselves. It rejects the idea that, whatever the problems inherent in it, there is something deeply humane in the attempt to transcend those differences.

The recourse to insider authority takes us back to the question of historical and cultural stasis I mentioned previously. As Fabian has observed, in its initial anthropological construction, "culture" floats independent of time and thus of historical change. NAGPRA's language suggests that an object made in one cultural context at a particular historical moment retains the same meaning and importance for people in an utterly different cultural and historical moment. It might be useful to draw on literary critic Mikhail Bakhtin's concept of the "chronotope" to clarify this point. The chronotope (literally, if awkwardly, "time/space") describes the way time and space in any novel are inextricably linked: there a specific literary time can only unfold within a specific kind of literary space, and conversely a specific literary space shapes the kind of time experienced in the novel. To understand a novel's chronotope is one key to understanding its meaning. Cultural objects too have their own chronotopes, meanings that are shaped by their creation at specific moments in time and space. We can struggle to understand what those meanings might have been, but we can't, in the end, re-create those moments.[50] Yet at one level, that is exactly what repatriation attempts to do. NAGPRA represents an attempt to turn back the clock, to restore things (literally and figuratively) to their prelapsarian condition, to undo the past.

There is a romantic, indeed utopian, impulse here, but it requires that history be denied and replaced instead with "heritage." NAGPRA participates in what David Lowenthal has dubbed "the heritage industry." He summarizes the difference between heritage and history this way: "History tells all who will listen what has happened and how things came to be as they are. Heritage passes on exclusive myths of origin and continuance, endowing a select group with prestige and common purpose. . . . History is for all, heritage for ourselves alone. . . . Heritage reverts to tribal rules that make each past an exclusive, secret possession. Created to generate and protect group interests, it benefits us only if withheld from others. . . . We exalt our own heritage not because it is demonstrably true but because it *ought* to be."[51]

Anthropologist Michael Brown largely agrees, and he sees the dilemma rooted in the strange career of the concept of culture. He writes, "Culture was an abstraction distilled from behavior and shared understandings. It served as a shorthand way to talk about the habits and attitudes that give each society a distinctive signature. It was, in other words, a useful analytic device and nothing more. But in promoting the concept of culture anthropologists inadvertently spawned a creature that now has a life of its own. In public discourse, culture and such related concepts as 'tradition' and 'heritage' have become resources that groups own and defend from competing interests."[52]

Even if the return of human remains and cultural material can succeed in reconstituting specific tribal identities, that project ignores some of the risks inherent in the attempt to rewind the past. As Jonathan Friedman has astutely pointed out, "The history of Western expansion is littered with examples of the combined destruction of cultural identity and its psychological aftermath. But the construction or reconstruction of identity is just as violent and dangerous a process for all involved. The emergence of a cultural identity implies the fragmentation of a larger unity and is always experienced as a threat."[53] Packaged as heritage, in Lowenthal's sense, cultural identity is seen only as something warm and fuzzy and sidesteps these thorny issues altogether. Things usually aren't that straightforward.

Historian James Clifford, though not discussing repatriation, also points to some of the complications that arise when fashioning identities. Drawing on the work of Richard Handler, Clifford writes, "Identity, whether cultural or personal, presupposes acts of collection, gathering up possessions in arbitrary systems of value and meaning. Such systems, always powerful and rule governed, change historically. One cannot escape them. . . . In Handler's discussion the collection and preservation of an authentic domain of identity cannot be natural or innocent. It is tied up with nationalist politics, with restrictive law, and with contested encoding of past and future."[54]

The control of cultural meaning may be the ultimate significance of NAGPRA, and the real value of repatriated objects. As Georg Simmel observed years ago, the value of commodities is created through the act of exchange. Repatriated objects become valuable when they are forced back into the medium of exchange, from Native group to museum and then back from museum to Native group. Similarly, the value of these objects comes not because they mean something specific necessarily, but because the power to define that meaning has shifted, from museum to tribe, from non-Native to Native.

At the very least, repatriation risks robbing objects of their own biographies. Certainly objects don't have agency apart from their creators and users. Yet as Igor Kopytoff has perceptively pointed out, objects do accumulate their own histories over the course of time, permitting us to ask questions about objects of the sort that we ask of people whose biographies we want to know: How has the use, perception, value, and significance of this object changed over time? What of the pivotal moments in that history? What do the answers to those questions tell us about the changing social, cultural, political, and economic contexts in

which this object has existed?[55] Repatriating an object might well constitute the latest chapter in that object's biography, but perhaps at the cost
of erasing several of its previous chapters.

NAGPRA may have settled these questions at least for the moment,
but it hasn't, I think, solved them altogether. I suggested earlier that we
ought to look at repatriation from the point of view of the objects themselves, to acknowledge that objects have their own cultural life and their
own biographies. To do this hints at considerable complications for the
premises of NAGPRA and repatriation.

Consider the copper kettle.

As Canadian anthropologist Laurier Turgeon tells its story, the hum-
ble copper kettle arrived in the New World with Europeans in the six-
teenth and seventeenth centuries. Kettles appear to have been widely
adopted by a number of Native groups living in what is now the Great
Lakes region of Canada, and these groups made different uses of the
kettle. As Turgeon writes, summing this up, "The copper kettle became
the rallying point for individuals and groups, because its force of attraction was stronger than that of any other known object. Around the kettle
people gathered for festivals of life and death; around the kettle they
reflected on the community and what they wanted it to become; around
it too they rekindled such hopes."[56]

The kettle interests us precisely because of its intercultural nature, the
way it was borrowed, refashioned, reimagined, and reused from one set
of cultures by other cultures. I think Turgeon is right when he concludes, "The copper kettle served as a catalyst for identity formation
because it was an appropriated object. The act of appropriation, more
than the object itself, produced the creative tension involved in identity
formation. It is as if the acquisition of European objects through trade
allowed Amerindian groups to consolidate, extend their alliances, and
distinguish and reinforce themselves in relation to other Amerindian
groups."[57]

Or consider the "Raven Cape." Made of feathers braided into plant
fibers, this extraordinary cape or breastplate was purchased for the University of Pennsylvania Museum by Louis Shotridge in 1923 as part of a
collection of objects from the Tlingit village of Angoon, on the west
coast of Admiralty Island. The cape had been used by the Deisheetaan
clan in a variety of ways, though by the time Shotridge purchased it the
cape had passed out of clan possession.

Once it arrived in Philadelphia, museum director George Byron Gordon pressed Shotridge to learn more about the origin of the piece. It
clearly hadn't been made by the Tlingit or any other indigenous group
in the region. The first thing to give that away was the plant material
used as the backing of the cape. The feathers are held in place with

coconut fibers, and the village of Angoon sits about eight thousand miles from the nearest coconut tree. There are coconut trees aplenty in the Society Islands in the South Pacific, however, and this turns out to have been where the object was originally made.

Several of Shotridge's informants knew that the cape had come from somewhere else, though no one could recall for sure. Shotridge quoted some old men as saying to him, "We show our esteem for the Raven Cape, before the people, because it is the work of the people of another world." Asked how long the object had been with the Tlingit, another informer, who was roughly one hundred years old, estimated "the thing must have been in our possession for nearly a hundred and fifty years."

That would put its arrival on the Northwest Coast in the 1770s, at exactly the moment when European explorers began visiting the region regularly. Indeed, through a combination of archival research and more oral history interviews, Gordon became convinced that the piece had been brought to the Northwest by Captain Cook himself. Several Tlingit insisted that the piece had been brought by the "first white man" to visit them, and that distinction traditionally belongs to Cook. In 1778 Cook made his third voyage to the Tlingit region shortly after spending four months in the South Seas.

Regardless of whether Cook or George Vancouver or some other eighteenth-century European sea captain brought the piece, Tlingit informers also stated that it may have come to them from another indigenous group. They remembered that as the object became recognized as a clan object, it acquired important status, was stored in a white frame house, was worn on occasion by Tlingit dressed in Western clothes, and was used in rites of the Russian Orthodox Church in which Tlingit participated.[58] The remarkable biography of this object tells a story of trade and cultural interaction, of the nature of "globalization" in the eighteenth and nineteenth centuries, and of the marvelous adaptability and promiscuity of culture itself.

But for our purposes here, who could claim ownership over objects such as these? The Native group that last used it? The Native group from which the last group got it? The European group who introduced the kettle or the cape in the first place? If cultural appropriation is the key to the formation of cultural identity, does that hopelessly complicate the idea of exclusive ownership? Is "ownership" even the right question to ask?

All of which is to say that objects, then, because of their stability and their perseverance over time, stand—paradoxically—as evidence that any given culture is constantly in flux, that it is formed in reaction to, through the appropriation of, and by the inspiration of other cultures. Likewise, the meaning of objects, like any accidental fragment of the

Figure 8. The "Raven Cape" or Taumi. Made originally in the South Pacific, the breastplate was traded to a European explorer in the eighteenth century, traded again to a Native group in the Northwest, and collected by Louis Shotridge in the early twentieth century. Given its remarkable travels over 150 years, what culture can be said to own this object? Courtesy of the Penn Museum, object NA9476, image #150182.

past that exists in the present, comes both from the sense that they connect us directly with the past and from the way our contemporary concerns enable us to ask new questions about that past. People in the former Soviet Union used to joke that the future was certain but that the past changed all the time, and in a profound way they were right. The past does change all the time, despite the fact that the objects themselves do not.

Repatriation, conversely, is grounded in the notion of cultural isolation, purity, and stasis. Many cultural objects stand as eloquent if mute refutations of that idea. As Kwame Anthony Appiah points out, "If the argument for cultural patrimony is that art belongs to the culture that gives it its significance, most art doesn't belong to a national culture at all. Much of the greatest art is flamboyantly international; much ignores nationality altogether."[59] Good artists borrow, Picasso is alleged to have quipped, great artists steal, and so it is with cultures too.

The final irony about repatriation is that, framed as it is at the moment, it may wind up denying objects their voice to speak in the multiple cultural languages that shaped them to begin with. Being claimed as the sole possession of one group and its culture may mute their capacity to speak to us all.

Chapter 3
Where Is the East?

Three years after winning the Pulitzer Prize for his literary history *The Flowering of New England,* Van Wyck Brooks followed it up with a sequel. *New England: Indian Summer* told the story of American literature between the Civil War and the First World War, albeit as the title suggests, this version centered on New England. In setting the stage for his literary characters, Brooks noted that in the late nineteenth and early twentieth centuries, "Oriental art was the vogue among Bostonians" and remarked that "they were filling the region with their great collections." He made an interesting distinction among these Asiaphiles: "Some of these collectors were detached observers. . . . But others were enthralled by Oriental thought; they were seekers of salvation in the Buddhist way."[1]

That difference between "detached observers" and "seekers of salvation" nicely captures the two strategies that have been employed in American museums to represent Asian cultures and societies with objects. On the one hand, those detached observers tried to fit Asia into the sort of scientific taxonomy that they had developed for other kinds of knowledge. On the other hand, the seekers wanted something other than a "scientific" encounter with Asia—call it romantic or spiritual or escapist—and for those people objects in museums functioned more to convey experience than knowledge.

That museums at the turn of the last century couldn't settle on one method of displaying Asia should come as no real surprise. How to understand Asia confounded Americans across the nineteenth and early twentieth centuries (some would argue that it still does). As I discussed in the previous two chapters, museum anthropology borrowed its techniques from natural history, treating non-Western peoples as largely part of the natural world. Only by the mid-twentieth century did anthropological objects jump into the category of art, driven there by both political imperatives and an intellectual crisis within the discipline of anthropology. But Asia never quite fit into the frameworks of that early anthropology and was largely ignored by American anthropologists. At the same time, while Asia clearly had produced great civilizations, these weren't related to Western civilization, and as I have observed already, "art," at least initially, was solely the product of Western civilization. Where then would one find the East in an American museum? And in what kind of museum, and exhibited under what circumstances?

This chapter looks at the two ways in which Asia has been displayed in American museums. First I trace the way in which Asian objects became seen as art, displayed in art museums, with the apparatus of art historical knowledge. Then I will look at the counterpoint to that strategy—the use of display to allow visitors the experience of Asia—by focusing on one of the very first such exhibits, the Buddhist Temple at the University of Pennsylvania Museum, and on its creator, Maxwell Sommerville.

I don't mean to suggest that these two approaches are contradictory or mutually exclusive, nor do I think one is necessarily right or wrong, better or worse. Indeed, as we will see, the career of Ernest Fenollosa, the Bostonian-turned-Japanese Buddhist, demonstrates that they can happily coexist. Instead, I am interested in the tension between the way museums strove for categorical order and how Asian objects did not fully cooperate with that enterprise.

Asian Objects Become Asian Art

In 1929 Benjamin March published the results of a national survey he helped conduct at the behest of the Carnegie Corporation. March was curator of Asiatic art at the Detroit Institute of Arts, and his study inventoried collections of Asian objects displayed in American museums.[2] Given his institutional position, March chose, not surprisingly, to focus his attention on collections in *art* museums, ostensibly because of "the increasing interest among them in the Far East."[3] He was pleased with what he found. From tiny collections, such as the thirty-three objects at the Baltimore Museum of Art, to Boston's Museum of Fine Arts (MFA) collection of more than ninety-two thousand pieces, March reported Asian objects in museums large and small, in cities of all sizes from coast to coast.

March's survey, however, reveals something else as well. What March called "undoubtedly the most distinguished general collection of Chinese material in the country" was found not in an art museum at all but in the Department of Anthropology at Chicago's Field Museum of Natural History. In addition, the "preeminent" assemblage of Chinese sculpture in the country, according to March, sat in the galleries of the Museum of Anthropology and Archaeology at the University of Pennsylvania. And nine thousand Asian objects resided in Ann Arbor at the University of Michigan's Museum of Anthropology—a collection larger than all but those at a very few art museums.[4]

The choice March made to focus on art museums was not as innocent or self-evident as it would appear. By doing so, he had taken sides in a debate, almost one hundred years running, over whether Asian objects—especially those from China and Japan—should be categorized as fine art, anthropology, or something else altogether. Objects from Asia had presented American museums with significant conceptual problems throughout the nineteenth and early twentieth centuries. As Craig Clunas has pointed out, " 'Art' is not a category in the sense of a preexistent container . . . rather, it is a way of categorizing, a manner of making knowledge."[5] Choosing sides in this debate meant sorting out questions such as what kinds of objects should be collected and displayed, how those objects should be organized and arranged, and within what intellectual frameworks those objects (and by extension the cultures that produced them) should be understood.

Beyond the institutional question of which types of museums would display these objects lay the much more vexing question of how the cultures that produced the objects would be represented through the displays. Susan Stewart, James Clifford, and others have discussed how cultural identities are constituted through the acts of collecting and display.[6] This was particularly true in the nineteenth century, when Western societies were engaged in aggressive nation-building enterprises. To see Asian objects as anthropological meant understanding those cultures within the frameworks that were being developed primarily to understand non-Western and so-called primitive peoples. For those who classified Asian objects as art, who were dazzled by the achievements of Asian cultural production, Asian cultures could be understood in the same category as the great occidental civilizations such as those of Greece and Rome and their descendents. In the end, however, the frameworks of neither anthropology nor art history, which were the only two available at the time, worked completely when attempting to understand Asian cultural production. As a result, for American museum visitors, it was not at all clear where to find the East.

Asian Objects Become Fine Art

March would seem to have chosen sides wisely. By the end of the first quarter of the twentieth century, the debate about how to classify Asian objects had been resolved—though by no means entirely—in favor of fine art. There is a standard celebratory and largely teleological narrative that describes this triumph.

As traced by Warren Cohen, among others, the story begins in 1838 in Philadelphia, where Quaker merchant Nathan Dunn opened the first museum of Chinese objects in the United States.[7] By 1841 Dunn's Museum had folded (and relocated to London), and the narrative jumps to 1876 and the Centennial International Exhibition, also in Philadelphia. There, both China and Japan exhibited material—but in the main building, not Memorial Hall, which was the fine arts building.

Seventeen years later in Chicago, at the World's Columbian Exposition of 1893, Japanese objects (though not Chinese) were exhibited in the Palace of Fine Arts. The Japanese made an elaborate showing at the Exposition, as opposed to the Chinese, who were only represented by an exhibit of manufactures, and as one guidebook put it, "Of all the galleries in the Palace of Fine Arts few were examined with greater interest or closer scrutiny than those of Japan, a nation of artists in their way, no less than the French."[8] At long last, some Asian objects were being properly recognized as fine art; thus begins, in this narrative, what Cohen has called the "golden age of Asian art collecting."[9] With Boston's MFA taking the institutional lead, many American art museums began accumulating and displaying Asian objects, bestowing upon them the cultural status associated with fine art such as the Gainsboroughs and Rembrandts.

The process of placing Asian objects into the category of fine art reached a climax of a sort shortly after the First World War. In 1919 construction was completed on the new Freer Gallery in Washington, D.C., the first museum in the country with Asian art at its center—the first since Dunn's, at least. The Freer opened to the public in 1923 and was directed initially by John Ellerton Lodge, who had worked (and continued to do so) with the Asian collections in Boston.

The Freer's location on the Mall was heavy with significance. Located in the growing cultural complex of the nation's national museums and next to the Smithsonian's original Castle, the Freer signaled to Americans that Asian art as art had arrived. With Lodge presiding over a twin empire in Boston and Washington, "East Asian art [became] part of American culture."[10] March's conclusion in 1929 that most major and many minor art museums collected and displayed Asian objects has only been amplified over the course of subsequent years.

What this narrative stresses is the development of an aesthetic sensibility that gradually, but inevitably, permitted Americans to cultivate an appreciation for the masterworks of Asian art in much the same way that they learned to appreciate the finest works of Western art. Pioneers such as Charles Freer and Ernest Fenollosa (for a time, Asian objects curator at Boston's MFA) helped develop for Asian objects an apparatus of scholarship and connoisseurship similar to that upon which the study and evaluation of Western art depended. Once Asian objects had their own attendant framework—stylistic schools, chronological progressions—the objects themselves could be treated as art.

While this story is true, it is also too much a teleology. That is to say, whatever may have been the case at an earlier time, we now categorize Asian art as fine art proper. What remains to be explained, therefore, is how American museums arrived at that obvious and inevitable conclusion. Part of this narrative must address the fact that for Asian objects to come to rest in the category of fine art by the 1920s, they had *not* to be classed as something else. In the United States, as March's survey inadvertently reveals, that other choice was to classify the objects as anthropological or ethnological. As much as an evaluation of the objects themselves, the debate about where Asian objects belonged hinged on larger questions of how Americans perceived and "invented" the cultures that produced them.

Nathan Dunn's Collection of "Curious Things"

By all accounts, Philadelphia merchant Nathan Dunn had an extraordinary appreciation of Chinese culture. His business led him to Canton in 1818, and he did not return permanently to the United States until 1832. He claimed to have access to Chinese people and Chinese objects unparalleled for a Westerner. That access to an otherwise off-limits world came, at least according to reviewer E. C. Wines, because Dunn did not participate in the opium trade and was therefore trusted and respected by local Cantonese. "Most Americans," Wines told his readers, "who trade in China are more or less engaged in the opium traffic, which is contrary to the laws of the Empire. Mr. Dunn was never interested to the amount of a dollar in that illicit commerce."[11] Dunn was also a Quaker, and his aversion to dealing in opium may have been tied to his faith.

Dunn publicized his virtuous business endeavor doubtless to help portray his collection as an act of high-minded, cross-cultural understanding. In the 1830s there was considerable work to be done in that direction. As an anonymous writer observed in the *American Journal of Science and Arts*, "It would be difficult to name a subject that has puzzled the learned world so much and for so long, as the accurate delineation of the character of that wonderful and unchanging people, the Chinese." Dunn hoped to rectify the situation when he returned to Philadelphia, bringing with him his collection of roughly ten thousand objects. He spent fifty thousand dollars assembling the collection and then laid out an additional eight thousand to install it in a gallery. On December 22, 1838, Dunn opened his museum to the world. It holds the distinction of being the first systematic collection of Chinese material exhibited publicly in the United States.

Dunn's attention to system and classification distinguished his museum from the other large collection of Chinese material on view in the United States at that moment. The East India Marine Society had put its collection of objects accumulated from merchants and sailors on display in a museum in Salem, Massachusetts. But this "flood of objects, good, bad, and indifferent" amounted to a hodgepodge. The East India Marine Society's museum exemplified the complaints made by British traveler J. S. Buckingham about American museums generally. "In America," he wrote in 1842, "museums are almost always the property of some private individual, who gets together a mass of everything that is likely to be thought curious . . . the worthless generally prevailing over the valuable. The collections are then huddled together, without order or arrangement . . . and there is generally a noisy band of musicians, and a juggler . . . to attract visitors . . . and mere amusement, and that of the lightest and most uninstructive kind, is the only object sought in visiting them."[12] By attempting a synoptic, categorical museum, Dunn prefigured the museums of the late nineteenth century that tried to replace mere "curiosities" with system.

The results of Dunn's work astonished. From written descriptions, the museum was truly an impressive operation. Visitors entered a double colonnaded salon 160 feet long and 63 feet wide with enough objects to occupy "hours, nay days and weeks." The rest of the museum's galleries contained everything from paintings and furniture to models of boats and natural history specimens. Between these displays were "a street with sedan and bearers" and a "silk mercer's shop." As one reviewer gushed, Dunn had brought to Philadelphia "*everything* that was characteristic or rare, whether in the natural history, or natural and artificial curiosities and manufactures."[13] Though the museum has left scant historical traces—and the collection itself has long since been dispersed —we can deduce two things about Dunn's exhibition strategy. First, it is clear that his goal was to be encyclopedic. According to one journalist who toured the museum when it relocated to London in 1842, "On every side are works of art; the evidence of the idol worship of China, of her commerce, her manufactures, her paintings, her carvings, her silks, satins, embroidery, implements, coins—everything in short that can tend to illustrate her domestic or public life."[14]

This encyclopedic approach to collecting mirrored the model that had been developed by Charles Willson Peale when he established the nation's first important museum in 1764 in Philadelphia (and indeed, Dunn's collection shared space with the remnants of Peale's museum). What Peale reveals to us when he pulls back the curtain in his 1822 self-

CHINESE MUSEUM, PHILADELPHIA.

Figure 9. Nathan Dunn's Chinese Museum in Philadelphia from the outside. The first large-scale, systematic exhibit of Chinese objects in the United States. It didn't last long and moved to London. Courtesy of the Historical Society of Pennsylvania.

Figure 10. And from the inside. The exhibit of ten thousand Chinese things astonished visitors. Courtesy of the Historical Society of Pennsylvania, Kennedy Watercolor Collection.

portrait, *The Artist in His Museum,* is a diverse collection that includes everything from fossils to stuffed birds to portraits of the most eminent contemporaries. Dunn's collection of "everything that was characteristic or rare" and his attempt to use a museum as an encyclopedic repository were squarely within the most reputable museum practices of the early republic. Second, the response to Dunn's museum reminds us of the epistemological power that objects held for viewers in the nineteenth century. Simply put, knowledge about a variety of subjects inhered in the objects associated with that body of knowledge. As a writer reviewing Dunn's museum for the *Chinese Repository* (a journal published in Canton) described it, "There are several means employed to impart knowledge of distant and strange countries." One is to write narrative history; another is to exhibit a panoramic view. But the best way "is the one . . . which Mr. Dunn affords his visitors." By encountering actual objects, "the visitor must feel as if he were examining a country, where the breath of life and the noise of instruments had suddenly ceased, and every object animate and inanimate had been left unchanged and indiscerptible." As Dunn himself put it on the title page of his catalogue, "Words may Deceive, But the Eye cannot play the Rogue."[15]

Through an encyclopedic scope and a belief that objects were the source of knowledge about the larger forces that produced them, be they natural or cultural, Dunn made it clear that his ambition was to reproduce China metonymically through the museum, letting the objects stand for the culture whence they came, and a number of writers made excited note of this. A visit to the museum, according to Wines, was a substitute for a trip to China itself. In fact, Wines believed that the museum would give a better idea of China than a visit to the country because foreigners were permitted to see only a small part of Canton: "It is no longer necessary to measure half the circuit of the globe, and subject one's self to the hazards and privations of a six months voyage on distant and dangerous seas to enjoy a peep at the Celestial Empire. This is a gratification which may now be enjoyed by the citizens of Philadelphia . . . and by the citizens of other parts of the United States, at no greater peril of life and limb than is connected with locomotion by means of our own steamboats and railroads." The result, in Wines's estimation, was "China in miniature." Another writer told readers that he would "long remember our last Saturday evening's excursion to Canton," and still another enthused, "Mr. Dunn's collection at once transports us to China."[16]

It is hard, perhaps, for those of us who take relatively easy global travel for granted to remember how museum displays once functioned as surrogates for travel, even more so for China, where Dunn's degree of access would have been seen as extraordinary in the 1830s. Writing of his own travels in Asia a generation later, Englishman Robert Nicholas Fowler, clearly an adventurous type, described with some disappointment his Chinese experience: "There seem no facilities for traveling in the interior of China. . . . The roads are said to be very bad. . . . The inns are very poor, and are not in the habit of accommodating strangers. Hence, though nothing is easier than to visit the ports of China, to explore the interior would be an undertaking of very great difficulty. What is easily seen of China is seen from the deck of a ship and very few except missionaries have attempted to penetrate inland."[17] Dunn did attempt it; in fact, he was successful and brought back the evidence of his success to display, and as a result visitors to the museum could pretend they had visited China itself.

Dunn offered his museum as evidence on one side of the debate about how China and the Chinese should be viewed by Westerners. Americans certainly saw China through two sets of lenses. Through one, the Chinese were like most other non-Western people—backward, primitive, and unprogressive. This perception grew in the 1830s and 1840s, when events of the Opium War in China seemed only to prove that point. The Chinese, however long their empire may have lasted, had finally succumbed to the technological and commercial superiority of the West. While some might feel squeamish that opium had been the driving force behind Britain's defeat of China, most simply accepted that China could not compete with the West. For some, the Chinese had "all the self-complacent vanity of half civilization"; for others, Jesus was the cure for China's ailments, its "wretchedness and degradation" attributable entirely to a "false religion." For such Americans, "reception of Christian ideas and institutions alone is needed for their regeneration."[18]

Through the other set of lenses, this hierarchy of Western superiority and Chinese inferiority was confronted by troubling facts that could not be ignored. The sheer immensity of the Chinese empire astonished people, embracing "not far from one tenth of the land of the globe, and full third part of its inhabitants. It includes the widest range of climates . . . its commercial resources are incalculable." Beyond these physical facts, China had all the trappings Westerners looked for when they defined civilization; this much was obvious and unavoidable. The Chinese possessed a continuous record of their history far beyond any Western civilization, and they had produced dazzling works of art and literature. Their very language, then as now, simply left Westerners stammering. As one writer put it, "How the Chinese classics were ever written is a profound mystery; but 'there were giants in those days.' "[19]

What Wines called the three greatest inventions of civilization— printing, gunpowder, and the compass—all came from China, "whatever mortification the statement may inflict upon our vanity." Looked at this way, China was "interesting in its relation to the philosophy of human progress." As one writer reminded readers, "We see there the highest stage of civilization which has yet been attained by any nation independently of Christian institutions."[20] This, then, was the defining dilemma: Through which lens to view the Chinese? The problem vexed people in the 1830s, and it would continue to do so through the mid-twentieth century. Such were the parameters within which Americans sought to understand China and display Chinese objects in American museums.

It was in the midst of this discourse that Dunn's museum opened. By constructing China in miniature and by insisting that the objects on display were not ill-gotten through the opium trade, Dunn used an encyclopedic museum to argue that China deserved a place in the front rank of civilizations. For some this seemed obvious. The displays made clear that the Chinese deserved credit for considerable accomplishments in many areas. Remarking on the exhibit of "agriculture and other instruments," one writer mused, "Here is a study of Chinese manufactures perfectly novel to an American, who will be surprised to find that the most simple operation which he has been taught to believe can be performed only by an instrument of a certain form, is equally well executed by another of totally different figure." Wines agreed, concluding his review of the museum by asserting that "whoever attentively examines the immense Collection of Chinese Curiosities . . . will need no further proof of the ingenuity of the Chinese in arts and manufactures. In several branches of labour, both agricultural and mechanical . . . they have never been surpassed; and in some they are unequalled by any other people." Even Chinese law, a description of which Dunn provided in the museum, compared favorably to that in the West. Wines quoted an essay from the *Edinburgh Review* that certainly makes Chinese law sound appealing even in our own day, "We scarcely know any European code that is at once so copious and so consistent or that is nearly so free from intricacy, bigotry and fiction."[21]

But the encyclopedic display Dunn featured in his museum did not persuade everyone that the Chinese had produced art. Wealthy New York collector Philip Hone, who came to Philadelphia in January 1840 to see "the famous Chinese museum," viewed the museum as "an immense collection of curious things." Likewise, William Langdon, who published an expanded museum catalogue in London, believed that Dunn's collection demonstrated that the fine arts had not attained "the perfection that belongs to them in the enlightened nations of Christendom." What makes these criticisms particularly interesting is that Dunn had not intended his museum to be an art museum as such. Indeed, the art museum as we know it today in the United States is largely a product of the last half of the nineteenth century. Dunn's model was a synoptic, encyclopedic museum like Peale's; the Metropolitan and the Art Institute of Chicago belong to a later generation. Lawrence Levine has wonderfully demonstrated that the boundaries that delineate highbrow from lowbrow in American culture were fluid in the nineteenth century and only ossified in their current form at the turn of the twentieth century. The two-sided reaction to Dunn's Chinese objects—the impulse both to be dazzled and to denigrate—suggests that part of what may have helped define what constituted fine art in the nineteenth century was an ethnocentric reaction against Asian cultural production. As one writer concluded in 1848, "The genius, art, and taste of the classic ages have, indeed, left memorials by the side of which China has absolutely nothing to exhibit."[22]

Art, as the definition began to take shape in the mid-nineteenth century, would be seen to be exclusively a Western achievement. In Dunn's museum, visitors found that the Chinese could be credited with certain accomplishments, technical and otherwise, but not apparently with artistic achievement. To draw from Edward Said and others, though they have worked in a different context, the Occident defined itself as much as it defined the Orient when it created the boundaries of inclusion and exclusion around the category of art. Scholars through the century would develop a scholarly apparatus designed in part to reify this distinction between East and West.[23]

Dunn demonstrated that China could be constituted through the same encyclopedic techniques that Peale had used in the late eighteenth century to construct a museum image of the United States. But in so doing, Dunn's museum only raised questions about how Chinese culture and civilization would fit into the emerging framework of categorical knowledge. As the nineteenth century wore on, however, the model of knowledge as an encyclopedic whole dissolved and was replaced with one where knowledge was parsed into finer and finer disciplinary units. This only compounded the problem of where to fit Asians and their civilizations. As one writer put it, "In what category to place them must puzzle the psychologist."[24] It puzzled the rest of America as well.

Asia at the Fair: 1876 and 1893

Dunn's museum had a spectacular but brief life, both in Philadelphia and in London. By the late 1840s, Dunn was dead and the collection had been dispersed in ways that are still unclear. The museum had at least two American imitators: Peter's Chinese Museum in New York and Boston's Chinese Museum. Each drew on the prestige of Dunn's venture by claiming to be even bigger but were otherwise quite similar, at least to judge from the remaining descriptions. These museum ventures didn't last long either.[25] In addition, P. T. Barnum acquired a large Chinese collection for his New York museum but decided that exhibiting Chinese people would be an even bigger draw.[26] With these exceptions, however, Americans would have to wait until 1876 before they could again see a large, synoptic collection of objects from Asia.

Although both China and Japan made showings at Philadelphia's Centennial International Exhibition in 1876, the Japanese took the opportunity to bring themselves to the world's attention in a way that the Chinese did not. Consequently, although China's exhibits excited some "curiosity and interest," it was Japan's displays that drew the greatest attention. Japan's geopolitical position had shifted since the 1850s and the forced "opening" of the country by Americans. The Japanese were now willingly, and successfully, pursuing a progressive—that is to say, Western—course of development, and thus their cultural production was more sympathetically received. As a consequence, "many European and American arts and sciences have since been introduced." In

Figure 11. China at the 1876 Centennial Exposition. Courtesy of the Print and Picture Collection, Free Library of Philadelphia.

addition, "the youth of Japan have been sent abroad to America and to European countries to be educated."[27]

In his exhaustive research on the various ways Chinese culture came to the United States during its first one hundred years, John Haddad has demonstrated that there was not a uniformly contemptuous attitude about China and the Chinese. He argues that in many of these cultural interactions the Chinese themselves played an active role in their own representation.[28] Nonetheless, I think it is fair to say that the comparison to Japan, made for the first time in Philadelphia in 1876, allowed Americans to dismiss China while celebrating Japan. Indeed, the juxtaposition of exhibits made it possible, at least for some, to resolve the contradictions and conundrums China represented in the Western imagination. Japan could now be seen as a compatriot of Western nations, which made it that much easier to reject China for its obstinate refusal to westernize. One reporter from Cincinnati drew this conclusion in his report from Philadelphia to readers back home: "The Japanese Department . . . lies side by side with the Chinese. The oldest of Oriental Empires is thus placed in close contrast with the newest addition to the disciples of Western progressiveness. . . . Here is slow old China, with the bulk of her exhibit unpacked. . . . How different is it with the ambitious, striving, progressive Japan! She is all ready and obviously anxious to be seen. . . . On this side of the aisle all is life; just across the way, the almond-eyed Celestials have learned little since the days of Confucius."[29] Those Americans who had condescended, or worse, toward China needed the comparison made in 1876 between Japan and China to demonstrate that they had been right all along.

The Japanese government hoped in a deliberate and self-conscious way to make a big impression in Philadelphia and may well have been aware of the gain to be made by the comparison. They had made their first showing in an international exhibition three years earlier in Vienna; in 1876 they chose objects valued at roughly two hundred thousand dollars and spent another four hundred thousand dollars on their transport and display in Philadelphia. In addition, the Japanese commission to the fair published, in English, a forty-two-page primer on the history, cus-. toms, and politics of Japan for distribution at the exhibition. The result was a triumph. James McCabe wrote a large illustrated history of the fair, and the Japanese exhibits in the fair's main building left him breathless. Of a particular work in bronze, he assured readers that it "cannot be reproduced by the most skillful artificer in either Europe or America." Porcelain "attained perfection in Japan before it was known in Europe," and the display of porcelain pieces in Philadelphia "surpasses in beauty of form and ornamentation the combined exhibit of every other nation in the building." He concluded his tour through these galleries by telling readers that "the visitor who makes even a hasty inspection of the display . . . must amend his ideas of Japan. We have been accustomed to regard that country as uncivilized or half-civilized at best, but we find here abundant evidences that it outshines the most cultivated nations of Europe." At Philadelphia, as Neil Harris has observed, "the Japanese made their first entry into the popular consciousness."[30]

The 1876 Exposition, like Dunn's museum before it, provided a substitute for travel to faraway places, but unlike museums whose collections were not for sale, the Exposition provided a place for these ersatz travelers to purchase souvenirs. Both William and Henry Walters, the wealthy Baltimore collectors, "lacked either the time or the inclination to travel to the Far East. Therefore, international exhibitions remained for [them their] only opportunities to follow the Far Eastern art market." William Walters bought ten thousand dollars' worth of Japanese bronzes from the Centennial Exposition.[31]

Just as Japan's exhibits in 1876 reflected a newly ambitious relationship with the West, China's reflected a country still falling in Western estimation. The Chinese display in the main building was less than half the size of Japan's, and McCabe felt that "every part of the enclosure is of the gaudiest character." He acknowledged some "exquisitely carved articles in ivory" but was otherwise condescending in his assessment. Far from finding the Chinese the equal of European civilization, McCabe found them primitive and concluded by saying, "A number of almond-eyed, pig-tailed celestials, in their native costumes are scattered through the enclosure, and you may for a moment imagine that you have put the sea between you and the Exhibition and have suddenly landed in some large Chinese bazaar."[32]

By 1876 Japan's cultural stock may have been rising, both absolutely and in relation to China, but it had not yet reached the plateau of fine art. The exhibition in Philadelphia represented a snapshot of nineteenth-century industrial progress and reflected ideas about how the world should be classed or categorized. In addition to the exhibits from foreign nations and from each of the states, the fair included those of industry as separate from agriculture and fine art as separate from technology. In this schema, fine art did not include Japanese, or indeed any Asian, objects—neither in the fine art building and its annex nor in Frank Leslie's official guide, *Masterpieces of the Centennial International Exhibition*. Leslie could not quite resolve how to describe Japanese art. "The grotesque in art," he reported, "seems to be a part of the very nature of the Japanese . . . not only in the dragons and other unknown creatures delineated, but in caricatures of domestic life which are exceedingly comical." Japanese objects were certainly admired by visitors in 1876 but they were not exhibited in the same space as fine art.[33]

For Japanese objects, the final ascension to art would have to wait until 1893, in Chicago. Japan had been among the first countries to respond to the call for exhibits at the World's Columbian Exposition and eventually spent more than six hundred thousand dollars on displays. The Japanese built their own pavilion, and the country was fully represented in almost all of the major buildings in the White City, from mining to fisheries, including the Palace of Fine Arts. People certainly acknowledged that "the art exhibit of Japan differs, of course, from that of other countries," yet there it was, in room 24 of the Palace, between Spain and Holland. This is not to say that the Japanese were not subjected to sneers, racialist jibes, and other small condescensions. Still, the exhibits at the fair had the effect on many visitors of admitting the Japanese to the family of civilized nations, which was underscored by their inclusion in the fine arts building. The title character of the popular 1893 novel *The Adventures of Uncle Jeremiah and Family at the Great Fair* overhears two women discussing the Japanese exhibits: "I don't see the use of sending missionaries to Japan. I don't believe they are so very bad at all. I don't believe that anyone who could make such lovely things could be a very wicked heathen."[34] Such were the cultural stakes for Japan in 1893, and those attitudes would last. Just before the First World War, high school principal Emilie Jacobs published a set of lesson plans about Asia. Among the "12 Japanese Traits" students ought to memorize were "self-control; bravery and courage; patriotism; honest; politeness; hospitality; reverence; love of beauty." Given all this, it should come as no surprise that the conclusion to these lessons read simply, "The most progressive and intelligent nation of Asia: Japan."[35]

China, by contrast, smarting at the passage of the Chinese Exclusion Act ten years earlier, refused to sponsor an exhibit on fairgrounds proper but rather was represented out on the Midway by a reproduction of a Chinese village. Having spiraled into chaos and civil war by 1893, the country was described by some Western writers as an "empire in catalepsy," undergoing a "vivisection." One included China as one of three "rotten cultures."[36] From great empire to village, the display in 1893 stood almost metaphorically for what had happened to China in the eyes of the West by the 1890s.

With their public sanction in Chicago, Japanese objects became the vehicle through which American collectors first established Asian material as fine art, and Japanese culture became the avenue through which Americans would develop an appreciation for the whole region. The MFA in Boston took the lead in collecting and displaying Asian art, most importantly under the impetus of William Sturgis Bigelow and Ernest Fenollosa in the 1890s. (By contrast, the Metropolitan Museum of Art did not hire a specialist curator for Asian art until 1915.) It is surely not coincidental that Freer began his career as a collector of Asian objects in 1894 with a group of Japanese prints.

While Japanese objects were making their debut as fine art in 1893, the World's Columbian Exposition also presented the emerging discipline of anthropology to a broad public for the first time. Conceived as the scientific study of human culture, anthropology represented a new field of knowledge, growing from roots in history, archaeology, ethnology, and natural science. As the Smithsonian's Otis Mason exclaimed, "It would not be too much to say that the World's Columbian Exposition was one vast anthropological revelation." The discipline not only had its own building at the fair but also was the subject of a great International Congress of Anthropology there in late August. The fair offered anthro-

Figure 12. Japan triumphed in Chicago in 1893, while China was regarded as a degraded civilization. From Hubert Howe Bancroft, *The Book of the Fair* (Chicago: Bancroft Company, 1893). Image courtesy of the Paul Galvin Library, Illinois Institute of Technology.

pologists an unprecedented opportunity to present their work to the public and thus to legitimate the discipline itself.[37]

Anthropologists, in part emboldened by their triumph in Chicago in 1893, set about the task of creating large museum collections. The White City gave birth directly to the Field Museum of Natural History, which, at its founding, had a large anthropological section. Simultaneously, the University of Pennsylvania had formed its own museum of anthropology and archaeology in the 1890s. The Field Museum located anthropology under the larger umbrella of natural history, but the University of Pennsylvania's was the first major museum in the United States devoted exclusively to these fields. Both museums, and several other anthropological collections as well, included Asian objects. Chicago's 1893 World's Fair thus signaled the appreciation of Asian objects as both art and anthropology.

Art versus Anthropology

Benjamin March's 1929 survey suggests that the distinctions made in museums between art and anthropology were not simply a matter of choosing between different kinds of objects. Both the Field Museum and the Museum of Fine Arts in Boston collected approximately the same types of objects: jade, lacquerware, sculpture, ceramics, armor, and metalwork. This material could function, apparently, as both art and anthropology. However, the distinctions between the two were not obvious. At a superficial level, to find art in Asian objects might mean to appreciate aesthetic or, indeed, spiritual qualities, while to see those objects anthropologically might mean to see in them illustrations of the lifeways of those who made them. In fact, the MFA's Fenollosa and Boston collector Bigelow were both sufficiently drawn to the mystery and exoticism of Japan to convert to Buddhism. And Fenollosa used his knowledge of Chinese and Japanese art to elucidate Chinese and Japanese traits for readers of the *Atlantic,* a project with decidedly anthropological-sounding overtones.[38] Likewise, as I discuss shortly, Maxwell Sommerville, who donated his collection of Buddhist objects to the University of Pennsylvania's anthropology museum, took to dressing as a Buddhist monk and sitting in the midst of his collection to chat with museum visitors.

Put simply, Asian objects did not fit comfortably into the frameworks used for understanding art or for defining anthropology in turn-of-the-century American museums. Anthropologists of the late nineteenth century borrowed their understanding of human culture from the theories of natural sciences. Relying on the evolutionary metaphor, many who studied human culture felt that cultures, like the development of organisms from lowest to highest, went through a roughly evolutionary progression from barbarism through savagery to civilization. In part, this framework helped those in the West understand the astonishing variety of the world's other cultures—cultures they encountered with more regularity and with greater intensity through imperialist and colonialist adventures. But Western anthropology also insisted that the world's cultures be understood hierarchically and that the contemporary West represented humanity's highest cultural achievement. As John Haddad has put it, "Most cultural evolutionists regarded China as a colossal anomaly and shied away from serious study of it."[39]

Anthropology had its first institutional home in natural history museums, and the history of the Asian collections at New York's AMNH underscores the difficulty faced by those who built museums of exactly where to put the East. Franz Boas ran that anthropology department at AMNH and wanted to use the museum's collections and exhibits to illustrate his own ideas about cultural development. Boas, as is well known, rejected the ideas of the nineteenth-century cultural evolutionists and saw instead a more relativistic set of changes and adaptations. China, with its lengthy history and sophisticated culture, was for Boas an ideal society to prove his point that cultures needed to be understood on their own terms, not merely against the measure of the West. In 1900 he sent German anthropologist Berthold Laufer on an expedition to China, reminding him that the goal "is to bring home to the public the fact that the Chinese have a civilization of their own, and to inculcate respect for the Chinese."[40]

Things proved not to be so straightforward. By 1902, Boas was growing concerned about the kinds of materials Laufer was sending back to the museum. Laufer grew to have enormous respect for Chinese painting, writing that he believed "the best Chinese masters are not inferior to the artists of Italy and Holland," and thought that Chinese sculpture rivaled "whatever Greek sculpture brought to light." While comparing Chinese art to the best of the Western tradition might indeed foster Boas's goal to "inculcate respect" for the Chinese, it did not necessarily do so in an "anthropological" way. Boas wrote to Laufer urging him to collect more on "the industrial side" of Chinese arts and crafts. Boas worried that Laufer's own interests "center so much more towards the religious, literary, and artistic life."[41] Boas's ideas about anthropology broke from those of the nineteenth century, but he remained committed to the notion that certain kinds of objects had anthropological—that is, scientific—value, and "art" objects were not among them.

Back in New York, Boas's exhibits worried those who ran the AMNH. By concentrating so much on presenting the "science" of anthropology, Boas risked boring visitors who found little to hold their attention. As already mentioned, when museum president Morris Jesup toured the anthropology galleries, he announced, "I am not satisfied." The exhibits left him confused and frustrated. By 1908, with Boas gone, Jesup and the AMNH had decided that China "was not within our province at all."[42] Anthropology found a home in natural history museums provided it reinforced notions of cultural evolution, echoing the biological evolution on display in the rest of the museum, and reinforced the hierarchies that separated the "primitive" world, rooted in the natural world, from the civilized, which had transcended nature. On these terms, China was surely not within the province of the AMNH.

Things proved no less confusing at the nation's first museum devoted exclusively to anthropology. When the University of Pennsylvania's museum opened its permanent quarters late in 1899, visitors entered through two great wooden doors. Above those doors two figures carved in stone hold a medallion that is inscribed "Free Museum of Science and Art." The free part of the name was easy. Philadelphia mayor Edwin Stuart traded city-owned land to the university for the promise of a museum open to the public without charge. Science and art, which presumably defined what the visitor would find behind those wooden doors, proved to be more complicated. Passing through the doors of the new building, visitors found themselves on a landing. From the landing, they could ascend to the second floor, where, according to the museum *Bulletin*, they would find artifacts from the ancient Mediterranean world and objects secured by the museum's famous expeditions to the Near East. Should visitors choose instead to go downstairs, they would discover something of a hodgepodge: a collection of objects connected with Buddhism; "ethnological objects of Asiatic origin, material from central and South America"; and "collections illustrative of the life of the Colorado cliff dwellers, and other American aborigines and collections . . . recently brought from Borneo and adjacent islands."[43]

The symbolism in the design of the museum was not subtle: from the entrance landing, one *rose* to find the civilizations of the Near East and the Mediterranean but *descended* to find Native Americans from all parts of the New World, Buddhism, and objects from the primitives of Borneo. The division between the top floor, arranged with a geographic order, and the bottom floor, arranged randomly, was the difference between what was considered to be civilized and what was considered primitive. Rome, Greece, Egypt, Sumer—all had a direct, genealogical relation to the civilizations of Europe and the United States. These societies had a history, and their cultural products could thus be considered art. Other groups—those without any discernible connection to Europe and the United States—had no history, as Westerners defined the term, and their cultural products could only be studied by the new science of anthropology.

These distinctions and the hierarchies that they reinforced worked admirably well to explain the differences between Americans and the indigenous tribes they had conquered and between Europeans and the African groups they colonized. But how did the model explain the cultures of China and Japan? At the turn of the twentieth century Westerners continued to view the East with an admixture of awe and condescension, respect and contempt.

After all, the Chinese could lay claim to a legitimate history, punctuated with dynasties, major cultural epochs, political events, and all of the chronological markers that define what history means in Western terms. More than that, Chinese history stretched back continuously far beyond any society in the West; its sheer scope made Western civilization seem insignificant. Finally, Asian objects, as records of this long history, demonstrated a level of technical and aesthetic accomplishment that made much of Western art seem crude. Yet clearly this continued to cause some Westerners to chafe. As an anonymous reviewer put it in the *Edinburgh Review* in 1910, "No one, we suppose, will accuse the East of anything very remarkable in the way of intellectual development. . . . Eastern life has very little in it of what we call intellectual, save what it has occasionally borrowed from Western sources."[44]

In this way, China and Japan unsettled the easy dichotomies that formed the foundational core of early anthropology—dichotomies between those groups that had a proper history and those that had only an anthropological culture. Neither China nor Japan formed part of the Western lineage, and yet they clearly did not belong comfortably in the same category as the cultures from Borneo. Both societies struck Westerners as existing within the chronological bounds of history and in the timelessness of culture—what the reviewer of Dunn's museum had, years earlier, called the "unchanging" Chinese. Both produced objects of art and science. Viewing Asian objects through an anthropological lens did not adequately solve the categorical problems first posed by Dunn's museum.[45] China did not reside comfortably as either science or art.

Fine Art Triumphant

In 1915 Laurence Binyon authored "The Art of Asia," which appeared in *Atlantic Monthly:* "The art of Asia, with its revelation of so rich a world of beauty hidden so long from Western eyes, has in quite recent years assumed more and more of importance, and attracts new students and new lovers every day. It is a vast subject, as vast almost as the art of Europe." By the early years of the twentieth century, then, the discourse about Asian objects had shifted significantly since the days of Dunn. Asians were now seen as being capable of producing "beauty" and were being given credit for an art history almost comparable in its scope and breadth to that of Europe. Binyon at one point compares Chinese painting with that of "rather exceptional artists like Botticelli." By this time, several American museums of fine art were collecting and displaying Asian objects as art. When the first Walters Gallery opened to the public in 1884 it had an "Oriental Gallery"—more a corridor to judge from the photos—and when it moved into its new home in 1909, the Asian collection had grown large enough to warrant its own catalogue. The Cleveland Museum of Art, when it opened in 1916 had among its original fifteen galleries one each for Japan and China. The first issue of the

Cleveland Museum's *Bulletin* captured nicely the shift in attitude that had taken place by the early years of the twentieth century. Describing one of its stone statues, soon to go on public display, the *Bulletin* took the opportunity to make a larger case for Chinese art: "It has been said that the Chinese have no sculpture; that it is more like carving than anything we know by a higher name. Is there anything wanting in the dignity of this figure, in the grandeur of conception, in the sculptural effect, in the proportion, or in the adornments which so closely resemble the real? Here we have something concrete, and not merely a strange expression of foreign religious thought. We readily associate tenderness, compassion and mercy with this beautiful god."[46] By 1921, Asian art collector Worcester Reed Warner could write "Oriental Art, which was once the cult of the few, has recently come to be the interest of the many. Fine examples of it are now to be found not only in museums but in the hands of numerous private collectors around the world."[47]

Yet perhaps the most dramatic institutional manifestation of the arrival of Asian objects in the category of art was the creation of the Freer Gallery in Washington, D.C. Freer had amassed an amazing private collection. Selected pieces from it had been put on display as the inaugural exhibit in Cleveland, where museum officials gushed, "How great is our debt to him may be easily comprehended, when it is said that from no other collection on this continent, still less in Europe, could such a selection have been made."[48] Donated to the nation by Charles Freer in 1906 (after some distasteful squabbling), the Freer collection opened finally to the public in 1923 and signaled the ultimate acceptance of Asian objects into the category of fine art. The only collection to rival it was at Boston's MFA. According to journalist Agnes Meyer, the Freer "was the only place in the world where the entire development of Chinese pictorial design may be studied." Meyer also insisted, evincing a nationalistic pride born of years of feeling culturally inferior to Europe, that "if European scholars must now come to America to see the finest examples of Chinese painting, Chinese jades and bronzes," it was because of Freer. As Grace Dunham Guest, assistant curator at the gallery in 1927, stated in a series of articles for the *United States Daily*, "It is as a museum of Oriental art that the Freer Gallery takes its place among the few centers devoted to scholarly research in that field."[49]

Needless to say, the location of Asian objects more squarely in the category of fine art was not inevitable, nor was it complete. To the suggestion that Freer's gift might be used as the core of a new, national museum of art, Charles Moore, who was involved in redesigning the Mall, wrote dismissively to President Theodore Roosevelt, "Mr. Freer's collection is a special one. It can have no possible relation to such a general and indeterminate thing as a National Art Gallery."[50]

The aesthetic movement that flourished in the United States in the 1880s and 1890s was an important point of entry for Asian objects into the American artistic consciousness. In 1882 Oscar Wilde made a celebrated tour of the country preaching the gospel of aesthetics to enthusiastic crowds. Enlisting artists such as John La Farge, Louis Comfort Tiffany, and Candace Wheeler, American aesthetes sought to spread beauty and art throughout the land, hoping that its effects would soften the edges of a hardened, industrial nation. James Abbott McNeill Whistler was a towering figure in the movement, and his admiration for Japanese art was tremendously influential. In fact, it may be fair to say that Whistler was among the first Western artists to incorporate Japanese motifs and elements into his work. Following Whistler's lead, a handful of aesthetes—Fenollosa and Freer prominent among them—shaped a discourse that insisted on seeing Asian objects as art. As Jeffrey Nunokawa has stated about this cultural moment, "In an early instance of Japanese exceptionalism the land of the rising sun was apprehended by Western eyes as a palace of art."[51]

Among other things, these scholars and aesthetes created around Asian art the same scholarly apparatus that had developed around Western art in the nineteenth century. As Binyon sketched it, Japanese and Chinese painting "has developed within itself movements, corresponding to the movements in Western painting, and where a surprising amount of work that is centuries old seems modern in feeling and contemporary with ourselves." As I have suggested, the lines around the category of art were drawn in the nineteenth century to exclude Asian cultural production. Binyon suggested that those lines could be straightened and drawn parallel. Such collectors, critics, and aesthetes also helped to change the political context for discussing China and Japan. Japan could more easily be seen by the West as progressive because of its aggressive and successful campaigns of modernization. China, as we have already noted, languished in civil war and therefore in the estimation of the West at the turn of the century. Indeed, the Cleveland Museum of Art, which included a gallery of Chinese art when it opened, took the opportunity for a dig at China's recalcitrance in its inaugural catalogue. Describing the 172 Chinese objects on display, the catalogue complained, "There is scarcely one subject upon which it is possible to be sure that our position is impregnable. The chief of many reasons for this uncertainty would seem to lie in the reluctance of the Chinese themselves to permit anything in the way of excavation."[52]

Still, art appreciators reminded Western readers that Japan owed a great cultural debt to China, and for this reason, if for no other, China was worthy of a cultural reappraisal. A writer for the *North American Review* could casually toss off that "nobody ever claimed for the Japanese originality of thought or religiosity of temper." For these writers, China could play Greece to Japan's Rome in the cultural construction of the West. "In a sense," wrote Binyon, "Japan owes everything to China."[53]

Beyond rescuing the reputations of Asian civilizations in the eyes of the West, Western Asiaphiles had another agenda that was better served by locating objects in the category of art rather than in anthropology. Implicit in the intellectual constructions of anthropologists was a stress on difference and distance. By studying exotic and primitive cultures and by putting those cultures on display for the public in museums, anthropologists underscored a sense of otherness and the notion that evolutionary progress had brought the West a great distance from its primitive origins. These stresses were, as I suggested earlier, part of what made it difficult to place China and Japan within anthropological frameworks.

Those who promoted Asian objects as art wanted quite explicitly to emphasize sameness, commonality, and especially cultural cross-fertilization. Ernest Fenollosa was "an outspoken advocate of an East-West synthesis in the arts."[54] In a 1962 biographical sketch of Fenollosa and his ideas about Japan, cultural critic Van Wyck Brooks stressed the sense of closeness and familiarity Fenollosa felt with Japanese culture and that he tried to foster in others. Worried that as a result of rapid modernization the Japanese themselves had "ceased to treasure their traditions and their heirlooms" and that "the old native arts were regarded as barbaric," Fenollosa saw himself in the role of Ruskin for Japan: "Fenollosa found, in his travels, a condition that was much like Italy's as Ruskin described this in *The Stones of Venice*." Brooks closed this appreciation of Fenollosa by quoting a letter Fenollosa had written to his friend and colleague Edward Morse: "I cannot see why my work this summer was not just as important at bottom as much as that which the world's archaeologists are doing in Greece and Turkey. Of course people don't see the practical importance of Eastern civilization for the world with the same vividness as they do that of Greek culture. . . . But from the point of view of human history as a whole it is absolutely indispensable."[55] Art helped Fenollosa and others link Japan firmly in the traditions of Greece and Rome in its significance to the history of civilization.

His ideas about the connections between East and West shaped the way Freer organized his collection. Freer seems to have developed an enthusiasm for Eastern thought and culture and to have believed that elements of both could be beneficial to the West. As Meyer wrote, Freer "derived boundless happiness from his contact with Oriental lore" and "began to discover profound value for our turbulent era in the calm acceptance of the world which the Chinese sages possessed." His "definite ambition," she continued, was "to bring to the Occident and particularly to Americans the great philosophical, moral and aesthetic contributions which he discerned in their noble art traditions."[56] Son of the bustling industrial city of Detroit, Freer offered the timeless wisdom and calm of the East as an antidote to the hurly-burly of American life.

Freer did not necessarily view his assemblage as one primarily of Asian art. By the time he donated it to the nation, it was probably most notable for its group of works by Whistler, who was already an art-world celebrity. When the gallery was under construction, newspaper readers kept up with events through stories with headlines such as "Nation Is Heir to Works of Whistler's Genius" and "The Freer Gallery Opens with Important Whistler Collection." In fact, much of the Chinese material in Freer's collection was added after Whistler's death in 1903, as if Freer used those objects to fill out the collection of paintings by his now-dead friend. Meyer, writing in 1927, just four years after the museum opened, claimed that the whole museum was "a memorial to the great friendship which existed between these two men, a memorial such as no painter and but few other human beings have ever been given." According to scholar Linda Merrill, "The Asian objects were meant to enhance the Whistlers."[57]

The significance of Freer's collection and the museum he gave to the nation, then, may not be that it signaled the elevation of Asian objects to the lofty position of fine art equivalent to European painting. Rather, his purpose seems to have been to use Asian objects as a way of demonstrating a fundamental aesthetic connection between a handful of American painters—Whistler first and foremost, Dwight William Tryon, Thomas Wilmer Dewing, and Abbott Handerson Thayer secondarily—and the art of Asia. Freer always saw his collection "as constituting a harmonious whole." More than that, he may have surrounded his paintings with Asian objects as a way of giving the former a legitimacy and a pedigree of sorts. In this sense, his attraction to Asian art bears a resemblance to the fascination European modernists had for the primitive sculptures of Africa in the early years of the twentieth century. In both cases, non-Western artistic traditions served not only as the source of artistic inspiration—Japanese paintings for Whistler, African masks for Picasso—but to give definition to modernist aesthetics. And in both cases the definitions that emerged from the connection to non-Western traditions traded on a set of long-held stereotypes about those other cultures. Picasso's modernism was seen to be infused with the raw energy associated with the primitive; for Freer, modernism meant drawing on the harmonies, mysteries, and timeless qualities perceived to be at the heart of the East. As Binyon observed, "We feel no veiling interval of time between the most typical Chinese paintings of a thousand years ago and ourselves. Of how much European art can we say this? How modern in spirit are the Chinese paintings."[58]

By displaying Whistler's paintings and Asian objects together, Freer demonstrated that Whistler's painting, whatever its relations to the art historical traditions of the West, was rooted in the history of art and thought in the East. As Freer told Smithsonian secretary Samuel Pierpont Langley in a letter, "My great desire has been to unite modern work with masterpieces of high civilization harmonious in spiritual and physical suggestion, having power to broaden aesthetic culture and the grace to elevate the human mind."[59] Freer's collection illustrated Binyon's point about the modernity of ancient Asian traditions and demonstrated that Whistler had connected with these spirits.

Freer used his museum to define a certain kind of modernism—one where Western painting, tired and hackneyed by the nineteenth century, would be reinvigorated through contact and inspiration from Asia. According to Fenollosa, the Freer collection "illustrates the most conspicuous fact in the history of art, that the two great streams of European and Asiatic practice, held apart for so many thousand years, have . . . been brought together in a fertile and final union." In Fenollosa's estimation, nineteenth-century painters (the Barbizon school, the impressionists) had made only a "superficial and unsystematic study" of Asian art. The deeper truths to be learned by students following Freer's lead might well help develop a "new canon to supplant our gray, academic traditions."[60]

At the Freer Gallery, Asian art could be appreciated on its own terms, but that was not apparently what Freer intended primarily. Rather, seen as a context for contemporary American paintings, it pointed the way for a new artistic movement, embodying the essential truths of both East and West. His solution to the problem of how to categorize Asian objects was in fact less a solution to the larger question than it was an idiosyncratic way of institutionalizing a particular vision of American art using a particular vision of Asia.

As fine art museums took over the primary role of exhibiting Asian objects to the American public, the scholarly work of studying these objects moved, in the twentieth century, to departments of art history. There, Chinese and Japanese cultural production are taught, studied, and therefore legitimated in the same institutional context as Western painting and sculpture. With the exception of archaeological remains, the study of Chinese and Japanese material culture is now conducted largely by art historians.

That fine art won the day over anthropology in the debate over where to place Asian objects reflects only partly a resolution to the categorical debate that had been ongoing since the 1830s. It reflects as well anthro-

Figure 13. Asian art arrives on the Mall. The Freer Gallery shortly after it opened. Courtesy of the Freer Gallery of Art and Arthur M. Sackler Gallery, Smithsonian Institution, Washington, D.C.

pology's movement away from the study of objects altogether as we discussed in Chapter 2. Most of the prominent ethnologists/anthropologists in the last quarter of the nineteenth century—Franz Boas, Frederick Putnam, Stewart Culin, to name three—had connections to museums, and in those museums they shaped the study of an anthropology that was dependent on objects.

By the first quarter of the twentieth century, anthropology was leaving its museum nest and roosting more and more in university departments, particularly under the influence of Boas. By the First World War, according to Curtis Hinsley, the concerns of museums and academic departments had drifted far enough apart to make interactions between them "rare." By 1920 roughly half of the professional anthropologists in the United States made their institutional home in college and university departments, and that was the direction in which the traffic would continue to flow. In short, anthropologists ceased to be much interested in objects of any kind.[61]

Further, neither China nor Japan proved to be fertile anthropological fields in the late nineteenth and early twentieth centuries. For example, none of the papers published from the 1893 anthropological congress at the Columbian Exposition in Chicago dealt with Asia. Perhaps because neither China nor Japan existed in direct colonial relationship to a Western power at this time, or perhaps because early anthropologists preferred to study cultures that were more easily and recognizably primitive, Western anthropologists did not much venture into the Asian field.

Thus Asian objects became more thoroughly the province of art museums and art history departments. This was so, not necessarily because those places were intellectually more hospitable, but because anthropologists had ceded them and moved on to other concerns. And as a consequence, as Clunas has noted, objects that once were seen to embody anthropological information were now discussed in terms of "influences and trends": "Objects transferred from the domain of 'ethnography' to that of 'art' typically find diachronic links privileged at the expense of connections with others that have failed to make the transition." By the First World War, even the University of Pennsylvania's anthropology museum had conceded that its Asian objects were no longer in the category of anthropological "science" but had jumped across the divide into the realm of art. Echoing the ideas of Freer and other aesthetes, authors of a new handbook of oriental art told visitors that schools of Asian art were "destined to exert a steadily growing influence upon the esthetic ideals of Occidental lands." And it concluded, if the point needed to be made, "It is for this eminently practical reason, as well as for its own intrinsic interest, that the field of Oriental art is so important to us."[62]

By the time March published his survey in 1929, art had won the debate. Although anthropological collections still contained significant numbers of important objects, art museums became the primary home for Asian sculpture, ceramics, jade, and the like. In the foreword to March's book, E. C. Carter was quite clear about the political implications of this victory: "Our museums, in holding up before the American people a true picture of the life, the art, and the techniques of the orient, are fulfilling an educational purpose much needed in our day by providing 'a reminder that these orientals are no sinister barbarians but a race founded in deep wisdom and culture.'" He went on to commend American art museums for encouraging "a sympathy . . . toward the oldest of living civilizations."[63]

The institutional decision to place Asian objects in art museums reflected an intellectual shift in the way Americans viewed the cultures that produced those objects. By conferring the status of fine art on the objects, American museums thus elevated Asian culture and helped shape a popular view of Asia that, while surely not equivalent to that of the West, was more elevated than that of the rest of the world's non-Western people.

Such were the stakes in the contest between art and anthropology. To be associated with art meant wisdom and culture, for which the American public ought to have a sympathy. These were the virtues that anthropology could not necessarily bestow upon the creators of these objects. But neither category of knowledge could comfortably embrace Asian cultural production. If an anthropological understanding did not do justice to the civilizations of the East, then an art historical system of meaning that stressed aesthetic and formal qualities did not, perhaps, leave room for an understanding of the people and social forces that created the objects on display. In the end, art became an effective way of transforming the Chinese and Japanese from the barbarians of the nineteenth century to civilized, if still exotic, players on the world stage by the end of the twentieth century.

Asian Objects as Asian Experience

In December 2003 I had the opportunity to see the exhibit "Circle of Bliss: Buddhist Meditational Art" at the Los Angeles County Museum of Art (LACMA). The show had received strong notices in all the right places, and I entered with no small level of excitement and anticipation. "Circle of Bliss" was an exhibit of objects, mostly from Nepal and Tibet, illustrative of that particular kind of Buddhism called Tantric.

The show, at least as it was installed at LACMA, had a certain lushness to it—lots of deep red walls and seductive lighting. But after a few galleries I had to confess to my companion that I found the whole exhibit quite strange, though I couldn't quite put my finger on why.

Perhaps, she said, irritation evident in her tone, I was annoyed because nothing in the show suggested any connection between the iconography of the objects on display and the older traditions of Hinduism from which most of these stories, myths, and figures came.

No, I thought, that wasn't it, because I know absolutely nothing about the iconography of Hinduism, though this was probably the source of her annoyance, my friend being a Hindu, or rather a lapsed Hindu, who now felt some obligation to stand up for the religious tradition in which she, as a Southern Californian born and bred, otherwise had little interest.

My friend, her Hindu nationalism newly inflamed, was certainly right, however, and not just about the Hinduism displayed in the show. There was very little of the sort of historical context one has come to expect from broad survey art exhibits—not much to explain where Tantric Buddhism came from in the first place, or where the nation of Nepal came from (no mention, in fact, that in the nation of Nepal, only 10 percent or so of the population are practicing Buddhists).

Even at a level more internal to the subject of the show, there wasn't much by way of historical context. No time spent tracing the evolution of styles, schools, techniques, or influences. Nothing to answer the most basic historical question: How has Tantric Buddhism changed over time, in response to any number of changing political, social, economic, military, and cultural circumstances? In the individual galleries, this fundamentally ahistorical approach to the subject meant that objects from the seventeenth century shared space with objects produced quite recently, without any sense that specific temporalities might matter. As portrayed by the "Circle of Bliss," Tantric Buddhism is what it is, is what it always has been, and is what it always will be. Simply put, it has no history.

These may only be the small, parochial concerns of a historian. In fact, the exhibit worked deliberately to break free of the usual and conventional art historical questions. Indeed, as John Huntington, one of the co-curators, puts it in the catalogue introduction, "*The Circle of Bliss* is part of an emerging trend to design exhibitions along thematic lines that reflect the cultural concerns and values that they represent rather than Western-based art historical taxonomies."[64] Thus the exhibit depicts Tantric Buddhism as Tantric Buddhists would have it, and in this sense "Circle of Bliss" reflects the anxieties over representations of non-Western culture as discussed in Chapters 1 and 2. It may be interesting to exhibit Buddhism in ways "that reflect the cultural concerns and values that they represent rather than Western-based art historical taxonomies," but it isn't self-evident that it will be, and doing so only replaces one set of vexatious questions with another.

At the same time, "Circle of Bliss" seemed an almost perfect illustration of Susan Stewart's description of "the collection," even if in this case the collection in question exists only temporarily. "The collection," she writes, "seeks a form of self-enclosure which is possible because of its ahistoricism. The collection replaces history with *classification*, with order beyond the realm of temporality. In the collection, time is not something to be restored to an origin; rather, all time is made simultaneous or synchronous within the collection's world."[65] And if not quite classification, in this case, certainly "thematization."

One could be forgiven, especially on a casual stroll through the exhibit, for concluding that "Circle of Bliss" simply recapitulated the central Orientalist trope of the "timeless and unchanging" East. Yet while it struck me as remarkable that such troping would still go on—one cannot imagine, for example, an exhibit on Lutheranism that commingled objects made in 1677 and 1977 without any attempt to explain the differences between then and now—this was not, ultimately, the reason that I found "Circle of Bliss" so odd.

The organizing principle of the show was to display the constituent parts of Tantric Buddhist worship. Thus, by the time I got to the end of the show, I couldn't help but feel that I had just walked through a well-illustrated, three-dimensional how-to manual. This, I learned later when reading the catalogue, was just about how I was supposed to feel. As Huntington puts it at the very beginning of the book, in a way that struck me as reaching more for Zen koan than Tantric enlightenment, "When is an exhibition not an exhibition? When it is about the beauty of the idea behind the art. *The Circle of Bliss: Buddhist Meditational Art* exhibition has been designed to highlight the aspirations and ideals that inspired this remarkable body of works of art."[66] By the end of the show, one did not learn much about Tantric Buddhism as a world historical phenomenon, but one might have absorbed quite a lot about how to be a Tantric Buddhist (though I confess I did not pay quite enough attention to have achieved this Nirvana by the time I reached the gift shop). "Of course," my angry Hindu friend responded, "this is LA—half the people here already claim to be Buddhists and the other half think they ought to be."

I found the thrust of the show to be just as remarkable as the "timelessness" of everything on display. After all, one can't imagine that our hypothetical exhibition on Lutheranism, curated, say, by Garrison Keillor, would be organized around teaching people how to be Lutherans (one gallery devoted to the making of casserole dishes, another to the organizing of rummage sales, and so on).

In this way, "Circle of Bliss" participated in the other tradition I mentioned at the outset of this chapter. If some museums tried to act as "detached observers" by trying to fit Asia into established taxonomies and frameworks, then others functioned as "seekers of salvation." In this tradition, museum and exposition displays employ Asian objects in order to convey not simply knowledge about the exotic East but also some sense of Eastern spirituality and mysticism, those "aspirations and ideals." Through displays of objects from Asia, Western museum visitors might not only learn information about these cultures but, more, gain some measure of esoteric wisdom. These museums attempt to combine the visual with the experiential and, in so doing, these exhibits—of which "Circle of Bliss" was merely the latest—have allowed visitors to "go native," so to speak, at least for an afternoon.

As we have already seen, this sort of installation has a genealogy that can be traced back into the nineteenth century and the very first exhibits of Asian material in the United States in the 1830s and 1840s. It informed the way people reacted to the Chinese and Japanese displays at the 1876 Centennial Exposition in Philadelphia, and it was at the heart of the Buddhist Temple installed at the Free Museum of Science and Art when it opened at the University of Pennsylvania in 1899. Nathan Dunn's Chinese Museum opened in Philadelphia in the 1830s but closed within a few years; the Centennial's exhibitions were necessarily temporary. The Buddhist Temple at the University of Pennsylvania's museum was thus among the first American exhibits of Asia installed during that first golden age of museums. The goal of the temple was to convey the experience of Asia—of Buddhism more specifically—and to invite visitors to put at least one foot into an exotic and faraway world. Rather than creating a "scientific" order out of Asia through classifying and categorizing Asian objects, the temple claimed to present Asian Buddhism on its own terms. Rather than westernizing the cultures it represented, the temple attempted to easternize those who came to visit.

By going native at the University of Pennsylvania's Buddhist Temple, visitors occupied a space somewhere between a doctrinaire aestheticism, sterile academicism, and a reactionary retreat from the modern world. In the remainder of this chapter, I explore the University of Pennsylvania's Buddhist Temple in this cultural middle ground and suggest that for most Americans, then and now, the phenomenon of using museum galleries to enter the imaginative and spiritual world of Asia was really a search for what I'll call a "usable Asia."

The Professor and His Temple

The Free Museum of Science and Art, the brainchild of the university's provost William Pepper, had been in the works for roughly a decade before it opened. Pepper, who like Charles Eliot at Harvard University, Daniel Coit Gilman at Johns Hopkins University, and William Rainey Harper at the University of Chicago, turned the University of Pennsylvania into a modern, research-driven university, had enormous ambitions for the museum. At his most imperial moments, he imagined nothing less than an American version of the British Museum.[67]

That ambition would be achieved in two ways: first through sheer scale. The original plans for the museum envisioned an institution roughly four times the size of what it is today. The second method was through its intellectual scope. As I discussed earlier, the University of Pennsylvania's museum tried to fill the intellectual space described by the Smithsonian's George Brown Goode as *Kulturgeschichte* and defined as "the natural history of civilization, of man and his ideas and achievements," a space between science and art.

But we have already seen how when the new building opened in 1899 the collections that gave some physical embodiment to the term *Kulturgeschichte* did not accommodate Asia comfortably. That upstairs-downstairs division between the civilized and the savage, between Babylon and Borneo, meant that Asia could be both, or neither. In the midst of this categorical confusion, Maxwell Sommerville built his Buddhist Temple.

It was a personal and single-handed project rather than an institutional endeavor. Sommerville amassed and assembled his temple in time for the museum's opening, and he presided over it as his personal terrain in the museum until his death in 1904. However we might finally want to characterize it, the temple was the only one of its kind in the nation. In fact, if Harry Dillon Jones is to be believed, it was "the most complete and elaborate representation of a Buddhist house of worship ever set up outside of the countries where Buddhism is the prevailing religion."[68]

Sommerville has proved an elusive figure given how prominent he once was, at least in Philadelphia circles. Born in Virginia in 1829, he moved to Philadelphia as a child and graduated from the city's famous Central High School (whose graduates include, among others, painter Thomas Eakins, Albert Barnes of Barnes Foundation fame, and Alain Locke, the central intellectual figure behind the Harlem Renaissance), which was the extent of his formal education. After graduation he went into the printing and publishing business, the success of which allowed him to accumulate great wealth. That money enabled him to travel extensively—he really does seem to have gone around the world—and to add items to his growing collection. In Jones's purple eulogy, "Now and then the prosaic world of money grubbers is given pause by the career of some public-spirited mortal who consecrates his days, his money, and his strength to the fulfillment of a plan that promises no personal gain, but only the heightened welfare of the community."[69]

The professor's first claim to fame was his collection of engraved gemstones. Indeed, it was that collection—also on display at the University of Pennsylvania—that earned him his "professoriate" as the world's first, and I suspect last, professor of "glyptology." (In fact, Stewart Culin, who worked at the museum at the time, later reported sardonically, "It was on this occasion, it was said through the intervention of the President of the corporation with the Editors of the Dictionary that the word glyptology was added officially to our language.")[70]

But according to Culin, the Buddhist Temple was "in every respect" the "crown of [Sommerville's] life." After an extensive tour through

Figure 14. Maxwell Sommerville presented as the proper Philadelphian he was.
Courtesy of the Penn Museum, image #152271.

much of Asia, Sommerville returned home, and with eager anticipation the press followed his progress from San Francisco back to Philadelphia, loaded as he was with "six tons" of material from the Far East. The *Evening Telegraph* explained to its readers the origin of the temple: "In his travels, and the Professor has traveled extensively for years in Eastern Asia, India, China, Japan, the Southern Pacific islands, and Africa, Dr. Sommerville made a searching investigation of the religions and superstitions of the Orientals, and about five years ago he decided to purchase the treasures of shrines in various parts of Asia, his purpose being to bring them together to form a Buddhist Temple." Writing to Provost Pepper from Asia during his collecting trip, Sommerville requested 2,100 square feet of space in the new museum.[71]

The press were not disappointed when they got to see the temple for the first time on May 3, 1899. The next day the *Philadelphia Times* described "a scene of Oriental splendor, the glare of the searchlights bringing out the glistening effect of the golden deities, the richly embroidered panels and the highly colored hangings," while the *Philadelphia Press* explained, "To the casual observer the interior of the temple is a confusion of Oriental color, gods, shrines, ritualistic paraphernalia and weird and rich embroideries. Deities of brass, wood, stone, great and small, and all ugly are scattered here, there, everywhere."[72]

To judge from the extant pictures of the temple, it is indeed possible that Sommerville may have squeezed six tons of objects into the exhibit. The temple seems to have been almost a caricature of Victorian clutter—things truly scattered "here, there, everywhere." In fact, this great confusion was a deliberate cross-cultural hodgepodge. As Sommerville himself explained in the gallery guide to his display: "The temple is not Corean, Tibetan, Chinese or Japanese, nor of any one Oriental nation."[73]

Yet while Sommerville's collection was certainly displayed ahistorically, without geographic specificity, and within its own "self-enclosure," to borrow from Susan Stewart, he did not quite replace history with classification, at least not the sort of classification that usually governed the organization of museum objects. The order with which Sommerville replaced temporality was religious, or quasi-religious. As he described it in his gallery guide, "It has been installed at the University of Pennsylvania that all may form an idea of such a place of worship."[74]

Conveying this "idea," then, was Sommerville's primary objective in creating and installing the only Buddhist temple in the United States. Sommerville was not interested in Buddhism with much chronological or even geographic specificity. His guidebook begins with brief descriptions of what is on display but then moves quickly to treat those objects as metonyms for the religion itself. So, for example, his discussion of a sculpture of Binzuru spends no time on the object itself but rather focuses on the importance of the deity:

Binzuru, the deity to which the faithful come for help in all their ailments. Buddhists know Kileso to signify pain. Sin is expressed by the combination of that word Kileso and Akusala. Binzuru, being a perfect saint, was believed to be free of Kileso. He knew no pain; his condition was nishklesa. The counsel that Binzuru is supposed to give to those who pray to him is, Do righteously and escape suffering. In whatever part of the human frame there may be suffering, a corresponding part of Binzuru's person is rubbed by the devotees. In many cases relief ensues. Their cry is, "I go for refuge to Buddha." Such is faith![75]

In other words, though Sommerville's temple sat inside an institution devoted to a new scientific discipline, he did not want to treat Buddhism as a subject of scientific or historical interest. Rather, Sommerville wanted his temple and the things that filled it to serve as a conduit for experiencing or even practicing Buddhism. Indeed, Harry Dillon Jones claimed that "Buddhists frequently visit the temple and spend hours there."[76] As Sommerville's gallery guide continued, "Through its completeness Mongolians and Buddhists generally will recognize a shrine where they may perform their accustomed acts of devotion." The press seized on Sommerville's purpose immediately. The reporter for the *Philadelphia Times* concluded, "Nothing is lacking and the most devout follower of Buddha could worship just as well at the University of Pennsylvania as he could in Thibet." The *Evening Telegraph* helpfully told readers that "for a small fee the novice is permitted to make a pilgrimage in this room, being assured that at the end of the experience he will have faith in Buddha."[77]

This all sounds a bit hyperbolic, and we don't really have any way of knowing whether Buddhists really did come to the museum for their "acts of devotion," but in 1903 the *Philadelphia Inquirer* covered a small incident at the museum that might make us check our skepticism. "A devout Oriental," the paper reported, "who visited [the museum] was so enraptured with the Buddhist temple and the opportunity there presented for him to commune with the deities of his country that it was necessary to forcibly remove him from the building." The nameless "Oriental" was tossed out of the building by "two husky colored porters," but not before he "became very much excited" and had prostrated himself in front of "one of the images of Buddha" reciting "prayer after prayer."[78]

The experience of visitors was further heightened by the good professor himself, who frequently gave lectures on Buddhism and who could often be found sitting in the middle of his temple dressed in Japanese

Figure 15. Among the features of the temple was Sommerville himself, who spent Sunday afternoons dressed as a Buddhist monk and gave lectures for the edification of visitors. Courtesy of the Penn Museum, image #174644.

Figure 16. Maxwell Sommerville's Buddhist temple was a great hodgepodge of objects he had collected on a tour of Asia at the end of the nineteenth century. Courtesy of the Penn Museum, image #175434.

clothes, an outfit Sommerville also wore when he entertained at his house and when he walked about town. Sommerville was almost as much a fixture in his temple as any of the objects, and Jones, in his extended obituary, reported that "nothing so crushed the spirit of the gentle old professor as the indifference of some visitors to this priceless nature of these curios . . . to see some jaunty individual step within the sacred confines of the Buddhist temple, gaze around with indifferent eyes, and walk out without making a single inquiry."[79]

Indeed, Sommerville seems to have viewed his own performance as a Buddhist as integral to the appreciation of the temple. Culin wonderfully, if sarcastically, described this performance at the opening of the temple in 1899:

A slight hitch occurred at the opening exercises. The Professor insisted that as the temple was practically holy ground the guests should remove their shoes and enter in their stocking feet. A kind of truce was patched up although the Professor was far from satisfied by their failure to prostrate themselves before the image of Buddha, a ceremony at which he himself set an example. . . . Costumed as a priest in a robe of parti-colored brocade . . . he marshaled his guests down the aisle past the rinzo and the images of the sixteen Lohan on one side and the shrine of the Buddha on the other. . . . . The success of the affair was prodigious. The Professor was so elated that it was evident from our conversation afterwards he would have been willing to have shared the honors of the occasion with the founder of the religion himself.[80]

In this way, the temple became a stage and Sommerville its leading man.

This Buddhist theater did not enjoy a long run. After Sommerville's death in 1904, no one stepped forward to fill his kimono and sit in the temple, nor did anyone volunteer to give lectures about the meaning and practice of Buddhism. The temple itself was quietly dismantled not long afterward. Still, despite the amusingly eccentric figure Sommerville obviously cut at the turn of the twentieth century, the results of his collecting were not altogether frivolous. Recall that in 1929, Benjamin March, curator of Asian Art at the Detroit Institute of Arts, called the University of Pennsylvania's museum's collection of Chinese sculpture the "preeminent" such assemblage in the United States.[81] Some of that, at least, was collected by Sommerville.

Antimodern Asiaphiles

But how are we to understand the cultural role Sommerville and his temple played and the cultural milieu out of which they both came? At one level, we can place Sommerville with a larger group of American artists and intellectuals who, in the late nineteenth and early twentieth centuries, also went native to one degree or another. Anthropologist Frank Hamilton Cushing, for example, traveled to the American Southwest to conduct field research on the Zuni early in the 1880s. He returned east—to "civilization"—dressed as a Zuni, having been initiated into the Priesthood of the Bow, a Zuni secret society. From 1882 on, Cushing was often portrayed in his Zuni costume, including, most famously, in the full-length portrait of him by Thomas Eakins completed in 1895.[82]

Other Americans—among them architect Ralph Adams Cram and historian Henry Adams—found a kind of refuge from the modern world in the imagined harmony of the Middle Ages. Few, however, took this infatuation as far as Boston architect Henry Hobson Richardson. Richardson, whose most significant buildings derive from the heavy Romanesque style of middle Europe, took to clothing his increasingly heavy body in the robes of a medieval monk.

Picking up where Ruskin, Pugin, and others left off, these turn-of-the-century Goths saw in the premodern Middle Ages an antidote to all the ills afflicting the industrial, modern world. In a medieval world remarkably free of repressive authority, periodic famine, Black Death, and peasants crying, "Bring out your dead!" Adams, Cram, and others saw order instead of chaos, community instead of alienation, unity instead of fragmentation. In this sense, the retreat to the thirteenth century was part of what historian T. J. Jackson Lears has described as the larger phenomenon of "antimodernism" in the years surrounding 1900. Lears defines antimodernism as "the recoil from an 'overcivilized' modern existence to more intense forms of physical or spiritual experience" and sees the impulse as linking a wide range of cultural phenomena across the landscape of American culture—from the American arts and crafts disciples of William Morris to these neo-Goths.

More often than not, according to Lears, the source of that elusive "spirituality" was the Middle Ages and/or the Orient.[83] Asia, and especially Japan, provided a premodern escape for those who found themselves burned by the corrosive acids of modern America. In the mid-twentieth century, critic Brooks looked back on this generation and noted, "Numbers of Boston and Harvard men were going to Japan and China in a spirit that was new and full of meaning." He went on to characterize the mood and motive of these Bostonians: "The optimism that John Fiske and William James maintained in Cambridge was foreign to their mood and offended their taste. It justified the restless striving that had lost all meaning for them. They longed for quiet, solace and escape. Sad and fatalistic, feeling that life was empty, they found a natural haven in the teachings of Buddha. Blessed for them was Nirvana, where illusion ceased, where the trials, the expiations and the whirlwind of life were calmed and silenced and ended in absolute truth."[84]

William Sturgis Bigelow certainly fit this bill. A wealthy Bostonian, he journeyed to Japan in the late nineteenth century looking to fulfill some yearning. According to his friend Margaret Terry Chanler, "He had never, before going to Japan, had any spiritual experience whatever. He knew more about the mountains in the moon than he knew about his own soul." He found what he was looking for by studying and converting to Buddhism. The result, as described by Lears, was dramatic: "To most of his visitors and correspondents, Bigelow seemed profoundly at peace; he had embarked on a serious and satisfying Buddhist pilgrimage, foreign to all his American experience. . . . Now he was far from the demands of the achievement ethos and deep in the lore of esoteric Buddhism."[85]

A bit of this antimodernism permeates Sommerville's temple. I discussed earlier the stress Sommerville placed on Buddhist spirituality in the description of his temple. That sense of longing for a premodern world infuses his discussion of Buddhist priests as well:

The priest, like the people, is inwardly convinced that before he can arrive at Nirvana it is probable that his will should be tried by other phases of metampsychosis. . . . The sentiment is a beautiful one—a period of probation in which the baser instincts will be consumed and the better qualities refined. These holy men are generally very earnest in their prayers. They become so absorbed that they seem not to be of the world of worshippers about them. One can observe an expression of exaltation on their countenances as they appear to come nearer and nearer to the loved deity whom they are imploring for help.[86]

Beauty, earnest love, total absorption—these resonate as the opposite of the ugly, avaricious, alienated West.

For those looking for "quiet, solace and escape," Asia and the Middle Ages shared some important characteristics. Each was "premodern," meaning, largely, preindustrial, and yet despite this—or precisely because of it—each produced complex and beautiful art and architecture. Each society was held together by a set of values and ideals quite different from those of contemporary American society, and the remoteness of those ideas in both time and space only heightened their appeal. And, it goes almost without saying, Asia and the European medieval past constituted slates blank enough that Americans could inscribe whatever they wanted onto them. No coincidence that Cram, who designed the very Gothic graduate school complex at Princeton University, also wrote a book about Japanese architecture.[87]

Still, even Lears acknowledges that the American fascination with Asia at the turn of the last century is more complicated and cannot fully be explained as an antimodern reaction. He attributes it as well to what he terms "a more diffuse aestheticism."[88] Certainly aesthetics played a role in the attraction that both the Middle Ages and Asia had for Americans. After all, architecture, more than anything else, was what chiefly enthralled Cram, Adams, Richardson, and others about medieval Europe. But the Western consideration of Asian aesthetics moved in a quite different direction by the beginning of the twentieth century. Indeed, for many influential cultural figures, Asian aesthetic ideas pointed exactly toward the modern. The pivotal influence in this development was Ernest Fenollosa, another Bostonian who traveled to Japan and immersed himself in that world.

Asia and the Modern

Fenollosa, a "Yankee-Spaniard" born in 1853, grew up in Salem, Massachusetts and thus in the shadow of the Asian trade that had come through that port during its heyday earlier in the century. He also, therefore, probably saw the displays at the East India Marine Hall. The East India Marine Society was founded in 1799 by ship captains and supercargoes; membership was restricted to those who had traveled around one of the Capes. They traded maritime information and brought back artifacts and curiosities from their voyages. These formed the basis of a museum of sorts, and by 1825 the society built the Marine Hall to put them in. It amounted to an accidental cabinet of curiosities in an age when such things had largely disappeared. Antebellum writers who visited the Peabody Museum, as it became known, complained about the randomness both of the collection and of its display, and they noted how few people ever seemed to visit the museum. In fact, the latter observation was just how the members intended things. In the 1830s, by resolution of the society, visitors were restricted to people personally introduced by a member.[89]

Whether or not Fenollosa spent much time in this museum, he surely grew up with a consciousness of Asia. As Brooks described it, "The Far East seemed closer to Salem than to any other American town" in the mid-nineteenth century.[90] Fenollosa had developed sufficient interest in Japan to make his first trip there in 1878, after having graduated from Harvard and immediately after his marriage. He went there to fill a teaching post at the University of Tokyo, teaching philosophy, and stayed through most of the 1880s.

He came to Japan at just the moment when that country was embracing Western modernization. This is one reason why the Japanese were received so warmly by Fair-goers in 1876. Indeed, Fenollosa's invitation was a part of that process. But he fell in love with the older Japan, with the art and the Buddhism that that society, uncontaminated by the West, produced, and he took it upon himself to rescue these artistic traditions from the oblivion into which modernization seemed to be casting them. This required, as I observed earlier, creating art historical categories, hierarchies, canons, and theories for Japanese art that simply had not before existed.

Having "taught" the Japanese to appreciate their own artistic production, he then took it upon himself to act as a cultural interlocutor on behalf of the East to an ignorant West. He did so by advising Americans—Bigelow perhaps most importantly—on the purchase of objects, and when he returned to the United States he found an institutional base of operations by taking a position as curator at the Boston MFA in the 1890s (Bigelow's collection formed the core of the MFA's Asian holdings) and by working with Charles Freer.[91]

We get a wonderful sense of Fenollosa in his role as Asian aesthete and advisor from the letters that Henry Adams wrote to John Hay. Adams went to Japan in 1886 with artist John La Farge, and Hay had asked him to buy Japanese art. Fenollosa often served as host and guide for such Americans, and he did so for Adams. Adams reported back with his characteristically caustic sense of humor:

Fenollosa and Bigelow are stern with us. Fenollosa is a tyrant who says we shall not like any work done under the Tokugawa Shoguns. As these gentlemen lived two hundred and fifty years or thereabouts, to 1860, and as there is nothing at Tokio except their work, La Farge and I are at a loss to understand why we came; but it seems we are to be taken to Nikko shortly and permitted to admire some temples there. On secret search in Murray, I ascertain that the temples at Nikko are the work of Tokogawa Shoguns. I have not yet dared to ask about this apparent inconsistency for fear of rousing a fresh anathema. The temples and Tokugawas are, I admit, a trifle baroque. . . . Some of the temples are worse than others, but I am inclined to let Fenollosa have his way with them, if he will only let me be amused by the humor.

Later, when Adams found some paintings that he liked, he wrote wickedly to Hay:

I fear that Fenollosa . . . will say that they are Tokugawa rot, and will bully me into letting them go. He is now trying to prevent my having a collection of Hokusai's books. He is a kind of St. Dominic, and holds himself responsible for the dissemination of useless knowledge by others. My historical indifference to everything but facts, and my delight at studying what is hopefully debased and degraded, shock his moral sense. . . . He has joined a Buddhist sect; I was myself a Buddhist when I left America, but he has converted me to Calvinism with leanings towards the Methodists.[92]

Fenollosa's most enduring written works remain his long poem "East and West," delivered as a Phi Beta Kappa address at Harvard in 1902, and his essay "The Chinese Written Character as a Medium for Poetry," drafted sometime around 1904. The latter remained unpublished at Fenollosa's death in 1908 but was edited and published in 1919 by Ezra Pound. His posthumous influence on Pound, and on the artists Max Weber and Georgia O'Keefe, has made it easy to see Fenollosa and his aesthetic ideas as foundational for American modernism, and we have already discussed the connections Fenollosa saw between East and West through modern art.[93] Finding refuge and/or inspiration in things Asian, therefore, leads us to both modernism and antimodernism. After all, not only the Gothic Ralph Adams Cram but also Frank Lloyd Wright, the avatar of twentieth-century American modernism, could each find inspiration and fascination with Japanese architecture.[94]

Looking for a Usable Asia

Neither modernism nor antimodernism, I think, fully explains Maxwell Sommerville and the experience he hoped his Buddhist temple would provide.

Nothing in Sommerville's work suggests any interest in or connection to the somewhat rarified currents of Euro-American modernism. He strikes me as thoroughly middlebrow, a man who made a fortune publishing thoroughly middlebrow books—encyclopedias and such—and whose most important association was as a member of the Masons. Nor, frankly, did he pose as a truly persuasive antimodernist either. While he did resort to the stereotypes of Eastern spirituality, and while he did sit in his temple dressed approximately like a Buddhist priest, he seems to have been playing a part rather than living a life. As one newspaper was careful to report on opening day at the temple, "The Professor then paused to observe that although he had been deeply interested in his work of investigating the religions of the Orientals, he wished it to be understood that he was a Christian."[95]

Sommerville and Brooks do not seem ever to have crossed paths— Sommerville was an old man when Brooks was establishing his reputation; Sommerville was a Philadelphia man of business while Brooks was a cultural critic and writer steeped thoroughly in the world of New England letters. But Brooks may help explain, inadvertently, how Sommerville's temple functioned.

If Brooks is remembered at all today, it is for his 1918 essay "On Creating a Usable Past."[96] Brooks was primarily interested in the traditions of American literature. Writing in the shadow of the First World War, and the countless other dislocations of the modern world, he was convinced that the past might be mined to help Americans make sense of the present. "Look back," he told his readers, "and you will see, drifting in and out of the books of history . . . all manner of queer geniuses, wraith-like personalities that have left behind them sometimes a fragment or so that has meaning for us now."[97] But Brooks was interested generally in those Bostonians who were drawn to Asia, and he was interested in Ernest Fenollosa quite specifically. Late in his life, Brooks published a book of biographical portraits that took its title from the book's first essay: "Fenollosa and His Circle."[98]

The piece is a breezy, entertaining account of Fenollosa's life and career, and it appeared a year before William Chisolm's full-length biography. Just as interesting, for our purposes, are two of the other sketches Brooks included in his book. The fourth chapter is a study of painter George Catlin, and the last of the eight portraits is devoted to philosopher Randolph Bourne.

Catlin belonged entirely to the nineteenth century and was dead before Brooks was born. In the mid-nineteenth century he enjoyed tremendous celebrity, both in the United States and in England, for his paintings of Indians. In the 1830s, Catlin journeyed to the trans-Mississippi west to capture the lives and faces of Native Americans on canvas. Catlin's accomplishment resided not simply in the paintings themselves, whose quality is, to put it generously, uneven, but also because Catlin ventured to go where few Americans had gone. He lived among the Indians, witnessing their daily lives and their rituals.

In short, he went native, and as a result he became a strident critic of the federal government's policy toward American Indians. He saw himself as their champion and as their historian in a way similar—I don't think the analogy strains too much—to how Fenollosa saw his role as an interpreter of Japan. In the midst of certain doom—"for they are 'doomed' and must perish"—Catlin believed, "I have flown to their rescue . . . phoenix-like they may rise forth from the 'stain on a painter's palette,' and live again upon canvas."[99]

That Brooks should have been drawn to these two Americans who went native and championed the cultures of other people can perhaps be explained by his inclusion of Randolph Bourne as part of *Fenollosa and His Circle*. Bourne had been a colleague and friend of Brooks's in the heady years before the First World War. Two years before Brooks published "On Creating a Usable Past," Bourne wrote the essay for which he is probably best remembered, "Trans-National America," which appeared in the *Atlantic* in July 1916.

Bourne's essay, published as World War I raged in Europe but before the United States entered the conflict, responded to the xenophobia that had arisen as a backlash against thirty years of unprecedented immigration. To those especially old-stock Anglo-Americans who feared that the nation would be buried under a tide of foreign influences, Bourne wrote, "The foreign cultures have not been melted down or run together, made into some homogeneous Americanism, but have remained distinct but cooperating to the greater glory and benefit, not only of themselves but of all the native 'Americanism' around them." As Europeans were busy tearing themselves apart, fueled by nationalist and ethnic rage, Bourne noted, "In a world which has dreamed of internationalism, we find that we have all unawares been building up the first international nation."[100] Brooks presumably saw Fenollosa, Catlin, and Bourne as kindred spirits, sharing a cultural temperament of the sort that would facilitate the creation of Bourne's transnational America. A "circle" not because these men knew each other and shared a friendship but because they all moved across and between cultures.

It is easy enough to dismiss the activities of people like Fenollosa, Adams, and Sommerville as variations—even amusing ones—of Edward Said's Orientalists. At another level, however, this is too easy. Arif Dirlik has asked us to see Orientalism not simply as a discourse of power exerted in one direction but as resulting from a set of interactions and relationships, taking place—and here he borrows from Mary Louis Pratt—in a variety of cultural "contact zones." As he points out, "In its practice, orientalism from the beginning took shape as an exchange of images and representations corresponding to the circulation of intellectuals and others—first the circulation of Europeans in Asia, but increasingly with a counter-circulation of Asians in Europe and the United States." And in the provincial case of the United States, it is probably right to say that at least as many Asians circulated in America as Americans circulated in Asia. There was or is nothing comparable in China, after all, to the populations of Chinese living in the United States. Indeed, as Dirlik reminds us, in addition to participating in a discourse of imperial power, "orientalists have also been responsible for introducing elements of Asian cultures into their societies, for their use of the 'orient' in self-criticism, as well as in the critique of Euro-American modernity."[101] In these "contact zones," Dirlik believes, "the orientalist . . . is 'orientalized' himself or herself in the very process of entering the 'orient' intellectually and sentimentally."

So, for example, Fenollosa's poem "East and West," according to Lawrence Chisolm, "revealed the world's dialectical progress toward a new global civilization as an unfolding of Spirit. The unfolding was Buddhist, Hegelian, and Emersonian, cosmopolitan in a transcendental mode."[102] If we reject out of hand the careers of Fenollosa, Catlin, Frank Hamilton Cushing, and even Maxwell Sommerville as simply examples of American cultural imperialism, we deny the real and profound effects those "other" cultures had on them as individuals, and through them on all of us as well. Maybe we aren't so far from Bourne's dream after all.

Surveying the burgeoning immigrant cities of the industrial age, Bourne believed that transnational America would happen in the city. Whatever the novelty of Sommerville's temple, even in Philadelphia it was not the only "contact zone" between East and West at the turn of the twentieth century. A Japanese garden graced the grounds of Fairmount Park as one of the few permanent remains of the 1876 Centennial; in 1905 a gate from a seventeenth-century Buddhist temple was added to that site. In 1897, the *Philadelphia Inquirer,* in a man-about-town squib, reported, "Under the supervision of a Japanese artist a miniature Japanese garden has been erected on the beautiful grounds of John H. A. Klauder at 1513 Allegheny Avenue. A miniature Buddhist temple, waterfalls, hanging baskets and other features make the garden attractive. The designer is Teitoko Morimoto."[103]

Philadelphia's "Chinatown" dates to the second half of the nineteenth century. It included its own Buddhist temple on the second floor of a commercial building. In 1895, that temple hosted a three-day set of ceremonies to support the Chinese war effort against the Japanese. (I suspect those Buddhists who may have come to Sommerville's temple were Japanese. While the Chinese population had its own place of worship, the Japanese would certainly not have been welcome there.) The press estimated that several thousand Chinese participated. It also reported that "few Caucasians were admitted to the ceremonies," except those who "had for years interested themselves in Chinese affairs and were trusted accordingly."[104]

A Japanese teahouse in the city's largest park, a Japanese garden designed by a Japanese artist in a largely industrial section of the city, and a handful of Caucasians admitted to a Chinese religious ceremony—these are intriguing fragments, giving us a small glimpse into a world of cultural interactions that suggest at least the possibility of cultures at play envisioned by Bourne. Stewart Culin viewed Sommerville as "a fraud and an imposter," and his descriptions of the temple drip with sarcasm. But if we read through that sarcasm we might give Sommerville some credit for trying to create one of those cultural contact zones at his temple. Describing Sommerville's lectures, Culin wrote:

On Sunday afternoon the Professor would hold services to which the Japanese students in the college were invited. On these occasions he would deliver an invocation in the Unknown Tongue, or it may have been Sanscrit, after which he would preach a kind of sermon and urge toleration for current beliefs in the light of the example set by the Lord Buddha. I never heard of Japanese students attending but I did hear of his corralling a number of ladies who were being entertained at a tea in another section of the building. He always conducted visitors personally and encouraged them to ask questions, taking his self-appointed position of Buddhist Chaplain . . . very seriously.[105]

A joke for Culin to be sure, but perhaps not for everyone who came to the temple.

Here, then, was the purpose of going native for many Americans at the turn of the twentieth century. For the most high-minded among them, immersing oneself in the culture of the East promised the kind of cosmopolitanism that made Bourne so optimistic about a transnational America.[106] Others, less sophisticated or rhapsodic perhaps, searched for a "usable" Asia to fulfill whatever needs they had. Brooks, again inadvertently, had hinted at just this in his 1918 essay: "The spiritual past," he wrote, "has no objective reality; it yields only what we are able to look for in it."[107] For Americans coping with the wrenching changes that greeted the dawn of the twentieth century, Asia represented both the spiritual and the past.

If this, then, was what those who went native hoped to accomplish, it is worth pausing briefly over how they tried to achieve it. At the risk of stating the obvious, for Americans the connection between Asian spirituality and wisdom and the dilemmas of the modern West came through the collection of objects. Maxwell Sommerville, William Sturgis Bigelow, and Henry Adams all went east first and foremost to collect. Fenollosa too, while he was a poet, philosopher, and aesthete among other things, started his interest in Japan by collecting. (Adams was again characteristically naughty in describing the collecting impulse in Bigelow and Fenollosa in a letter to Hay: "I have still to report that purchases for you are going on, but more and more slowly, for I believe we have burst up all the pawn-brokers' shops in Japan. . . . Bigelow and Fenollosa cling like misers to their miserable hoards.")[108]

We might see the collection—some might use the term *appropriation*—of exotic souvenir objects, as Stewart does, as part of the nostalgic impulse we have already discussed. As Stewart puts it, "The double function of the souvenir is to authenticate a past or otherwise remote experience and, at the same time, to discredit the present. The present is either too impersonal, too looming, or too alienating compared to the intimate and direct experience of contact which the souvenir has as its referent."[109]

As compelling as that analysis is, in this case I think it may be incomplete. In using objects as the primary way to find what they were looking for in Asia, these collectors did not rely upon that "object-based epistemology" that I described in the introduction in quite the same "scientific" way as other museum collectors did.[110] Those who assembled the great museum collections of the late nineteenth century did so with the assumption that particular bodies of knowledge inhered in the objects associated with that body of knowledge. Further, that knowledge could be gleaned through the careful collection, classification, and observation of those objects. These collectors, however, and Sommerville particularly, modified this object-based epistemology when they collected objects from Asian cultures. Their goal, as we have described, was to provide visitors with the experience of Asia, rather than with taxonomic clarity about it. Objects remained at the heart of what they wanted to accomplish because they believed the best way to experience the esoteric, mysterious, and inscrutable world of Asia was to surround oneself with the objects produced by those people, even if those objects were not organized into a system.

Visitors to Sommerville's temple certainly found themselves surrounded by objects, and their particular history, geography, and provenance was secondary to the larger effect Sommerville hoped to achieve. As Fenollosa put it in an essay written for the *Golden Age*. "Thinking is *thinging* to follow the buds of fact as they open, and see thought folded away within thought like so many petals."[111] This relationship between things and thought, between objects and understanding, lay at the heart of the phenomenon of using museum galleries for the experience of Asia.

A year or so after he died, rumors began to circulate about Maxwell Sommerville's collection. Some of the objects—maybe many of the objects—Sommerville had given to the museum, including a number of the carved gems and Buddhist relics, might not be authentic. "Doubtful treasures," the *New York Tribune* called them and insisted that honesty and reputation demanded that the university museum investigate the matter and remove any of the objects that might be found to be "spurious."[112]

While these accusations doubtless embarrassed the museum, they were not altogether unusual. A number of objects and collections acquired in the late nineteenth and early twentieth centuries turned out to be something other than what they were originally advertised to be. Some of this can be chalked up to fraud and fakery. As more and more Americans—Europeans as well—tried their hand at collecting, some of them were simply snookered. And so it is even today.

At another level, however, the fate of the Sommerville collection reminds us that ideas about authenticity were changing precisely just as and probably because so many people were amassing collections. Further, those ideas meant changing attitudes about what kinds of objects belonged in museums. The curiosities and exotica that were the staple of antebellum dime-store museums and Barnumesque display had been dismissed in favor of objects that had a legitimate pedigree. Gone too, banished to the basement, were the casts and reproductions that had once filled art galleries. Handmade objects took primacy over mass-produced items in art museums and anthropological collections. Sommerville might well have been duped on his buying trip through Asia, but he might also have held an older notion of what kinds of objects were worthy of collecting in the first place. He was a man of the nineteenth century, and his collection, viewed with such suspicion at the beginning of the twentieth century, may simply have reflected an earlier sensibility.

After all, at the same moment that Sommerville was installing his Buddhist hodgepodge in a museum of anthropology and archaeology in order to present "Buddhism," art museums such as those in Cleveland and Boston were installing Asian objects in roughly the same way they displayed Western art and developing the intellectual trappings of styles, schools, and provenance that help define "art" in the first place. In this sense, Sommerville's temple harkened back to an older exhibitionary tradition. Nathan Dunn's museum of "Ten Thousand Chinese Things," when it opened in Philadelphia in 1838, attempted to give visitors an accurate and largely sympathetic presentation of Chinese culture and to give them an immersion experience. Ten-foot Chinese lanterns illuminated the exhibits, including panoramas and dioramas of China to give visitors a better sense of the context from which the ten thousand things came. From the few press reports we have, people were stunned.[113] In a similar way, Sommerville tried to convey knowledge through experience.

Or he might not have cared much one way or the other.

At some point in their acquaintance, Sommerville made a confession to Stewart Culin (or so Culin claimed). Shortly after the temple had its grand opening, Sommerville told Culin that, in fact, the structure itself was a fake. "However, being a man of strict veracity," Culin went on, "he had constructed the entire material fabric of the temple from pieces of board packing boxes which had come from China filled with porcelain and bric-a-brac. He was able to say therefore, with absolute truth that every stick in the structure had come from the East." As Sommerville allegedly explained it to Culin, "He told me he had brought no Buddhist temple from the East; nothing more in fact than the idea."[114]

Which brings us full circle. When, to paraphrase John Huntington, is a temple not a temple? When it is the idea of a temple. Sommerville's temple tried to convey the idea of a temple; he filled it with objects intended to convey the idea of Buddhist ritual practice rather than objects that had some significance and authenticity in and of themselves. And through all that, he tried to convey the very idea of Buddhism itself. For Sommerville, the experience of going native centered around a set of mysteries, wisdoms, and truths that might be experienced through the immersion in objects. Facts, in this experience, were entirely secondary. In this sense, Sommerville and some of the other late nineteenth-century "seekers" Brooks referred to kept alive an earlier distinction between fact and truth.[115]

And if we are to believe the press reports of the time that some small number of Buddhists did use the temple for worship, and if we acknowledge that at least some number of visitors opened themselves up to the possibility of being themselves "orientalized," then in some way Sommerville succeeded.

Without question, we now recognize the category of Asian art, and what seems remarkable is that Americans once did not. There is certainly an anthropology and an archaeology of Asia, but for museums, Asian objects reside in the world of art. The project of creating an art historical apparatus for Asian objects that Ernest Fenollosa started has blossomed. Virtually all the major and many of the minor American art museums have departments of Asian art, staffed by curators trained in the field; likewise, university departments of art history teach the field of Asian art and train graduate students in it.

And yet the fit of Asian objects into the category of art, defined as it originally was in specifically Western terms, is by no means snug in the American museum. In the twentieth century, as comprehensive art museums increased their holdings of Asian objects, they tried to arrange them into their own evolutionary display strategies. Depending on an individual museum's holdings, objects are usually arranged so that visitors can follow the progressive development of art from the ancient Mediterranean (Egypt, Greece, Rome) through medieval Europe, the Renaissance and baroque periods, and so on, concluding with impressionism, postimpressionism, and modernism.

The Philadelphia Museum of Art (PMA), which opened in 1928, may be the best example of this model. As designed by director Fiske Kimball, the museum was to showcase an evolutionary understanding of art history created by walking on a "main street" through the galleries. This "Pageant of Art" would illustrate "European art from the time of Christ onward to the most vitally modern of contemporary work, or, in Asia, from the austere beginnings in India and China down to the last flowering of the delicate art of Japan," giving visitors "a vivid panoramic history of the art of all ages." The evolutionary metaphor, according to Kimball, stood behind this method of organization, which complemented the period rooms. "It seems to me that the evolutionary order, and the placing together of all products of a single civilization and art, reinforcing one another by their cumulative effect, is interesting and advantageous."[116]

Such a neat and comprehensible narrative enables visitors to walk through the history of art. But once again, in museum practice, Asian art tends to confound this arrangement. Asian art cannot necessarily be placed into the same chronological, formal, or stylistic categories used to organize Western art. It also does not necessarily fit into the same categories of media. Ceramics, for example, are generally viewed as decorative art when made in the West but as high art when produced in Asia.[117] While Kimball included Asian art in his evolutionary vision, in fact, the Asian galleries at the PMA sit at the end of one wing, thematically disconnected from the rest of the collection.

So while American art museums have expanded the definition of art to include Asian material, in many cases Asian art remains in but not of the art museum project. The Freer Gallery, therefore, stands as a different solution to the problem of where to find the East. Built to house an individual collection, it has grown to become, along with the Sackler Gallery, which opened on the Mall in 1987, the National Museum of Asian Art. So too, in the early 1990s, the Seattle Art Museum moved into its new home and created the Seattle Asian Art Museum to occupy (wonderfully) its old building. Even more recently, in 2003, the Asian Art Museum of San Francisco opened in the building that used to house the city's main library. Until 2003, the museum had existed as a wing of the larger M. H. de Young Memorial Museum.

In other words, while the comprehensive art museums at the turn of the twentieth century decided to incorporate Asia as one category of

Figure 17. The Sackler Gallery shortly after it opened. Courtesy of the Freer Gallery of Art and Arthur M. Sackler Gallery, Smithsonian Institution, Washington, D.C.

their larger collections, more recently in Washington, Seattle, and San Francisco, Asian art has been disaggregated and been given its own physical and institutional space. If museums a century ago were conceived as great three-dimensional encyclopedias, then some have now decided that Asia requires and deserves its own separate volume.

Chapter 4
Where Have All the Grown-Ups Gone?

When the Wellcome Collection of scientific and medical artifacts opened in its new London digs in June 2007, seventy-nine-year-old Nobel Prize winner James Watson—of Watson and Crick fame—was present as a guest of honor. Looking out at the new exhibits in their new building, Watson took the occasion to chide American museums: "We have a large number of fine art museums, [but] we don't have the equivalent number of science museums so congratulations." He wasn't finished: "The United States is a disgrace. There is not a first-rate science museum in the whole country."[1]

That would seem an extraordinary complaint given that by the turn of the millennium, according to one estimate, the nation counted roughly three hundred science museums from coast to coast, and those places attracted upward of 115 million visitors per year. Further, that figure represents a tripling of the attendance from just ten years earlier.[2]

I suspect that what Watson meant by his caustic remarks was that there weren't any science museums designed as serious, adult places comparable to the art museums he mentioned. I suspect he meant that most of those many millions of visitors were children and that science museums exist largely for them at their level of understanding. And in this sense, Watson's charge may well be right, sweeping though it is. By and large, we view science museums as the domain of kids. Natalie Angier, in her recent book on scientific literacy, for example, takes this as a given. She describes a transition when children grow up and out of the science museum and into the more sober places like art museums and the theater in not altogether charitable terms: "The differential acoustics tell the story. Zoos and museums of science and natural history are loud and bouncy and notably enriched with the upper registers of the audio scale. Theaters and art museums murmur in a courteous baritone. . . . Science appreciation is for the young, restless, the Ritalined. It's the holding pattern fun you have while your gonads are busy ripening. . . . Childhood, then, is the one time of life when all members of an age cohort are expected to appreciate science."[3] Watson and Angier have identified a genuine dilemma in American public life.

Science museums are surely the place where many people encounter science as something other than a gruesome set of school exams. But those science museums cater almost exclusively to schoolchildren. They have largely abandoned the adult audience. On the one hand, art museums, designed primarily for adults, challenge children with a raised bar and make no particular accommodation for kids in their permanent galleries or temporary exhibitions. Science museums, on the other hand, offer the chance for adults—parents of visiting children mostly—to dumb down.

It wasn't always thus.

In the nineteenth century, natural history museums expected a mixed audience. So, for example, way at the back of the Long Gallery at Peale's museum, at least as portrayed by Peale in his famous 1822 self-portrait, a father lectures his son about exhibits that are decidedly not kid-friendly. That dynamic remained unchanged, as far as I can tell, through the early years of the twentieth century. The exhibits at natural history museums—all those glass cases stuffed with various specimens—were not designed specifically with children in mind. While museums that received some public funding at the turn of the twentieth century, either from city or state sources, often had to demonstrate their utility to schoolchildren or their teachers, I think it is fair to say that this didn't fundamentally alter the way in which these museums used exhibits to convey science. As these museums evolved throughout the twentieth century, however, those who worked in museums increasingly divided the children from the grown-ups in their educational programming strategies and exhibitionary strategies. In so doing, science museums focused more and more on children as their primary audience.

Before charting the disappearance of adults from the halls of science museums I need to elaborate on a distinction Angier hints at in the passage quoted earlier and that I mentioned in Chapter 1. We can group science museums into two broad categories: natural history museums and museums of science and technology. The former, at least in the United States, came first. Natural history museums can trace their origins back to Peale's museum in Philadelphia, where natural specimens, including the famous Mastodon skeleton, shared gallery space with portraits of famous Americans. Peale's collection didn't survive in its original form for very long. It closed in Philadelphia and relocated to Baltimore. But Philadelphia also produced the Academy of Natural Sciences, which stands today as the oldest natural history museum in the nation (and the place where the nation's first dinosaur skeleton made its public debut). During the late nineteenth century several other cities, including most famously New York and Chicago, built large museums of natural history.

Museums of science and technology, or science and industry, came a generation or so later. Certainly people talked about the need to establish museums of science and technology. Americans clearly had a taste for such museums, because they thronged to see the temporary exhibits of technology that formed the centerpieces of the periodic world's fairs of the late nineteenth and early twentieth centuries: 1876 in Philadelphia, 1893 in Chicago, and 1904 in St. Louis. Yet, for whatever reason, Americans did not set about building large-scale, permanent museums of science and technology until the 1920s.

So in this chapter I look first at natural history museums, using New York's AMNH as my case study, and second at museums of technology, with a focus on the Franklin Institute in Philadelphia and the Museum of Science and Industry in Chicago, to explore how science museums struggled over changing definitions of research and education, how they reconceived how exhibits could function in the museum, and how children became the primary audience for science museums of both kinds.

Natural History Research and Natural History Education

With the Second World War over, the president of the AMNH took a moment to survey the damage at his museum. The result, published in the museum's 1945 *Annual Report,* was sobering. "The old halls are still there," he sighed, "with few exceptions." He found that "the building itself is in a shameful state of disrepair." More worrying still, he reported, "Our financial situation is very disturbing." Three years later, things had gotten no better. The president stated, with stunning candor, "The past year has been a period of extensive crisis for the American Museum of Natural History. Those responsible for its administration have been faced with a series of problems which threatened the very survival of the institution."[4] All in all, a bleak assessment. Shocking, too, given that the AMNH was arguably the nation's premier natural history museum, and unarguably among its three most important.

The war was only indirectly responsible for this state of affairs, of course. The four years of American involvement capped a fifteen-year period of stagnation and disinvestment that began with the Great Depression. On top of that, in 1933, just as the worst of the Depression had set in, Henry Fairfield Osborn stepped down as museum president. Under Osborn's stewardship, AMNH had assumed its international prominence in the world of natural history museums and had established preeminence in several areas of research, particularly paleontology.

The AMNH thus entered the postwar period on the verge of institutional collapse. In 1942, in the midst of the war, the museum had hired Albert Parr to put things right. Parr struck some as an unlikely choice: he was only forty years old, came from academia (Yale) rather than from the world of New York institutions, and was an oceanographer, a field not even covered by the museum. Still, Parr recognized quickly that the crisis at the AMNH was not simply one of flaking paint and budget deficits. Parr believed that what the natural history museum did and how it did it needed to be reinvented. That reinvention entailed confronting difficult questions about the relationship between research, exhibits, and public education. Those questions, in turn, had a profound effect on who came to see the exhibits and what they learned from them.

The AMNH that Osborn had shaped exemplified how museums were intended to work at the turn of the twentieth century. Built around a notion of what Osborn called "naked-eye science," the AMNH created exhibits of specimens carefully classified and arranged.[5] Thousands of specimens. While the exhibits were designed to illustrate an evolutionary narrative, to demonstrate the relationship between species, and to give categorical order to the natural world, the sheer quantity of specimens on display also served to portray the abundance of nature, on the one hand, and in the case of rare and exotic specimens, the ingenuity of the museum's collectors, on the other. As the venerable Joseph Henry put it in an address to the crowd gathered to lay the cornerstone of the museum in 1874: "It is to be a temple of nature in which the productions of the inorganic and organic world, together with the remnants of the past ages of the human family are to be collected, classified and properly exhibited."[6]

That model of museum display—the long galleries crammed with glass cases stuffed with specimens—had already come under attack from many in the museum world by the 1920s and 1930s. Those protesters had come to the conclusion that these exhibits were dull, enervating, and drove potential visitors away. Just as troubling to the scientists at these museums, the science on display in these old exhibits grew more and more out-of-date. Turn-of-the-century museums aspired to an encyclopedic completeness in their collections and displays and believed that their exhibits could and should hold a mirror to creation, well-ordered and unchanging. These museums, while they might illustrate how nature had changed over time, had a much more difficult time demonstrating how scientific understanding changed as well. As Parr politely pointed out, "It has been the general practice of most natural history museums to strive for a degree of permanency in their exhibits that leaves them in large proportion out of date at all times." The Plan and Scope Committee, created in 1942 to evaluate the museum and plot its future, gave Parr a mandate when it concluded: "No exhibit can accurately be termed permanent."[7]

The financial squeeze of the Depression years made it difficult for many museums to change their older exhibits, and thus that permanence felt even dustier. With the war over and museum finances stabilized, Parr set out to remake the exhibits. He hoped to move away from the display of classification and systematics and toward exhibits that focused on the human relationship to and interaction with the natural world. "The traditional method of displaying museum objects according to their academic classification rather than their dynamic relations in nature," Parr explained in 1942, "tends to produce in the minds of visitors a feeling of remoteness between museum interests and contemporary problems of mankind." This was not a complete repudiation of the old museum practices. The AMNH would still recognize that "collecting specimens for research, classification and exhibition is a basic function of museums." Now, however, the museum acknowledged that "just as the days of the endless corridors and cases filled with oddities for the spectator to gawk at are fast fading, so the days of helter-skelter collecting of specimens are past."[8]

So, for example, the 1942 *Annual Report* noted quietly that the systematic exhibits of birds had been abandoned to be replaced with new, more lively ones. The new exhibit program was announced officially in 1947, and the museum worked diligently to create new exhibits throughout the 1950s. The first of them, the Felix Warburg Hall of Man and Nature, opened in May 1951; the Hall of the North American Forest opened in the following year.[9] These new exhibits all aspired, following Parr's lead, "to bring man and nature together." Parr also realigned the educational programs run by the museum's education department under the theme "The World We Live In," so that the exhibits in the galleries and the lectures and classes offered by the museum reinforced each other.[10] "The World We Live In" programs lasted at least until the mid-1960s.

Parr and the museum's board doubtless had several reasons to renew the exhibits. Parr surely wanted exhibits to reflect the world of natural science, from which he had come, more accurately. New exhibits would also generate publicity and a sense of novelty that would help attract more visitors and donations. But Parr also believed that new exhibits, organized along the lines he envisioned, were the only way that the museum would fulfill its educational mission. As he put it bluntly early in his tenure, "Only a national institution could hope to approach us as

Figure 18. Albert Parr believed that the exhibits at the American Museum of Natural History should draw the connection between humans and nature. AMNH Image #320861, © American Museum of Natural History.

a sportsman's museum and a museum of rare or spectacular specimens. But it takes more than excellence in scattered subjects before the museum can also become a first class educational institution."[11]

"Sportsman's museum" must have stung at an institution whose patron saint was Theodore Roosevelt, given that spectacular dioramas, featuring big game stuffed and mounted in dramatic and artistically magnificent vignettes, were among the AMNH's most famous, and beloved, exhibits. The dioramas were leftovers—created under the tenure of Henry Fairfield Osborn and now regarded as scientifically out-of-date. Worse, the Plan and Scope Committee believed that their chief appeal was aesthetic rather than scientific. "What is now realized," the committee concluded, "is that they have become ends in themselves.

The beauty of the composition and not the natural history content is what the visitor sees. It has been suggested that such groups are 95% art and 5% science."[12]

In this focus on public education, the museum reflected a larger discussion in American society brought on by the war and the political events that preceded it. Taking stock of those events, a number of American writers, educators, and policy makers believed that a reinvigorated educational system would prevent the madness into which the world had descended. As the museum's president wrote in 1942, "The Museum believes that the reconstruction of our educational system will be one of the great tasks for the new world." The museum was certainly not alone, and its president, F. T. Davison, wanted to make sure that the museum would be a part of that reconstruction. "The Museum," Davison insisted, "is particularly interested in educational problems. Universal education and enlightenment in an atmosphere of free thinking and free expression is fundamental to the American ideal."[13] In the postwar world, Parr trumpeted education as the antidote to totalitarianism, and he saw the museum as a central bulwark against it. In a 1947 essay he wrote, "The greater the mental confusion of the times, the greater the challenge to education, and the greater the value of teaching properly conceived and directed toward the elucidation of the problems which disturb the world. . . . In a world beset by hostility and want, the natural history museums have an opportunity, never before equaled, to serve the development of peace and of a better life for all."[14]

Parr's rededication to the educational mission of the AMNH stood as an implicit indictment of the museum's long history as an educational institution. It also put him at odds with the research mission of the institution, which many at AMNH also regarded as central. In his grim assessment of the museum in 1945, the president also reported the "bad news" that "the scientific staff has been drastically and seriously cut as to numbers."[15] Parr had told the board as much, and in more detail, in a confidential report he prepared when he assumed the directorship. "The economic careers at the museum have long compared unfavorably with the careers in the leading institutions of higher learning in the New York region," Parr wrote. While that must surely have heartened the underpaid research staff at the museum, what followed most surely did not: "Under the circumstances the American Museum must consider itself lucky not to have fared worse than it has, but there have been a sufficient number of opportunistic, second-best selections of personnel to add inferiority in prestige to the inferiority in economic reward now attached to a museum career."[16]

Though Parr was evaluating his new place of employment, he really described a much wider phenomenon. Museums founded in the late nineteenth century, especially museums of natural history, could claim to be at the forefront of scientific research and the production of scientific knowledge, specifically when that forefront was located in the world of systematics and taxonomy. Colleges and the nascent universities were only just emerging as centers of knowledge production. The AMNH's own staff illustrates the shift dramatically. When he came to the AMNH to build its paleontology department, Henry Fairfield Osborn left a professorship at Princeton, believing that only in a great museum could he assemble the raw material necessary for his scientific researches. Less than a generation later, as I have already mentioned, the anthropologist Franz Boas, who began his career first at the Field Museum of Natural History and then at the AMNH, left the museum world to establish the anthropology department at Columbia University. From that post he exerted an enormous influence on how the discipline would develop in the twentieth century.

By the mid-twentieth century, universities had established their primacy as research institutions. Experimental biology had replaced the older, specimen-based natural history at the frontier of the natural sciences, and microscopes replaced naked eyes as the way science proceeded. As historian Ronald Rainger has described it, "Conceptually and methodologically, the study of fossil vertebrates was peripheral to the most important work being done in the biological and geological sciences." Consequently, the museum-based work with specimens had become increasingly "a marginal subject at institutions of American higher education."[17] Given how influential paleontologist Osborn had been for so long at the AMNH, this was a fact Parr forced the museum to confront. Except in the areas of anthropology and paleontology (and I believe Parr was wrong about anthropology, as I suggested in Chapter 1), both of which still relied on objects to some extent for their researches, "it becomes obvious that a museum career has little attraction for the best scientific talent developed by our educational institutions."[18] Parr ultimately proposed a major internal reorganization of the scientific departments within the museum to accommodate that institution's financial situation and the realities of scientific work as he saw it.

In dedicating the AMNH to a new, more expansive educational mission, while simultaneously acknowledging that the museum could not also be at the forefront of scientific research, Parr articulated a central dilemma not only for museums but for universities as well. At the latter, the dilemma has been reduced to a shorthand: teaching versus research, and never the twain shall meet. While universities continue to agonize over how to marry the two, Parr believed that the museum's future lay with education rather than with research. "What we need," he wrote in an essay on research, "is quite simply a policy that will secure for us the necessary scientific talent for our other purposes." In other words, scientists who educate rather than research. "That any wisely defined policy will also result in research being carried on on the side is gratifying, but we have a long way to go before we need to debate whether another position should be added in a determination to engage in research for its own sake."[19]

Parr voiced his opinion even more bluntly at a conference in Buffalo in 1953. To those who insisted that museums needed to carry on research precisely so that they could better educate the public about science, Parr responded, "I don't think research in itself, other than identification, is essential to a museum. To say there can't be education without research would be to condemn most school systems. A science teacher can be excellent without being a research scientist."[20] From his perch atop one of the most important natural history museums in the world, Parr saw museums as science teachers first and foremost and as places of scientific research only secondarily.

If Parr's tenure at the AMNH helps us track the shift in the role of the museum as a site of knowledge production, it also helps us trace the educational shift in those museums away from a vaguely defined, general audience to one focused more specifically on children.

Charles Willson Peale imagined that his natural history museum would be of use to the farmer, the mechanic, and the merchant. He did not mention children. Fifty years later, in an age when formal school institutions were only just becoming established and widespread, the founders of the AMNH envisioned that it would serve as an educational center for adults as well as children. In that 1874 cornerstone ceremony, Parks Commissioner H. G. Stebbins told the audience that "it is our purpose to provide such structures as shall furnish agreeable entertainment to the general visitor, while at the same time offering valuable aid to common school education."[21]

Fifty years after that, museum president Henry Fairfield Osborn hung on to his nineteenth-century conception of natural history and the natural history museum, even as he inadvertently acknowledged its changing constituency. Osborn stubbornly clung to the idea that a well-organized natural history museum presented nature in an unadulterated, transparent way. "Whereas teachers and books may differ in their counsels," Osborn insisted, "Nature is the visible expression of the divine order of things, and her facts are immutable." He went on to summarize the educational purpose of the AMNH, at least as he saw it, as restoring "to the human mind the direct vision and inspiration of Nature as it exists in all parts of the world and as it is becoming known through all the sciences, thus to discover and encourage predispositions and tastes, thus to arouse ambitions, to overcome all resistance, and to return books and learning as the handmaids and not the masters of education."[22]

Hopelessly out-of-date as this view of natural history was, the museum leadership was coming to recognize that the educational assumptions made in the nineteenth century needed to be replaced, because, as I discuss further in the last chapter, the nature of the public and its expectations were changing. A 1931 fund-raising publication described "special educational guides" who took visitors through the galleries "to all sorts of places [to] open up all sorts of vistas within the confines of one building. In fact, only by wearing a blindfold and stopping your ears could you be led through any section of this Museum without learning something surprising and thrilling."[23] Being led by trained staff through the galleries was a far cry from the way the museum had expected its visitors to learn in the past. Education in the galleries could no longer be taken for granted and now required not only exhibits and objects but also people to explain those exhibits. Naked-eye science now needed a supplemental lecture.[24]

Osborn also recognized that by the 1920s primarily children benefited from all this "vision and inspiration." In his 1924 essay "The American Museum and Education," he sounded a bit defensive, noting that while the New York City schools taught just over a million pupils with twenty-nine thousand teachers, the AMNH taught six million students with just five. Osborn still believed that a visit to the museum would inspire adults too, writing that "on coming for the first time into direct vision of the wonders and beauties of Nature, not only boys and girls, but men and women, young and old, feel a thrill which they may never have experienced before."[25] Men and women may well have experienced that thrill, but there is a hint of wishful thinking in the way Osborn constructed the sentence, a lament that there were not, in the end, very many men and women in the galleries. And quoting the figure of six million—and this figure includes those children who came to the museum and those whose classrooms had a visit from museum staff—Osborn made it clear who the primary audience for the museum was becoming.

A 1931 fund-raising promotional echoed both the museum's desire to reach adults and the gnawing sense that, really, it didn't. "Education is too often considered a prerogative of the young," the brochure claimed, then responded, "To which the Museum offers an emphatic NO. . . . Here is a place where without expense to you and in your spare time the essentials of a current education may be had—and pleasurably." In an inadvertent glance back to the older conception of natural history, this booklet described a taxonomy of education, classifying the different audiences based on their educational needs: "Education in the Museum is divided between the general public, teachers and higher students, and the pupils of elementary and high school."[26] Note that the "general public" constituted only one group in this five-part division.

Six million seems an extraordinary number. But by 1945 the museum had hit upon a new method of accounting: "pupil hours." The museum calculated this figure by multiplying the total number of students in a given class by the number of hours a museum employee spent in their class with one of the museum's traveling exhibition cases. The number of pupil hours in 1945 reached 18.5 million. Even so, some in the museum complained that they ought to do more: "We must also expand our educational services to children," thundered one *Annual Report.* By the end of the 1940s, the museum confidently claimed that "practically every school child within our community receives during each year a substantial measure of cultural enrichment from this institution."[27] So it went throughout the rest of the twentieth century, driven in no small part by public funding sources to pursue this work. While the amount of work the museum did with student groups in school buildings ebbed and flowed with the vagaries of funding sources, children, whether with their classes or with their families, remained the largest share of the audience who came through the museum's doors. To cite a typical year, in 1971–72 three million visitors came to the AMNH, of whom two million were children.[28]

If we recognize that a large proportion of those one million adults in the museum came towing those two million children, either as parents or as teachers, we can see that the museum's galleries had become even more kid-centric. That 1971–72 *Annual Report* noted that in the 1940s the museum's primary audience had been "largely family groups." Further, those family groups, according to the report, "did not require or expect much in the way of professional educational assistance," implying that, thirty years later, more museum staff would be necessary to keep up with the educational demands made by a new generation of parents and their children. Likewise, while AMNH staff energetically took the museum out to city classrooms in the mid-twentieth century, much of the adult programming that took place within the museum was geared toward schoolteachers. "The museum did not take for granted," AMNH officials reported in 1950, "that its work was completed when it taught children. It took the lead in making sure that the teachers of our children, as well as the children, have a firm basis on which to continue the work begun by the museum." Fifteen years later the museum proudly reported that it offered twenty-five different accredited courses for schoolteachers.[29] By the last quarter of the twentieth century, the museum had largely completed the transformation envisioned by Albert Parr from an institution committed to a nineteenth-century conception of natural history and museum practice to an institution that saw its primary public role as contributing to the science education of children.

The AMNH continued to carry on an active research program, to be sure—and still does—despite Parr's contention that original research was not a necessity for a natural science museum. Still, even AMNH officials had a difficult time explaining just where research fit into the museum's public role and mission. In 1972, the *Annual Report* confessed, "Although the AMNH *is* a science museum and has been engaged in scientific research for over a century, its role as a scientific institution and a rationale for its support of research had never been stated in writing."[30]

In fact, as early as 1885, AMNH president Morris Jesup had suggested that "perhaps the Museum should begin to aid original research in a more active manner." Concurrently, the museum never really articulated what it meant by "education" in the late nineteenth century either. As John Michael Kennedy has described it, "The trustees never tried to define how the Museum performed its educational functions. They simply assumed that examining the specimens was a good thing for the people."[31] And a good thing for research too. That older conception of natural history, predicated as we have already discussed on naked-eye science, made the connection between research and public display appear seamless. Scientists conducted their original researches by observing and classifying specimens in the same way that museum visitors did, only more thoroughly and carefully. Thus what museum visitors saw in those galleries represented the fruits of that study.

At the same time, these nineteenth-century museum exhibits resonated with at least some number of visitors who were themselves amateur collectors and natural scientists in an age where the division between amateur and professional had not yet been drawn sharply. Museums often relied on amateurs and local enthusiasts for specimens from the field, and these "volunteers" often helped inside the museum as well to prepare, to classify, and to arrange the results of these collecting expeditions. In the age of the amateur naturalist, natural history museums reinforced the activities of weekend hobbyists.

By the mid-twentieth century surely, and probably even earlier, that kind of research had been eclipsed by laboratory experiments and microscopic investigations, and universities displaced museums as the places where much of that new research was carried out. As Kennedy has pointed out, despite Jesup's interest in promoting research at the AMNH, the museum never reorganized itself along the lines of the new institutions that placed primary emphasis on original research.[32] Museums simply could not afford as many staff, nor were they central to training graduate students, except in a few areas of speciality. As the

Figure 19. Albert Parr in the role of teacher. Parr also believed that the museum should target children specifically. AMNH Image #2A2944, © American Museum of Natural History.

twentieth century wore on, the tension between museum functions and research functions grew more acute, especially in contests over institutional resources. The AMNH was certainly not alone in facing this dilemma: all of the nineteenth-century natural history museums—whether in Boston, Philadelphia, or Chicago—confronted the same problem.

In conceding scientific research to the universities, natural history museums also conceded an adult audience as well. The move away from research and toward education at the AMNH mirrors the growth of children as the primary audience for museum exhibits. One consequence of this, however, has been that most adults do not or cannot keep up with the scientific research that issues from university labs either, and thus for many of us, our only exposure to the ideas of natural science come when we take our own children to the museum and look at exhibits designed primarily for them.

As a postscript, I should reiterate what I discussed in Chapter 1, that the scientific relevance of these museums and their collections began to reemerge in the 1960s. While the vast majority of research in the life and earth sciences goes on in university departments and medical centers, the fields of ecology and environmental sciences have found homes in natural history museums as well. To be fair, as Mary Anne Andrei has demonstrated, exhibits in at least some natural history museums had been promoting the idea of conservation since the early years of the twentieth century. As early as 1915, A. R. Crook, curator of the Illinois State Museum, offered a paper titled "The Museum and the Conservation Movement."[33] Still, for a host of reasons, questions of conservation reemerged with unprecedented urgency in the 1960s, and in 1966 the AMNH acknowledged that "many of the studies pursued by our staff come under the heading of systematic biology, a field that has often in the past been treated as a step-child, but which is now being developed [along] broad new lines."[34] By the end of the twentieth century, a number of scientists had taken as their research the charge Parr put to the museum: to explain and explore the connections between humans and the natural world. Natural history museums now stand poised to be centers of both research and education in an age of climate change, collapsing biodiversity, and unprecedented strains on natural resources.

Then, of course, there are the dinosaurs. When the first dinosaur discovered in the United States went on display at the Academy of Natural Sciences in Philadelphia just after the Civil War, officials there worried that the building would collapse under the crush of all the visitors. Little has changed since, though presumably the floors of natural history museums have been reinforced. Dinosaurs—and all manner of extinct creatures—have always been and remain a central attraction for natural

Figure 20. A newer generation of exhibits at the Field Museum. These are even more visually exciting than the exhibits Parr envisioned at the American Museum of Natural History, employing new technology and theatrical techniques. © The Field Museum, #GN90960_098d.

history museums. In the last quarter of the twentieth century, I think it is fair to say, the field of paleontology experienced a revolution and entered a second golden age (the first, I would offer, occurred in the last quarter of the nineteenth century when the field emerged). Improvements in excavation and survey techniques, and most importantly advances in the way genetic material can be studied, have transformed our understanding of ancient life in countless ways, and this, in turn, has made the collections assembled by natural history museums more important and revealing than ever.

Science and Industry, Science and Technology, Science and Kids

Given the spectacular rise of the American industrial economy in the late nineteenth and early twentieth centuries, and given how much faith Americans have always had in the power of technology to make our lives better, it is surprising that no group of industrialists or enthusiasts bothered to build a comprehensive museum of science and technology in one of the nation's booming industrial centers during the great age of museum building. Certainly there were such museums in Europe: in Vienna, London, Paris, and mostly importantly in Munich. This despite the fact that the periodic world's fairs of the era showcased industrial and technological developments first and foremost. Perhaps Americans had grown so accustomed to seeing technology at those world's fairs that they felt no real urge to create a permanent museum of it. Yet while the 1876 Centennial Exposition served to found the Pennsylvania (later the Philadelphia) Museum of Art, and the Field Museum of Natural History resulted from Chicago's 1893 World's Columbian Exposition, none of these grand expositions spawned a big, permanent institution dedicated to the collection and display of science and technology.[35] In 1925, Charles Richards, the former director of the American Association of Museums, issued a cry for just such a place. Reminding his readers that "we are today one of the foremost industrial countries of the world," Richards begged, "Can we afford to omit from our educational program the story of what has made us? . . . we need the industrial museum."[36] Richards wrote thirty years after the Smithsonian's George Brown Goode called for just such a museum in his essay.

A few art museums at the turn of the twentieth century, notably those in Philadelphia and Boston, hoped to improve American industrial design standards by highlighting the relationship between art and industrial production in the way that London's Victoria and Albert Museum did, but at those two places that mission had receded in importance by the early twentieth century. It was not until the 1920s and 1930s that the American cultural landscape finally included a museum of science and technology. Two, in fact—one each in two of the nation's most important industrial cities, Philadelphia and Chicago. (A third one in New York was organized at roughly the same moment, but it did not survive very long.)

Most of the institutions in this country that call themselves science museums, or science "centers"—there is some contention within the museum world over whether many of these places should be classed as museums at all—were founded in the second half of the twentieth century. Given that, they postdate the era when museums saw themselves as integral to the production of knowledge, when museums, to borrow from Morris Jesup, were supposed to engage in "original research." Thus American science museums have not had to negotiate the tensions between the scientific community and the wider public, between research and exhibition, that faced natural history museums.

With the exception of the Franklin Institute. It alone among contemporary American science museums—at least as far as I am aware—began in the nineteenth century as a place of research, teaching, and information gathering and became a public museum only in the 1930s. Examining the twin histories of Philadelphia's Franklin Institute and Chicago's Museum of Science and Industry, then, provides us with an opportunity to trace how science museums have come to cater almost entirely to children and how they have come to see themselves competing not so much with other museums as with other sources of entertainment—movies, computer games, Disney World—for that audience.

The Franklin Institute stands as a rare survivor from the early Republic. Few institutions founded before the Civil War, with the notable exception of liberal arts colleges, have lasted into the twenty-first century. And while the nineteenth-century history of the Franklin Institute, and of mechanic's institutes and libraries generally, has not yet been thoroughly explored, the broad outlines of the Franklin Institute's history are generally well known.

Founded by University of Pennsylvania professor William Keating and Philadelphia office clerk Samuel Merrick, the Franklin Institute of the State of Pennsylvania for the Promotion of Mechanic Arts adopted its constitution in 1824 and moved into its new building in 1826. It would stay in that home for the better part of a century. Its name suggests pretty clearly its purpose: "to advance the general interests of Manufactures and Mechanics by extending knowledge of mechanical sciences to its members, and others, at a cheap rate." This the institute did by offering public classes, courses, and exhibitions of new inventions; running a laboratory; and accumulating a tremendous library. And all this was available to a wide and diverse population of members. Not a gentleman's club in the eighteenth-century sense at all, the Franklin Institute served the city's workingmen and "mechanics" as the city's industrial economy flourished in the nineteenth century.

Surprisingly, Bruce Sinclair's 1974 book about the early years of the Franklin Institute remains the best study we have of this remarkable and influential place.[37] No surprise, therefore, that there are all sorts of questions that remain to be explored by historians. The Franklin Institute sits at the fascinating intersection between the development of American science, debates over democratic education, and the role of knowledge and innovation in nineteenth-century economic development.

By all accounts, the Franklin Institute pursued its work with great energy and to much acclaim throughout the nineteenth century. However, by the end of that century it found itself at a crossroads. Much of its educational role had been adopted by city schools, and its centrality to the development of applied science had been usurped by university research agendas and by other national organizations. As the twentieth century began, the Franklin Institute found itself in some ways the victim of its own success.

It also found itself hopelessly overcrowded in its building on 7th Street, just below Market. Institute employee Walter Pertuch, looking back in 1955 on his half-century career at the institute, reminisced, "When I first saw the Institute, it appeared to be a very dismal place. Everything was old and run down. Even the building looked tired and weary."[38] As early as 1906, a committee began to contemplate a new location and the task of raising money for it. It was, apparently, a somewhat desultory effort. But while the institute remained where it always had been until 1934, the Franklin Institute's Board of Trustees made three fateful decisions in the 1920s. In 1922, it agreed to refashion the institute as a grand public museum of science and technology, in 1923 it announced the closure of its schools that had been operating for nearly a century, and in 1925 the board hired Princeton physicist and dean Howard McClenahan both as the institute's new secretary and as the founding director of the new museum. Hired the same year that Charles Richards issued his challenge to Americans to build an industrial science museum, McClenahan brought the Franklin Institute's museum to life.

At almost exactly the same moment that the Franklin Institute began its transformation into a museum of science and technology, Sears, Roebuck magnate Julius Rosenwald founded the Museum of Science and Industry in Chicago. Rosenwald put the museum in the former Fine Arts building of the 1893 World's Columbian Exposition and filled it initially with an estimated $5 million worth of exhibits all donated by area businesses. Rosenwald hired Dr. Waldemar Kaempffert, science editor of the *New York Times*, to direct the museum.

The founding of the Franklin Institute Science Museum and the Museum of Science and Industry parallel each other in several ways. Each museum exhibited the basics of broad scientific principles and the application of those principles to useful things. In this sense, both museums referred to "industry," "technology," and "applied science" more or less interchangeably. The goal in both places was for visitors to see the connection between basic science and everyday life. In his 1932 study of city problems, Yale professor Maurice Davie cited the Chicago Museum of Science and Industry and Philadelphia's Franklin Institute as "outstanding examples" of museums that brought "the fundamentals of science, engineering, and industry to the people."[39]

There is no evidence that Rosenwald and McClanahan ever crossed paths, but they drew their museological inspiration from the same place: the Deutsches Museum in Munich. The Society of German Engineers founded the Deutsches Museum at their annual meeting in 1903; the first exhibits went on display in a temporary facility in 1906, and the museum completed its move into its permanent home in 1925. Rosenwald and McClanahan both traveled to Munich to see the Deutsches Museum, both were dazzled by it, and both modeled their own institution on it to varying degrees. They weren't alone among Americans. Henry Ford was so impressed with the Deutsches Museum that he donated $1 million to it. For all those who cared about such things, the Deutsches Museum stood as the finest, most extensive, most exciting science museum in the world.

At one level, the Deutsches Museum reached for the same encyclopedic treatment of its subject that art museums and natural history museums did with theirs. The world of science and technology was broken down into its basic categories—a systematics of science and technology, if you will—and exhibits showed visitors the progress that had been made in each scientific or technological endeavor. As Waldemar Kaempffert, the director of Chicago's Museum of Science and Industry, put it, "What the art museum does for painting and sculpture the Deutsches Museum does for science and invention."[40]

The Museum of Science and Industry opened its doors to the public in 1933, to correspond with the "Century of Progress" exposition held in Chicago in that year. By that time, however, the museum was in a bit of disarray. Founding patron Rosenwald had died, and Director Kaempffert had resigned or been forced out (depending on your point of view). He was replaced by Otto Theo Kreuser, an engineer from General Motors, who presided over the opening of the museum, still unfinished and half empty. During the summer of 1933, Rufus Dawes was elected president of the museum. An influential businessman, Dawes was deeply involved in the "Century of Progress" exposition, and his position as president of the museum guaranteed that his organization would inherit some number of exhibits once the fair closed. Among the exhibits that moved into the museum were the "stratospheric gondola" and something called "The Epic of Meat," which began with a diorama of a cowboy surveying the range and ended with a variety of fancy cuts.[41] Carl Sandburg must have been proud.

The general manager of the "Century of Progress" was Major Lenox Riley Lohr. Lohr then went on to the presidency of the National Broadcasting Company (NBC), but he returned to Chicago in 1940 to take over the Museum of Science and Industry after Dawes died of a heart attack. Lohr, a teetotaler and butterfly collector, struck many as not entirely likable. One of his former colleagues at NBC told *Time* magazine, "He never took a drink, never talked about women, always made you feel he was a better guy than yourself."[42] But first and foremost he was a business executive from the new world of corporate entertainment, and under his leadership, the museum got its financial house in order, exhibits were added and updated, and the public started pouring through the doors.

Reinventing the Museum

As an explanation for why it took as long as it did for Americans to build these museums, Mike Wallace has pointed to a confluence of factors in the political economy and concluded, "Perhaps the industrial museum flourished in the twenties because it could now draw upon the resources of corporations, and of engineers who had made their peace with the corporate world."[43] This strikes me as persuasive, but incompletely so. On the one hand, while it is certainly true that by the 1920s the American economy had become fully corporatized, the desire to build such museums reached back before the complete corporate takeover of the American economy; on the other hand, these museums at least professed to link basic science with applied science in their exhibits. Exhibits of applied science lent themselves easily to corporate boosterism; exhibits of basic physics or chemistry less so.

Without question, many of the exhibits in science and technology museums served as advertisements for corporate interests and continue to do so—sometimes shamelessly and nakedly so!—but there is, I think, another reason it took Americans an extra generation to build their technology museums. While there was no argument about the importance of science and technology in American life, I do think there was considerable confusion about what to exhibit and how to exhibit it.

The older museums, whether of art or anthropology or natural history, were predicated on some version of an evolutionary narrative. How to create such a narrative for science and technology was not as easy to conceive for two reasons. First, the evolutionary link between basic science and applied science did not always present itself in an obvious way. Second, while it was surely possible to display the evolutionary progress of certain technologies—steam power, for example—by the end of the nineteenth century even that progress was not as linear and straightforward as it once had been. Rupture rather than continuity defined the development of technology and the forces it harnessed. For instance, when we looked at Henry Adams in the introduction, his "historical neck" had been broken in the Gallery of Machines at the Great Exposition of 1900. Histrionically, Adams underscored the exhibitionary difficulty posed by science and technology for the creation of a coherent, visual narrative.

By the time Americans did get around to building science and technology museums, those older, evolutionary narratives were loosening their grip on the display practices of other museums. Natural history museums had begun to replace their specimen-laden glass cases with attractive, visually exciting dioramas, and art museums created context for art by installing "period" rooms. By the 1920s, consequently, those who wanted to build museums of science and technology could begin to think about new ways of organizing and presenting their exhibits. Because it took a generation for Americans finally to build such places, therefore, the builders of science and technology museums drew upon the experience of older museums to rethink what a museum did and how it did it. The museum itself could be reinvented in several ways.

Earlier chapters have examined how the first generation of museums had been built largely for the display of objects and did little for visitors except to show them those objects. The new science museums started by focusing more on the experience visitors had when they moved through the galleries. "Back as far as 1916," complained F. C. Brown in 1928, "there was recognized such a thing as museum fatigue," and he was certainly not alone in believing that museums needed to rethink how they treated their audience. He continued, "If a museum is to be built for the lay public, the problem is, to a considerable extent, one for the practical psychologist to solve."[44]

Brown was associated with New York's Museum of the Peaceful Arts, a short-lived endeavor that was intended to launch a much larger museum of science and technology in New York City (what became of that project is something of a mystery). The Museum of the Peaceful Arts, in addition to generating support for the bigger, more permanent enterprise, gave museum builders "a demonstration museum" where new ideas about the museum experience could be tested. Brown insisted that "a museum should maintain itself on a lofty level," but he also believed the museum could "compromise with human nature to interest visitors in what we know is worth while." The innovations Brown and others at the Museum of the Peaceful Arts made strike us now as commonsensical and quaint for being so. Still, the earnestness with which Brown made his suggestions reminds us how novel they must have seemed at the time: "Chairs and stools should be thoughtfully interspersed throughout the exhibits and provision should be made for accessible dining and lunching as would enable the hungry visitor to lengthen his visit and encourage him to make frequent trips to the museum."[45] Thus was born the museum café.

Lenox Lohr accepted Brown's challenge when he took over in Chicago, according to his own report, at any rate. He spent some of his early days in the museum, notebook in hand, studying visitor behavior and jotting down ideas. Overhearing complaints about aching feet, Lohr carpeted expanses of the marble flooring; thanks to Lohr, the weary now had lounge chairs distributed throughout the museum, and the hungry could now eat in a cafeteria or in a "picnic room." But the first of Lohr's "startling innovations" came when he noticed how many men huddled outside to smoke. Immediately, the Major (the title came from his years in the Army Corps of Engineers, and he continued to use it) "took down the No Smoking signs and placed capacious ashtrays at convenient spots."[46] Some innovations have clearly proved more enduring than others, and Lohr would surely be disappointed today to find that smokers are once again huddled outside.

Beyond the addition of capacious ashtrays and commodious cafeterias, the biggest question the new science museums had to address was what to exhibit and how to do so. As I noted earlier, the evolutionary model presented some problems, not the least of which was the challenge of connecting technologies past with technologies present. Not to make that connection, however, meant that these museums risked simply displaying the history of technology. Several such museums did exist already, at least in Europe. The Museum of the History of Science at Oxford and the Museum of the Cavendish Laboratory at Cambridge, to name two, displayed "antique scientific instruments" and "relics," treating these objects, in a museological sense, like original works of art or like natural history specimens.[47]

Collecting and displaying original "relics" was decidedly not what the museum founders of the 1920s had in mind for their institutions, though the older ideas proved hard to shake entirely. Robert Shaw of New York's museum sounded very much like a nineteenth-century museum curator when he wrote, "An exhibition of science and its application may well be compared to a story, with the sections of the exhibit corresponding to the chapters, and the units of the exhibits to the paragraphs."[48] When Howard McClenahan outlined his vision of the Franklin Institute's new museum to the institute's members in 1928, he remarked to them that "there has come about a great change, a happy change in our conception of the purpose and the character of a museum." Calling the early museum "merely a depository for the collections of a man with an acquisitive sense," McClenahan announced that the museum "is no longer primarily a home for collections." Here then, as we mentioned in the Chapter 1, was the first example of a museum built without objects at its center. Instead, McClenahan went on, the new museum "shall be a place where the *principles* of science are emphasized, where the scientific fundamentals are displayed as they find application in industry, and where the growth of manufacturing and engineering processes are portrayed with the utmost possible clarity."[49]

Even so, McClenahan still imagined that his museum, like the older, evolutionary museums, would be a place where "growth from primitive

Figure 21. It looks like an art museum, but the Franklin Institute Science Museum helped reinvent the museum in an "interactive" age.
Photo: Steven Conn.

state to sophistication will become readily apparent." In that talk to the members in 1928 McClenahan drew a direct comparison between his vision of a science museum and the Philadelphia Museum of Art, which was just about to move into its new home. "The fine arts are there," he said, "looked upon as unitary. They are to be grasped as an inter-related whole, and not as a mere congeries of more or less disparate units. . . . Exactly the same purpose underlies the establishment which we are planning."[50] Henry Adams notwithstanding, McClenahan still believed that there was a unity and harmony in the world of modern technology and that the museum could display it.

This new conception of the museum also raised questions about how best to demonstrate the important connections between basic and applied science and between the history of science and technology and its present use. Just as worrying as building exhibits only to illustrate the history of technology was the concern that displays focused on the present would devolve into crass advertising for the corporations that sponsored the exhibits. Robert Shaw, for one, felt that the science museum would do best to exhibit things with which visitors already had some familiarity, "things he has already seen or with which he comes into contact during his daily life." In Chicago, Waldemar Kaempffert tried to connect past and present through illustrating social consequences of technology. He imagined an exhibit on the cotton gin that would then explain how it helped perpetuate slavery, or an exhibit on the skyscraper along with a discussion of urban crowding and other related ills.[51] Ideas such as those helped Kaempffert to lose his job at the Museum of Science and Industry in 1931.

In the end, Chicago's museum opened with exhibits sponsored by local businesses whose purpose was not to display the progressive evolution of technology but to celebrate the role of technology in modern life. Lohr was unapologetic about this. While insisting that the museum would not sell exhibits for ad space, he recognized that the age of philanthropic "angels" was over. As he put it, "income and inheritance taxes took care of that." In place of those donors, Lohr thought "the most promising source was big industry." The exhibits at the Museum of Science and Industry thus grew from such corporate sponsorships. In fairness, however, among the early, famous exhibits in Chicago was "The Miracle of Growth," a visually arresting—indeed, frank—display of human reproduction. As one reporter described it, "On a May Sunday I saw thousands of visitors of all ages waiting in line to file slowly through the hall. Family groups predominated. . . . Sex education of the young has long been a problem with school and church groups everywhere. Chicago seems to have made a good start toward a solution."[52] In the cultural climate in which I write, I wonder how many museums would have the courage to put up such an exhibit geared to adults, much less children, today?

The exhibits at the Franklin Institute's museum were less corporate focused, in part because the new museum building included an enormous memorial to Benjamin Franklin at its center and so concentrated more on the history of science and technology. But neither museum, I think it is fair to say, organized the world of science and technology as "an inter-related whole"; the exhibits, in the end, did constitute—again, more so in Chicago than in Philadelphia—"a mere congeries of more or less disparate units."

Instead of narrative coherence built with and around objects on display, however, science museums presented the public with an entirely new way of experiencing a museum. What had once been a primarily visual experience was replaced with an interactive one. Put another way, objects to be looked at were replaced with buttons to be pushed.

More than anything else, this is what impressed people like Rosenwald and McClenahan when they visited the Deutsches Museum. As McClenahan told Franklin Institute members, "In the old type of museum, the object most frequently seen was the 'Please do not touch' sign. That sign in the modern science museum is almost as rare as some of the exhibits. The visitor is expected, even urged, to handle, to operate, the exhibits. . . . And just so far as it is possible to do so, every exhibit is to be made active, be made 'to run.'" McClenahan recognized that his museum would have a fundamentally different relationship to objects. "In the institutions of the older type," he remarked, "the aim was always to get originals." In museums of the new type, however, "the originals are like salt on food—they add flavor and give distinction. But, as in the case of salt, a little goes a long way. A few great originals are enough."[53]

Given how ubiquitous push-buttoned interaction has become, it is worth remembering just how electrifying (pardon the expression) the experience was for that first generation of Americans to visit the new science and technology museums. Writing in the *Saturday Evening Post*, David Wittels called the Franklin Institute's museum a place "where every man's an Einstein"; a few years later Harland Manchester, also writing in the *Saturday Evening Post*, visited Chicago's Museum of Science and Industry and pronounced: "Museums don't have to be stuffy." Manchester opened his piece by drawing just the distinction the builders of the new museums had hoped to create: "To most people, a museum is a formidable edifice where serious people in their best clothes look at collections jealously imprisoned in glass cases by curators and guards. But this one is a carnival of science, a panorama of progress and a multi-ring circus of machines."[54]

Both writers enthused about exactly the things McClenahan had promised in 1928 that the new museum would be. "The Franklin Institute is one of the foremost scientific institutions in the world," wrote Wittels, "yet whole sections of it are deliberately set up so that they resemble penny arcades; and the forbidding PLEASE DO NOT TOUCH signs typical of museums are replaced by invitations to touch, feel and try." Likewise, in Chicago, "you push buttons and turn cranks, and things happen and the first thing you know you have learned something." Walking through the Museum of Science and Industry, "hundreds of shows lure you with the persuasiveness of side-show barkers." Rather than simply adding "science and technology" to the bodies of knowledge given museum form, those who built these new museums transformed what a museum could be and how visitors could engage with it.

That both writers used carnival metaphors—side-show barkers and penny arcades and multiring circuses—points as well to another fundamental difference between the old natural science museums and the new science and technology ones. The former reshaped themselves into

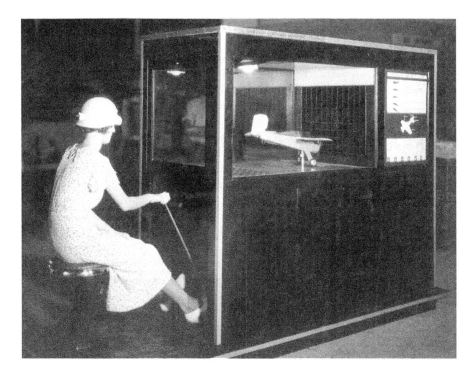

Figure 22. Go ahead, please touch. The new museums of science and technology created experiential rather than visual exhibits. Courtesy of the Archives, Museum of Science and Industry, Chicago.

institutions catering to children; the latter appealed to children from the outset.

This is clear from both of the *Saturday Evening Post* stories about Philadelphia and Chicago. Wittels recorded that "you just push the buttons and the exhibits go into their song and dance. . . . The kids are popeyed, also enlightened." Manchester, tongue firmly in cheek, recounted the adventures of one Mrs. Susson, a Chicago schoolteacher, as she stalked "hooky players . . . in a huge building on the shore of Lake Michigan. In a few hours she nabbed sixty happy vagrants. . . . Believe it or not they were caught red-handed visiting a museum."[55] The implication in these articles, and in others with similar tone, was that the science museum had found that happy middle ground between education and entertainment and that science museums were thus fun for kids and good for them. A writer for the *Christian Science Monitor* summed up the new science museum in this description of the Franklin Institute: "If it's new, if its [*sic*] got zip, get-up-and-go, if it's something so vitally important to everyday living that everyone should know about it, then it's a subject worthy of prominent display in the Museum of the Franklin Institute of Philadelphia. There in a few words you have the policy of a modern wonderland of science where . . . even the most intricate processes of applied research are explained in words or ways grammar school children can understand."[56]

At least one museum director remained decidedly unimpressed with the new "hands-on" ethos of the science museums. Albert Parr, who continued to write and think about museum questions after his retirement from the AMNH, was quite arch in his criticism: "'Audience participation' has been the catchword of museum educators for a good many years," he began one essay and continued, "Apparently the participation is thought of chiefly in physical terms. Turning a crank or pushing a button is supposed to make the visitor feel party to the events unfolding." Juxtaposing this phys-ed activity with "the true concept of learning by doing," Parr went on, "It seems high time to reestablish that man has brains if he would only use them, and that thinking is doing too. . . . A museum," he concluded in a way that must have offended at least some, "is not a gymnasium, not even for finger exercises with push buttons."[57] Parr tilted at windmills. These exhibits proved hugely popular and quickly created a large audience. Just after the war, in 1947, the Museum of Science and Industry recorded nearly 1.5 million visitors, more than double the number that came in 1940.[58]

It will not surprise anyone who has ever been to one of America's science museums to learn that most of those visitors were children, parents of children, or schoolteachers with their students in tow. Writing in 1947, Manchester observed in Chicago that "a large proportion of the visitors are grade and high-school pupils. Teachers all over the Midwest are using the museum to supplement science courses."[59] Much the same was true in Philadelphia, though on a proportionally smaller scale. In 1960, the Franklin Institute Science Museum broke its own attendance record with 440,000 visitors, of whom just over 325,000 were school pupils. By the 1990s the Franklin Institute received a million visitors, 60 percent of whom, by its own estimate, came in "family groups"; the rest were school groups. Fittingly, in 1950, the Franklin Institute played host to the first National Science Fair. As Michelle Tucker has summed it up: "While the old Institute had served adults, the new Institute . . . would be a source of science education for Philadelphia's schoolchildren."[60]

That these new, interactive science museums would appeal almost entirely to children was not a foregone conclusion. Many of those in the adult education movement, which blossomed after the First World War, saw museums—and specifically science museums—as central to the proj-

Figure 23. Children quickly became the primary constituency at the new museums of science and technology. Here, Linda and Doug Sneed in the Museum of Science and Industry's Hall of Elements in 1961. Courtesy of the Archives, Museum of Science and Industry, Chicago.

ect of adult education. Benjamin Gruenberg, for example, in his 1935 book *Science and the Public Mind,* saw great potential in the new science museums, "untrammeled by tradition," to teach adults. Ten years later, writing in the middle of the Second World War, Robert Morey believed that science museums could "build a barrier against rash judgments and actions" by helping people develop "critical habits of thought." He, for one, was convinced that interactive—what he called "functional"— exhibits could do just that: "When science museums construct functional exhibits that rouse curiosity, encourage the making of comparisons and tell the story of human progress in significant patterns of crucial facts, then the museum will become the university for the common man, helping to shape the thinking and the future of all the peoples of the earth." That tall order, Morey concluded, "is worth doing."

Indeed, just after the Franklin Institute Science Museum opened, only an estimated 25 percent of its visitors were children.[61] By the turn of the twenty-first century, however, I think it is fair to say that the science museums no longer saw their audience as "the common man."

Scientific Research, Scientific Education, Scientific Fun

Lenox Lohr was clearly an able administrator, a successful fund-raiser, and something of a museum entrepreneur. What Lohr was not, however, was a scientist. Indeed, he believed that much of the Museum of Science and Industry's financial difficulties resulted from its departmental organization where curators had final responsibility for all aspects of each department. Lohr regarded this as old-fashioned and too inflexible; he further believed that curators spent too much doing basic research.[62] In his reorganization of the museum, Lohr balanced the budget in part by sacking nineteen staff members, including many of the in-house scientists. In a crass, if honest, definition, Lohr saw the relationship between science and industry as simply "to supply better goods cheaper."

This outraged many in the Chicago scientific community, including Nobel Prize winner Arthur Holly Compton, who worked only a few blocks away from the museum at the University of Chicago. In response to Lohr's assessment of the role of science, Compton replied, "Faraday, as he discovered the laws of electricity, which are basic to electrical engineering, was not concerned with making better things cheaper. . . . A tragedy has occurred in the cultural life of our city."[63]

When Rosenwald hired him, Kaempffert imagined, and set about to build, an institution not unlike the older natural history museums with departments corresponding to the different fields of science. Likewise, Kaempffert believed that the Museum of Science and Industry ought to have a research library, laboratory facilities to conduct "original research," and a professional scientific staff to conduct that research and to present science to the public. He imagined an institution, in other words, not unlike the Franklin Institute.

As we have already reviewed briefly, the Franklin Institute was founded, in some measure, to promote and advance research in applied science, especially through its exhibits and through the work of its Committee on Science and the Arts.[64] Even as the Institute decided to build an enormous public museum, the Board believed that the institute could continue to function both as a center for scientific research and as a large-scale public museum.

At the end of World War I, in the middle of the institute's planning process for a new building and new museum, Philadelphia industrialist Henry Bartol bequeathed $1 million to the Franklin Institute for the creation of a research lab facility. The Bartol Research Foundation, which conducted work primarily in nuclear physics and cosmic radiation, operated first in a building at 19th and Race streets and then in 1928 moved to the campus of Swarthmore College, about twelve miles from the city, where it operated in partnership with the college. British physicist W. F. G. Swann was hired to run the Bartol Foundation.

Bartol was clear that the mission of his foundation was "for the conduct of researches in the physical sciences and for the investigation of problems of a scientific nature arising in the industries." Quickly, however, the foundation devoted itself to what we might call "basic" rather than applied research, sharing a consensus in the mid-twentieth century's era of "big science" that basic research would eventually yield practical applications. As the institute's Thomas Coulson described it in 1953, "It is abundantly clear by now that the fields of fundamental research are the incubating grounds for the ideas which supply the needs of industry."[65]

When he took the job at the Franklin Institute, Swann had already had an accomplished career in the academy. Trained in England, he had held academic posts in the United States at the University of Minnesota, the University of Chicago, and, just prior to taking charge of the Bartol Foundation, at Yale University where he directed the Sloane Labs. It reveals a great deal about the relationship between museums and their role in the production and dissemination of scientific knowledge that the Franklin Institute could first attract physicists from Princeton and then from Yale to administrative posts. At almost exactly the same moment that the Museum of Science and Industry in Chicago was shedding its labs and firing its scientists, the Franklin Institute was reinforcing its historical commitment to scientific research and stocking itself with scientists from the most prestigious places.

The Franklin Institute participated in the war effort during World War II in a number of ways, including optical and electrical research. The institute's research labs grew from nine thousand square feet to forty-three thousand during the war, and there is some evidence to suggest that this came at the expense of the museum. As one historian has described it, "The neglect of the Museum activities during . . . the war years clearly revealed the fundamental position of research in the Institute's self-image. Research had always come first."[66]

The institute continued to pursue scientific research vigorously after the Second World War in a number of different areas, under the consolidated name of Franklin Research Center. In 1951, the same year that the Bartol Research Foundation opened its ten-million-volt Van de Graaff nuclear accelerator, the National Asphalt Research Center was established at the institute.

By 1966, the Research Center built and moved into its own building, right across the street from the museum. Whereas the Science Museum stood as a late example of Beaux-Arts neoclassicism, the new Research Center building spoke the language of architectural modernism and reflected the success of the institute's research activities and the confidence with which it faced the future.

Essentially, the institute grew to become one of a small number of private research centers competing for and surviving with contracts either from government or from the private sector. By the 1970s, the Franklin Institute could boast of its research operations, "It is one of the ten largest not-for-profit, non-university affiliated contract research laboratories in the United States," an impressive, if highly qualified, achievement, with an annual budget of $20 million and a staff of six hundred to match. By 1980, the Research Center's budget had grown to $25 million, and it announced the creation of the Franklin Institute Policy Analysis Center "to study the impact of private and public policies involving science and technology on public health and well-being, and to communicate its finding to the public and to appropriate decision-making bodies." The Research Center's activities dwarfed "by far . . . all other activities of the Institute."[67]

The balance the Franklin Institute had created and maintained for nearly fifty years between its original research and its public museum was unusual, and it did not last. The *Annual Report* for 1983 announced somewhat bloodlessly that "research priorities" had been "reevaluated." The next year, the institute's board decided to close the Research Center and sell the building. Two years after that, the institute divested itself of its remaining stake in the Bartol Research Foundation, and the foundation became fully a part of the University of Delaware. The 1966 Research Center building has now been converted into an assisted-living residence for senior citizens—symbolic, however unintentionally, of what has happened to the Franklin Institute's research aspirations. By 1989, the board had committed itself fully to the Science Museum, and to expanding it. The goal was to "move from a regional to a national resource, from one that teaches the basics of science to one that champions the role of the individual in determining how technology may shape the future, from one that while considered an aggressive marketer among non-profits must now compete with major commercial attractions for its audience."[68]

To achieve this, the Franklin Institute embarked on a major expansion campaign that included adding ninety thousand square feet to its existing buildings, new exhibits, and an IMAX theater. In an irony he probably didn't realize, when the new "Futures Center" opened in 1990, *New York Times* architecture critic Paul Goldberger called the old

Figure 24. Inside the Franklin Institute's new wing, built after the institute closed its research arm. Photo: Steven Conn.

museum "venerable" and believed that the new addition "banishes stodginess."[69] This is, of course, exactly what people said when the Franklin Institute Science Museum opened in the 1930s.

The competition with commercial entertainment for audience share was one the Franklin Institute felt it could and can win. By closing its research facilities, however, the institute conceded that it could not compete in that realm. There are doubtless any number of institutional reasons behind that decision: research has become much more expensive, universities offer more professional prestige, and on and on. But another reason lies, I think, in the historical roots of the institute and how it envisioned the world of science. *The Journal of the Franklin Institute* began monthly publication in 1825, making it among the oldest scientific publications in the nation. Throughout the twentieth century it remained, in the words of one description, "one of the world's few non-specialized technical journals [publishing] technical papers on subjects ranging from human engineering and computer theory to zone refining of metals, submarines and satellites."[70]

What had been in the nineteenth century a great virtue of the *Journal* and of the institute's research more generally, its diversification, had become by the end of the twentieth anachronistic. Increasing specialization is the order of the scientific day, and there is less room in that world for the broad, encyclopedic, and integrative vision of science at the heart of the Franklin Institute.

Science and Citizenship

At one level, the takeover of science and natural history by children should be a cause for celebration. Children clearly love these places, and every time I go for a visit I am overwhelmed by their racket and their energy. There is nothing wrong, it seems to me, with children's claiming these museums as their own. Nor do I want to suggest a causal connection between the Franklin Institute's decision in the 1980s to get out of the research business and the Museum of Science and Industry's focus on children in its exhibits. Still, it seems more than merely coincidental. Without a research arm, the opportunities to engage with adults have been reduced; likewise, I think we are entitled to a certain skepticism about the science education on offer in Philadelphia, or in Chicago or any other place, given that these museums have chosen to focus not on the work of science but on its entertainment value.

At another level, we ought to be concerned that science museums have more or less given up on those of us over the age of eighteen. In so doing, science museums contribute to, or rather don't help to alleviate, our general scientific illiteracy. Natalie Angier is right, so far as I can tell, that for most of us "science" is a thing of our childhoods, and as adults we put it, along with other childish things, away. The Franklin Institute recognized as much at least as far back as 1969. Noting that "very few people visit the Institute from the time they finish high school until they have children," the institute's staff saw "a major programming need for the future, since it is this segment of the population most affected by the current [technological] revolution."[71] As far as I can determine, that need remains unfulfilled.

There is a genuine price to pay for that, even if one doesn't believe that a fluency in science ought to be expected of any educated person. More and more we are asked, in our role as citizens, to make judgments and shape policies that center on scientific questions: for example, the efficacy of stem cell research or genetically modified crops, the responses to climate change, or dwindling fossil fuels. The answers to these questions demand a familiarity with science that most of us simply don't have.

Science museums might help us with that, and some have moved in

the direction of being—to quote the title from a new program at the
Academy of Natural Sciences in Philadelphia—"town halls for science."
Albert Parr, for one, recognized this dilemma in 1943, and I'll give him
the last word. In an essay for *Natural History* Parr noted: "When science
was very young, the gap between scientist and layman was very
narrow. . . . As science advanced the gap widened. . . . We have come to
realize that this divorce between expert knowledge and public comprehension is one of the severest obstacles to the further progress of
civilization. . . . Our question is how to achieve a solution for the sciences
[. . .] through the medium of the public museums."[72]

The question has only grown more urgent.

Chapter 5
The Birth and the Death of a Museum

In 2003, wrecking crews arrived on Civic Center Boulevard in Philadelphia and began demolishing the Municipal Auditorium, which had opened in 1931 with much fanfare for its size and for its art deco elegance. Over the years, the auditorium had played host to any number of events, including national party conventions—in 1948 all three major parties, Democrat, Republican, and Progressive, nominated their presidential candidates there—trade shows, and high school graduations. The Beatles played the auditorium in 1964. The city had more or less mothballed the place by the 1990s, however, when a new convention center opened, designed to attract bigger, more lucrative conventions that had been passing the old auditorium by.

The auditorium, and a set of adjacent buildings collectively known to the locals as the "Civic Center," were being torn down to make room for several new hospital and research facilities for the Hospital of the University of Pennsylvania and the Children's Hospital of Philadelphia. As the crews went along, they also took down a small, frankly undistinguished neoclassical building immediately to the north of the auditorium. And while many locals carried fond and nostalgic memories of events at the Civic Center, few, I suspect, remembered what that small building once had been.

When the heavy equipment turned its destructive attention on the white terra-cotta façade, it demolished what remained of the Philadelphia Commercial Museum, and that institution vanished entirely from the physical landscape.

In fact, it had disappeared from the cultural landscape a long time ago. It was officially closed—padlocked actually—at the end of the twentieth century and had been a sad, forlorn, and increasingly shabby place for at least thirty years before that.

The Philadelphia Commercial Museum now exists only as a disconnected set of fragments: some archival material, a few dozen photographs, some ethnographic objects, including rare material from the Amur River region of Siberia, model ships from a once extensive collection of such things, and other miscellany. These bits and pieces have been duly dispersed and have found new homes in other cultural institutions around the city of Philadelphia.

To recall something we discussed previously: A number of museums were founded in the United States during the early Republican and antebellum periods. Most, such as those established by Peale, Dunn, and Barnum, did not survive beyond the Civil War. For a number of reasons, these early museums did not develop the intellectual rationales and institutional structures necessary to perpetuate themselves. By contrast, almost all of the large, public museums founded in the late nineteenth and early twentieth centuries did just that, and they have survived to the present. Some, certainly, are struggling, but many more are thriving. The Philadelphia Commercial Museum thus provides us with a relatively uncommon opportunity to study the fate of a museum founded at the turn of the twentieth century through its entire life-span—from birth, through its growth and flowering, and then during what proved to be its inexorable decline.

Most museums have undergone change and transformation over the course of their lives. Not too long ago, to take one spectacular example, Chicago's Field Museum of Natural History dropped the "Natural History" part of its name and is now simply the Field Museum. This change permits it to be something if not more than, at least other than, strictly a natural history museum. Few museums have actually closed, and certainly I can think of none in the United States that were of the size and significance of the Philadelphia Commercial Museum that have simply ceased to exist. My interest then is to examine why that happened. Why did the Commercial Museum fail to change and adapt? Why did its founding purpose and mission not survive past the first quarter of the twentieth century?

Institutions are each shaped and driven by their own—for want of a better term—institutional forces. Questions of funding, of constituencies, of leadership, of politics both internal and external define the parameters within which any institution must operate. At the same time, however, and this has been one of my central themes throughout this book, institutions—museums particularly—stand as the physical embodiment of a set of ideas and aspirations. Needless to say, ideas can't sustain institutions unless they can also attract money and inspire people. But I believe that the reverse is also true: Institutions can't survive without a coherent set of ideas, an intellectual purpose that is readily apparent both to those inside the walls and to those on the outside. In this sense, the demise of the Commercial Museum represents the death of the ideas that founded it.

I do not want to play Marc Antony precisely; I am not interested in either burying the Commercial Museum or praising it, but rather I want to offer a post-mortem, and in that autopsy perhaps to extract some final lessons about the relationship between museums, objects, and ideas in the twentieth century.

The Rise of the Commercial Museum

The "Philadelphia Museums"—the official name of what virtually everyone would refer to as the Commercial Museum—hatched in the mind of William Wilson, a botanist at the University of Pennsylvania, when he went to Chicago to visit the World's Columbian Exposition in 1893. The world's fair spawned one museum locally—the Field Museum of Natural History. That museum had a familiar area of focus and joined other such museums in other American cities. Wilson's idea for the Commercial Museum was, however, something new, at least in the United States.[1] With the Commercial Museum, Wilson attempted to give the world's fair itself a permanent home. In a sense, the Commercial Museum was Wilson's response to Andrew Carnegie's lamentation at the closing of the Chicago fair: "The great exhibition has come, triumphed, and passed away. . . . Our revels are ended. Prospero's wand has broken the spell."[2]

Not content with a broken spell, Wilson imagined his museum as the repository for the exhibits from Chicago and subsequent fairs as well. By the time the museum opened to the public four years later, in 1897, University of Pennsylvania provost and museum enthusiast William Pepper could confidently boast, "Our Commercial Museum possesses the most extensive collections of natural products in existence in any country."[3]

Measured in sheer volume, the growth of the Commercial Museum was staggering. That initial collection of material from Chicago—some twenty-five boxcar loads—was augmented the following year by exhibits from a fair in Liberia; in 1897 four hundred tons of material came from Guatemala after the closing of the Central American Exposition; five hundred tons of objects arrived in 1900 from the great exposition held in Paris. An obituary for Wilson praised his indefatigableness, commenting, "Always, whenever an exposition was held in any part of the world and there was an opportunity to enrich the collections of the Commercial Museum . . . Dr. Wilson was on hand to secure them."[4] By 1900, the museum housed more than two hundred thousand samples of foreign manufactured goods alone, to say nothing of the examples of raw materials and what we might call ethnological objects. An English critic wrote

in 1901 that the Commercial Museum "impressed me as much as anything I saw on the American continent, not excepting the Falls of Niag-
ara or the Congress Library."[5] Another visitor wrote to William Pepper
that "I had not the faintest conception of the gigantic scale on which
this noble enterprise has been planned. I wandered through those
rooms as in a dream."[6] In a few short years, the Commercial Museum
had amassed a major collection of material, and it impressed virtually
everyone who came through its doors.

Indeed, by the time of the Paris exposition in 1900, the Philadelphia
Commercial Museum had grown to be the largest such institution in the
United States. Actually, while it was indeed a huge operation, that distinction is less impressive than it sounds, because the Philadelphia Commercial Museum proved to be the only such institution in the United
States. While every large American city and even many small ones built
natural history museums and art museums, only Philadelphia had a
commercial museum. And that fact might be our first clue to the museum's eventual demise.

What, after all, is a commercial museum? The question isn't mine but
rather struck many at the time as requiring an answer. As Paul Cherington, who directed the museum's publications, put it, "The very name
'Commercial Museum' is a demand for a reconciliation between two dia-
metrically opposed ideas. What can a musty collection of specimens have
to do with commerce?"[7] What indeed?

To begin with, Wilson and Cherington would have insisted that their
museum objects were anything but "musty." Wilson founded the Commercial Museum with the same didactic faith in objects—that "object-
based epistemology" I mentioned earlier—upon which all other museums in the late nineteenth century were based.[8] Recall too that at virtually the same moment that Wilson established the Commercial Museum,
Goode outlined his six-part collection of museums that I have referred
to several times already. Goode included Commercial Museums as his
last among the six, along with museums of art, anthropology, history,
natural science, and technology. Thus Wilson could point to no less an
authority than the Smithsonian's George Brown Goode for validation of
this otherwise novel idea.

Objects, however, could only perform their pedagogic function if they
were systematically collected, classified, and arranged. Wilson explained
this to Edward Ayer of Chicago's Field Museum in 1894: "Museum material is worth nothing unless it is properly classified and scientifically
described." He went on, "all museum material should speak for itself
upon sight. It should be an open book which tells a better story than any
description will do. This it will do if properly arranged and classified."[9]
In this sense, Wilson saw no distinction between objects exhibited at a

natural history museum and those he put on display at the Commercial Museum. And just as objects were used to represent the natural world in a natural history museum, so too would commercial objects constitute the world of commerce.

By creating a systematics of commerce, Wilson believed that his museum would foster American commercial expansion around the world. Until quite recently, Wilson noted in 1899, American manufacturers had done virtually all their business domestically. But 1893 also witnessed a deep economic "panic," when, as Wilson went on, the American manufacturer discovered to his distress that he had "placed all his eggs in one basket."[10] The purpose of the Commercial Museum was to take American manufacturing international.

Wilson did not use the phrase "scientifically described" casually when he wrote to Edward Ayer. Wilson saw his museum as a scientific institution in the way that so much of late Victorian life was being refashioned as "scientific."

In the late nineteenth-century sense, "science" did not refer to a set of subjects or disciplines, nor even to a method, but much more broadly to the impulse to create system and rationality out of all aspects of human experience. Science became the way the late Victorians pursued their rage for order.[11] Certainly the new museums of the post–Civil War era in the United States were built around the intellectual framework of systematics, and not only in museums of natural science where this impulse to classification and arrangement first emerged. When Englishman David Murray boasted that the museum of 1897 was far in advance of the museum of 1847, he meant precisely that collections of dubious curiosities had been replaced by scientifically assembled collections of specimens, displayed in scientifically ordered exhibits. If you had been among the millions who visited the Centennial Exposition in Philadelphia in 1876, for example, and desired to see a watercolor done by the British artist H. M. Knowles titled "Interior of the Sistine Chapel," you would have found it in your guidebook under Department 4 (art), Group 41 (painting); Class 411 (watercolors). All that is missing here is the Latinate binomial nomenclature we attach to biological species, though in point of fact the classification system used by Centennial exhibitors was fashioned by a geologist.[12]

Science was at work ordering the world outside the museum as well. As historians John Hepp, Stephen Kern, and others have demonstrated, science reshaped the culture of time and space in both the United States and Europe in the years surrounding the turn of the twentieth century.[13] On November 18, 1883, for example, just ten years before Wilson would embark on the Commercial Museum project, Americans from coast to coast readjusted their watches and clocks from their arbitrary local time to a new, national standard time. In that same decade, libraries began to rearrange the books on their shelves in accordance with the new classificatory system invented by Melvil Dewey. Middle-class consumers shopped in carefully arranged department stores, whose order and regularity replaced the more haphazard world of the bazaar and dry goods shops, and made sense of a new and bewildering world of consumer goods.[14]

These changes transformed life—especially urban life—all over the Western world, but nowhere more so than in Wilson's own city of Philadelphia. In the 1880s, the University of Pennsylvania built the first college library in the United States designed around that new and rational Dewey decimal system. John Wanamaker, the city's king of department store princes and among the two or three most successful retail entrepreneurs of the age, organized his stores around what he called the "science of merchandising." In 1900 he addressed the American Academy of Political and Social Science at its annual meeting on the topic "the evolution of mercantile business."[15] Standard time, of course, was the invention of the railroads—responsible as much as anything for scientifically reorganizing time and space. In the late nineteenth century, the Pennsylvania Railroad, headquartered in Philadelphia, was not simply the country's biggest railroad but also its largest corporation, and it was referred to simply as "the Railroad." No surprise that leaders of the Railroad spearheaded the creation and adoption of standard time.

Philadelphia too led the nation in building an ensemble of museums—organized with this broad notion of science—whose purpose was scientifically to collect, classify, arrange, and display six different bodies of knowledge—from history to anthropology, to art to science, to technology to commerce. As William Pepper described the city's museum-building agenda in 1896, "Some years ago we began the serious task of developing in this community a complete series of museums. The controlling purpose has been the embodiment in each of the strict scientific and educational method. This implies the creation of a staff of experts of professorial rank; the establishment of laboratories for original investigation upon objects forming the collections; the formation of a library of references, and a bureau of publication to diffuse the results attained."[16]

This is the cultural context out of which Wilson's ideas grew, and he answered the question, "What can a musty collection of specimens have to do with commerce?" by creating a systematics of commerce. If systematics could be applied to everything from butterflies to books, why not commerce as well?

That systematics of commerce began, when visitors entered, with a history lesson installed in the main entrance. As described in a 1910 guide-

Figure 25. A taxonomic approach to commercial empire. The Commercial Museum's exhibits of Cuba early in the twentieth century. Courtesy of the City Archives of Philadelphia, Commercial Museum Collection.

book, the first exhibit "illustrates the history and development of commerce from the earliest beginnings to the present time. Serially arranged in uniform cases are the important products of commerce in the order of their entry into the world's demand, while maps in contemporary order show the development and changes in trade routes and the concomitant rise and fall of nations."[17]

With that history lesson as a frame, the rest of the museum's exhibits were, broadly speaking, arranged in two ways. As the museum's assistant curator described it, "First, geographic displays, which show all the resources of each country by itself, and second, monographic displays which present for comparative study products of the same kind from nearly every country of the world." For example, "the corn exhibit not only shows hundreds of Commercial varieties of corn and various foodstuffs made from corn but surprises the visitor by showing also corn oil and the dozens of useful things made from it, including such unexpected articles as rubber overshoes."[18]

Here, then, was Wilson's systematics of commerce. Exhibits organized around geography, paired with exhibits organized around products and materials, all illustrating the historical point that the rise and expansion of commerce was intimately linked with the rise and fall of nations.

Like all museum builders of the era, Wilson believed that his museum served the public in the widest sense, and he expected that everyone would come visit his museum. As the 1909 guidebook asserted, "The museum is much more than of local importance. Its ramifications extend into every quarter where human beings live and labor." There were series of public lectures held at the museum, and Wilson gave lectures to public schoolteachers on the topic of "commercial geography." He even pioneered educational outreach projects with primary schools by creating traveling "museums" and sending them out to those schools whose students couldn't make the trip to Philadelphia.

That was all well and good, but businessmen were Wilson's primary audience, and promoting American business activity overseas was the museum's chief goal. As he declared in 1899, "The Philadelphia Commercial Museum is endeavoring to increase foreign trade of the United States . . . with every nation of the world." The museum itself, in the words of one magazine report about it, served as "a school for American businessmen."[19]

And by all contemporary accounts—though they are hard perhaps to verify with numerical data—the Commercial Museum was a hugely successful institution. It promised to teach American businessmen—and future businessmen—how to navigate the largely uncharted waters of foreign trade, dominated thoroughly at this time by the European imperial powers. As Wilson lamented when an American businessman tried to branch out overseas, he "discovered his German and British competitors firmly entrenched in many markets."[20] In the face of this situation, Wilson's museum would provide what *Harper's* called "first aid for the exporter" as a way of leveling the playing field of global commerce. Capturing nicely the easy elision of commerce and imperialism at the museum, the writer asked, "Is it an American manufacturer of textiles who seeks to invade Central Africa? At the museum he will find samples of cloth made by the natives on hand looms. . . . Not only this, but the manufacturer may examine samples of goods made for the native trade in Germany and in England."[21]

In this sense, and Wilson repeated this point variously, the Commercial Museum also promised all the benefits of imperial expansion without any of the messiness that came with actual colonies. As Cordeiro da Graca, a Brazilian representative at one of the museum's international conferences, put it, "What I came here to admire today . . . is the very great conquest which you have made on this occasion. While Europe is armed to the teeth spending millions, sending soldiers to Africa, and all this only to acquire new colonies, this great country . . . makes the same conquest by promoting peace . . . Rendering the interchange of commerce of real and practical value by means of friendship." Perhaps an even greater compliment came in 1901 when the German minister of commerce proposed establishing a German commercial museum and pointed to Philadelphia's as the model to follow.[22]

The Commercial Museum Fades Away

Let me interrupt this narrative to put my scholarly cards on the table. Trying to trace the history and fate of the Commercial Museum after its founding period has proved remarkably frustrating. What I have constructed is pieced together from shadows and reflections, inferences and guesses, drawn from echoes and silences. Wilson himself seems to have left no cache of papers, at least that I can find. Perhaps his papers were part of a much larger museum archive that has largely disappeared; perhaps he never kept copies of anything. Who can know? Likewise, while Wilson and his museum were on cordial terms with the McKinley and Taft administrations—Wilson had been asked by Taft, who was then governor of the Philippines, to organize the Philippine exhibit at the 1904 World's Fair in St. Louis—I have found virtually nothing written to or from Wilson in the archives of official Washington. The Commercial Museum similarly disappeared from national publications as well. At the turn of the century, the museum was discussed regularly in journals and periodicals. In 1900 *The Journal of Political Economy* devoted an entire article to the museum. By midcentury the museum had vanished almost entirely from print, mentioned occasionally perhaps in articles detailing the history of American business.

Mindful then of drawing too many conclusions from too little evidence, I do think it is fair to say that by the end of the 1920s the whole enterprise was clearly on the wane. Several markers point to this decline.

Wilson himself died in 1927, and he took with him a founder's zeal and energy. The Library of Congress, for example, lists eighty titles published by the Commercial Museum; only ten of those appeared after Wilson's death. Almost before his body was cold, municipal officials began their plans to transform the facilities into something a bit different. Rather than expand the museum along the lines Wilson had proposed, those now in control started building a municipal auditorium and exhibition space to go along with it. That auditorium opened in 1931, and while the new "Civic Center" hosted a set of trade shows, it also functioned as an all-purpose gathering place for a whole variety of events. During the 1930s the Municipal Auditorium hosted political conventions while the rest of the facility attracted temporary exhibitions, such

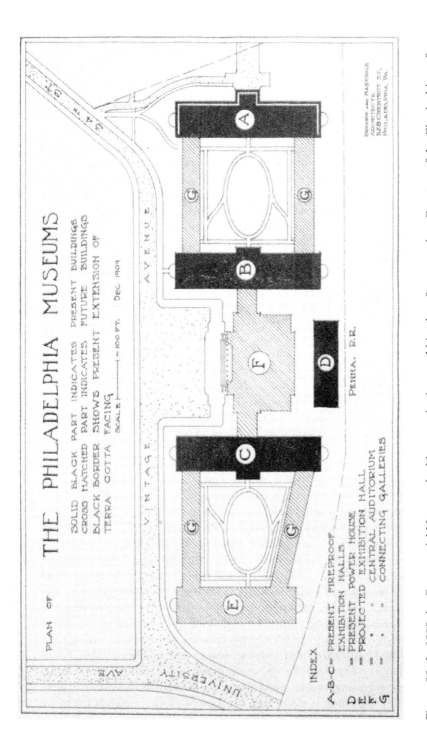

Figure 26. In 1909 the Commercial Museum had large aspirations and big plans for expansion. Courtesy of the City Archives of Philadelphia, Commercial Museum Collection.

as a meeting of the Dairy and Ice Cream Machinery and Supplies Association.

As the United States mobilized in earnest for the Second World War in 1942, the city proposed that the buildings of the Commercial Museum be turned into a temporary one-thousand-bed hospital for air-raid casualties. Forgetting for a moment that neither German nor Japanese planes ever made it as far as the eastern seaboard, the proposal might have made a certain sense, because the museum sat right across the street from the city's premier medical facility, the Hospital of the University of Pennsylvania. Still, such a proposal measures a kind of institutional weakness, suggesting that the most important war time contribution the museum could make was its empty space. By contrast, as we saw in the last chapter, the Franklin Institute put its research capacities to use for the war effort.

With the war over, the Museum resumed temporary trade show exhibitions, though they too suggest a diminution of the institution's ambitions and reach. Whereas once the museum promised to open international markets to American businessmen, the Foreign Trade Exhibit, which opened in the spring of 1946, claimed only that "the importance of Philadelphia in international commerce will be shown." A year earlier the museum had celebrated the end of the European conflict by hosting a traveling exhibit charting the development of women's stockings. A cheeky newspaper story proclaimed, "Now we know what made the Gay Nineties gay. It must have been those stockings. Such colors. Such stripes, dots and checks. Wow!" From dreams of an international commercial empire to the history of hosiery.[23]

In 1953 the city's Trade Board requested $1.7 million from the city to transform the museum into a "World Trade and Civic Center," though as far as I can determine neither the appropriation nor the World Trade Center ever materialized. Instead, the Commercial Museum's remaining building was remodeled and opened to the public in 1956. The description of this "new" Commercial Museum testifies to the profound change that had taken place in the space of thirty years: "The new building has four floors. . . . On the ground floor is the Philadelphia Panorama, a permanent exhibit on city planning. . . . The main floor has a large lobby and 15,000 square feet of exhibit space overlooking the Philadelphia Panorama. On the third floor are an auditorium, classrooms of the Commercial Museum's educational services, a large air-conditioned center for international visitors and another 20,000 feet of exhibit space. The fourth floor, completely air-conditioned, contains conference rooms, commercial library, a lounge and administrative offices. The building is decorated throughout with materials from the museum's collection."[24]

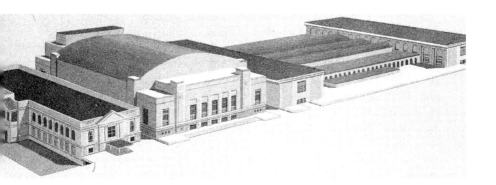

Figure 27. By the mid-twentieth century, the Commercial Museum had largely been replaced by a convention center known locally as the Civic Center. Here is a rendering of the center from the 1960s. Courtesy of the City Archives of Philadelphia, Commercial Museum Collection.

Figure 28. And from the 1970s. By this time, there were already suggestions that the center be closed and replaced with something larger and more modern. That happened early in the 1990s. Courtesy of the City Archives of Philadelphia, Commercial Museum Collection.

In the new museum, a city planning model occupied pride of place, and city officials showed it off to visiting dignitaries from other countries. Two years later, in 1958, the museum's journal *Commercial America* ceased publication after a run of fifty-four years. Such are the mile markers along the road to institutional oblivion. (And here too another mysterious vanishing: *Commercial America* had an international readership. At least initially it was published in both English and Spanish. By 1910 it had a circulation of twenty-thousand. Yet only eighteen libraries worldwide are listed as owning the journal, and far fewer have a complete set. My own university's library reports that it has lost *Commercial America* somewhere in the bowels of its book depository.)

A newspaper writer in 1960 finally, if inadvertently, described the changed and unsettled state of affairs by posing the question, "When is the Commercial Museum not the Commercial Museum?" He answered this question by parsing a definition:

> That question is a proper one because of the confusion among some citizens attending the unusually heavy schedule of events this month at the Trade and Convention Center. . . . Four years ago the North Building was rebuilt by Edward Stone (the Brussels Fair architects) and re-dedicated to a new series of international exhibitions. By terms of the original charter, all public events in this building are free of admission charges. Only this building properly can be called Commercial Museum. Exhibitors in other buildings who charge admission—for such events as the Home Show, Flower Show, Auto Show—have been asked not to use the name, but the habit persists. Eventually it is hoped, that [the] name Trade and Convention Center—or just Trade Center—will be established for the other buildings.[25]

By 1960, the Commercial Museum proper had become purely vestigial, and from the tone of this piece one gets the sense that it had become a source of annoyance to city officials. A generation later, annoyance turned to exasperation, and the doors were closed permanently. Ten years after that the bulldozers rolled in, and thus ended, after 110 years, the Philadelphia Commercial Museum.

Natural Science versus Social Science, and Objects versus Data

If that quick chronology traces what happened to the Commercial Museum, then I want to offer some speculations about why it happened. Again, I am perfectly mindful that institutional and political circumstances doubtless played a critical role in the decline. The Great Depression hit, after all, just after William Wilson died, and the city of Philadelphia clearly wanted a facility that would be more immediately remunerative for the city, not useful in some abstract sense to the whole nation. What I want to suggest here, however, is that even before the Commercial Museum died as a viable institutional entity, the ideas upon which it had been built had died, and that, in part, it was the lack of an intellectual foundation that caused the institution to crumble.

As far as I can determine, by the 1930s the museum had essentially stopped collecting new material, and if objects did come into the collection they certainly did not do so on the scale that they once had. Thus its exhibits were not updated or well maintained. Perhaps more than anything else, that signals a stagnation of the museum's purpose. The end of its active collecting might well have been the result of institutional constraints—tight budgets, cramped storage space, and the like—or it may have been a consequence of a larger change on the cultural landscape. Wilson began his museum with material brought back from Chicago's 1893 World's Fair, and he enriched it with collections from subsequent world's fairs.

Wilson died, as it happens, just a year after the 1926 Sesquicentennial Exposition was held in Philadelphia. As I have argued elsewhere, the Sesqui was the last of those fairs, in the United States at least, organized as a great comparative showcase of national industrial progress.[26] It punctuated a fifty-year fair phenomenon, dating back to Philadelphia's 1876 Centennial, which included expositions held in Chicago, St. Louis, and Buffalo, and it was by every measure and account a colossal flop. In the 1920s, as the United States made its transition from a producer-oriented economy to a consumer one, exhibits of raw materials and heavy industry no longer sparked the public's imagination. The fairs of the 1930s would instead feature the worlds of tomorrow created by America's large corporations and readily available for purchase by ordinary consumers.

Either way, the effective end of collecting must surely have had profound implications for the exhibitionary function of the Commercial Museum. At the very least, the distance between the ever-changing world of commerce and the virtually static exhibits at the museum would have grown every year. The end of collecting also reflected, I suspect, the failure of the objects themselves to function as Wilson intended them to. With his own intellectual background firmly in the world of nineteenth-century botany and natural science, Wilson attempted to create a natural history of commerce and put it on display much as plants and animals were displayed in natural history museums.

It isn't clear that he succeeded. On the one hand, the model of natural history was predicated on the fixity of species in a Linnaean system. The world of man-made commercial products changed all the time in ways that probably defied Wilson's efforts to create categories. Those changes only accelerated across the twentieth century as advances in everything from agriculture to material science made Wilson's groupings obsolete. On the other hand, as I discussed previously, by the early years of the twentieth century even natural history museums were reconceiving the way they could exhibit their specimens. Many recognized that the old form of exhibition—long galleries lined with glass cases, each filled with dozens of specimens—no longer appealed much to the public. Those who could afford it began to replace glass cases with more ambitious, lifelike taxidermy displayed in visually spectacular dioramas.

In 1939, T. R. Adam described, in overly stiff prose, the Commercial Museum's functions in a way that suggests it was still doing what it had done from the very beginning: "A considerable part of the energies of its staff are directed toward providing information as to the availability of required types of raw material and the likelihood of markets throughout the world for specific products."[27] Nothing in that description hints that the museum had altered its practice to reflect changes in the world of business. The Commercial Museum's comparative collection of cotton samples was doubtless unparalleled. Whether looking at all those samples was at all engaging or even remotely useful is another matter. Maybe the variety of products that could be made from corn oil no longer surprised and delighted visitors.

We can get some sense of the disappearance of objects from the museum's function by perusing the 1956 description of the newly renovated building. According to that article the new building had space for temporary exhibitions, not permanent ones. What remained on display from the museum's original set of objects seems to have been scattered about as part of the interior decorating. T. R. Adam could still write that "museums of commerce are a natural corollary to those of science and industry," but in fact Philadelphia's remained the only one in the United States, and by 1939 its time had already come and gone.[28] Despite Wilson's confidence, and despite the culture of scientific museums out of which his ideas came, he did not successfully produce an object-based systematics of commerce.

Another indication of the difficulty Wilson had creating a visually compelling museum of commerce is reflected in the audiences—such as we can determine them—who came to see it. A 1931 encyclopedia of Philadelphia still described the Commercial Museum much as Wilson would have: "The work of the Museum is conducted under three departments: An active museum for the entertainment and instruction of the manufacturer and the general public . . . a very extensive work in education for the benefit of the schools of the City of Philadelphia and the State of Pennsylvania . . . a Foreign Trade Bureau in which thousands of manufacturers are aided and furnished with information on all matters pertaining to foreign trade."[29]

In fact, by the 1920s, at least those first two had become much the same. As early as 1900, the Philadelphia Commercial Museum had developed a program to send portable, "traveling museums" to schools around the state of Pennsylvania. Described in 1921, "Each set contained several hundred specimens of important commercial products, and from 100 to 200 photographs. These collections were distributed not as a loan, but as a gift; so that the specimens were always available. The collections proved to be of great service, furnishing object lessons of much value in the study of geography and commerce."[30] That report came from the *Elementary School Journal,* and the museum did develop a reputation for innovative work with the public schools. Worthy though those efforts surely were, the connection between audiences of schoolchildren and the intended audience of American businessmen seems tenuous, and to judge by some of the extant photographs, as the twentieth century wore on, the Commercial Museum devolved into little more than an obligatory field trip destination for Philadelphia schoolchildren.

The "museum," however, was only ever one part of the Commercial Museum. When William Pepper described the constituent parts of a fully functioning scientific museum—a lab, a library, publications, and so on—Wilson followed his prescription almost exactly. In addition to the museum objects and exhibits, the Commercial Museum included a Bureau of Information, sometimes referred to as the "Foreign Trade Bureau" mentioned as the third area of operation by that 1931 encyclopedia, under which was a Publication Service, an Information Service, and a Translation Service for American businessmen whose language skills might not be up to the task. The bureau compiled information from around the world and published graphs, charts, and guides. As Wilson described his bureau: "It has served to give the business men of America an unusual opportunity to acquire, in a very short time, a great deal of information concerning the markets of the world."[31]

It also may have contributed to make the museum function of the Commercial Museum obsolete. In trying to develop a systematics of commerce in the 1890s, the Commercial Museum straddled an intellectual divide between an understanding of the world rooted in the nineteenth-century traditions of natural science and an emerging understanding shaped by the quantitative analysis of the new social sciences. By the time of Wilson's death and the subsequent demise of his museum, that social scientific way of knowing the world had supplanted a natural scientific way, at least in the world of commerce, and economics more broadly. The museum once boasted that it exhibited a "full series of all grades of Manila hemp, the most important commercial product of the islands, shown in hanks and in commercial

Figure 29. Books and exhibits. The Commercial Museum's library provided businessmen with books and data to help them conquer overseas markets. Courtesy of the City Archives of Philadelphia, Commercial Museum Collection.

bales," but once Philippine hemp production could be represented by a set of tables and charts, did American businessmen really need to see all those bales in order to get the information they needed about it? And if they didn't, would the rest of us be interested in looking at them?

The collections themselves reveal an institution caught betwixt and between different intellectual terrains. Collections of raw materials, such as timber, could comfortably sit in the world of natural science, but this was less true of processed natural products like textiles. Manufactured products might not belong in the category of natural science, but they were certainly part of the commercial world. Did the variety of ethnographic collections the museum possessed belong to commerce, and how so? W. M. Davis, for one, thought that the Commercial Museum housed "the greatest exhibition of the material basis for the study of industrial aspects of geography" in the United States. "Economic and

Figure 30. Publications and exhibits. *Commercial America*, the museum's journal, was published in English and in Spanish. Here the journal is advertised next to a diorama of a Brazilian sugar plantation. Courtesy of the City Archives of Philadelphia, Commercial Museum Collection.

Commercial Geography," then, were the object lessons this writer found at the Commercial Museum.[32]

As I mentioned, shortly after the Commercial Museum's remaining building re-opened in 1956, it mounted a display of African art, with a particular focus on objects from the Congo. As a newspaper review commented, "When [the Museum] was returned to active usefulness about two years ago the 3000 African art objects unearthed from its dust bins had among them some 200 items from the Congo basin."[33] Just about the last publication issued by the museum was a 1960 guide to its African collections. Note that these objects moved from the category of ethnography to the category of art without pausing in the category of commerce. There is no question that the Commercial Museum had amassed a large, fascinating collection, but it was, at some level, an incoherent one. The questions of what should or should not be displayed in a museum of commerce and in turn how those objects would define the field of commerce remained largely unanswered.

The loss of a rationale and the absence of a compelling intellectual coherence became apparent to the people charged with disposing of the collections when the museum closed officially in the late 1990s. The fates had not been kind to the Commercial Museum's collections, and it is hard to know whether the small fraction of objects that still remained in the museum faithfully represented the once-larger whole. Still, the final resting places for this material underscore the problem of categories I sketched earlier. The Independence Seaport Museum, a terrific museum of maritime history, took the ship models and examples of the kind of cargo that used to fill those hulls—bales of cotton and the like. The University of Pennsylvania Museum took the ethnographic objects, including those previously mentioned rare examples from the Amur River region. An assortment of local miscellany wound up in the Atwater Kent Museum, the small museum of Philadelphia history. And a significant number of pieces were claimed by the Philadelphia Museum of Art and incorporated into its permanent collection, including works by the African American painter William Johnson. Each of these lots made a certain sense in their new homes; they had made little sense all together, except perhaps as a museum of the museum.

The Museum versus "The Project"

If the museum found itself with a large collection of objects and a shrinking exhibitionary rationale, then its data and information-producing aspects also found themselves challenged and ultimately superceded by other institutions. When *Appleton's Magazine* called the museum "a school for American businessmen," it neglected to point out that it was the second such school to take up residence in Philadelphia. In 1881, roughly fifteen years before the Commercial Museum opened its doors to the public, the Wharton School of Finance and Economy of the University of Pennsylvania began offering courses as the first university-affiliated business school in the United States.

Joseph Wharton, who endowed the school that still bears his name, came not from the world of nineteenth-century natural science but from the first generation to make a huge fortune in the industrial economy. In 1854 Wharton got into the metal business and made it big in nickel and zinc. By 1879 his thoughts had turned philanthropic and he approached the University of Pennsylvania's trustees with what he called the "project."

The school's purpose, according to Wharton, was "to provide young men with special means of training and of correct instruction in the knowledge and in the arts of modern finance and economy." Wharton deserves to be quoted at length because it helps us understand some of the institutional and intellectual shifts taking place in the last quarter of the nineteenth century. He began with a quick description of the American educational landscape: "The general conviction that college education did little toward fitting for the actual duties of life any but those who purposed to become lawyers, doctors or clergymen, brought about the creation of many excellent technical and scientific schools." He went on, "Those schools, while not replacing the outgrown and obsolescent system of apprenticeship, accomplish a work quite beyond anything that system was capable of." "In the matter of Commercial education," he continued, "there was formerly a system of instruction in the counting-houses of old-time merchants which may fairly be compared to the system of apprenticeship to trades. Comparatively few examples of this sort of instruction remain, nor is their deficiency made good by the so-called Commercial colleges." And he concluded that "the existing great universities, rather than an institution of lower rank or a new independent establishment, should lead in the attempt to supply this important deficiency in our present system of education."[34]

One of Wilson's obituaries noted that while he was a professor at the University of Pennsylvania he "had witnessed the beginnings of the school of business instruction founded by the bequest of Joseph Wharton."[35] That much would seem unarguable. Yet beyond witnessing it—and here is one of the loudest silences in the strange history of the Commercial Museum—Wilson's museum and Wharton's school seem to have had little to do with each other, though they sat only several hundred yards apart.

In this sense, Wilson and Wharton both founded institutions to address the same perceived need: a systematic education for practical use in the new world of industrial capitalism, something more "scientific" than what went on in those countinghouses and apprenticeships.

Over the space of just a few blocks, the Commercial Museum and the Wharton School played out a much larger struggle for intellectual and educational primacy taking place more broadly between the museums of the late nineteenth century and the new universities growing at the same moment. In a report written in 1892 looking back on the first ten years of the Wharton experiment, Cyrus Elder noted perceptively that the school's "formative stages" coincided "with the new growth of social science and political economy, and new studies in history."[36] In other words, Wharton's success came because of its alliance with other emerging academic disciplines now making their professional home at the new American university. In 1894 the Wharton School began to develop a four-year curriculum to replace its original two-year course of study. That this happened in the year when Wilson set out to found the Commercial Museum may have been purely coincidental. However, it may reflect Wharton's understanding that its future success lay in hitching itself even more firmly to the larger university.

Needless to say, Wharton's model proved to be the more influential. There are no commercial museums in the United States anymore, but university schools of business continue to proliferate across the landscape, and they all trace their origins back to Wharton. In 1908, Paul Cherington, who had worked at the Commercial Museum since his graduation from the University of Pennsylvania and had directed the museum's extensive publications, left Philadelphia to take a professorship in the new business school at Harvard. He spent roughly thirty years there and became one of the founding figures of the academic field of marketing.

While the Commercial Museum could not compete with university business schools for the education of young businessmen, it also found itself in a losing competition with the expanding federal Department of Commerce. In 1899, the Commercial Museum organized the National Export Exposition with a budget of $750,000. Nearly half of that came from the federal government.[37] In 1903, the Department of Commerce opened, and in that year George Cortelyou, the first secretary of commerce, came to visit the Commercial Museum. In a speech he thanked the museum and its founder "for what they have contributed to the fund of our information upon commercial topics." He went on, "Some day the new Department of Commerce and Labor may find it advisable to have closer relations with these museums."[38]

That day, however, never came. The Department of Commerce remained a modest operation in its first decade. Its Bureau of Foreign and Domestic Commerce received a stingy $60,000 appropriation. After the First World War, however, the department was transformed, in no small part through the efforts of Secretary Herbert Hoover. When in 1921 English author B. M. Headicar gave advice to readers of the journal *Economica* about how to put together a commercial library, he insisted, "I would especially emphasize the need for a full supply of the consular reports and other publications and commerce reports issued by the United States Department of Commerce."[39] Though Headicar even suggested that such libraries might also have exhibits of objects, he never mentioned the Commercial Museum. Perhaps he simply didn't do his homework, or perhaps he recognized that the house that Hoover built was already eclipsing the museum.

The final speculation I have to offer to explain the demise of the Philadelphia Commercial Museum takes us back to those ice cream makers, because they remind us of the commercial nature of the Commercial Museum.

Museums in the last quarter of the nineteenth century, as we have already noted, were conceived of as purely "scientific" institutions and thus as disinterested public institutions serving a purely public good. In addition to answering what a dusty collection of objects had to do with commerce, the Commercial Museum had to satisfy people that a museum devoted to commerce could serve public rather than private interests. When he visited the museum in the early twentieth century, Oliver Farrington admonished that museums should stay away from "Commercial and advertising features" and should not display objects of "great money value."[40]

William Pepper put the problem bluntly in his address before the museum's advisory board in 1896: "The problem which gave the gravest anxiety was to secure a form of organization which would preserve the administration of the proposed museum from the taint of personal interest; would foster a true scientific spirit in all its work." Pepper, for one, was sure that this problem had been solved. The museum, he went on, had secured "public confidence in the integrity of our purpose, and in the strictly scientific method of our work."[41]

In the late nineteenth century, "science" functioned as a synonym for "disinterested," but no museum, needless to say, operates in a purely disinterested way. While museums of all kinds had (and have) social and political agendas that sometimes contradict, or at least complicate, that easy sense of public good, the Commercial Museum may have faced this dilemma more acutely than its companions in the early twentieth century. The museum's intended audience—and the source of much of its support—were businessmen with decidedly private interests in mind. Writer William Harvey put his finger on the dilemma, even if he didn't see it as one. The Commercial Museum, he wrote, "is a business institution run by businessmen, yet engaging in no private transactions, but depending solely on a public foundation enabling it to devote its energies to the fostering of the foreign trade of the United States." One can almost see him wink when Director Wilson, discussing the museum's National Export Exposition, concluded, "Unselfish as the character of the Exposition [is] the American manufacturer should require no urging to avail himself of its benefits. He is usually not blind to his own interest, and there is every reason to believe he will appreciate its direct commercial value to him."[42]

The distinction was a fine one. Individual business transactions would have violated the public spiritedness of the museum; fostering the collective business interests of the United States, however, constituted the public good. As late as 1932, Yale professor Maurice Davie singled out the Commercial Museum for particular congratulations on its educational work: "It is a public institution, supported by appropriations from the city of Philadelphia for its general work, from the State of Pennsylvania for its special educational work, and by subscriptions from manufacturers and merchants in the United States for special service along commercial lines."[43]

This tension also strained the way the objects on display functioned. Turn-of-the-century museum objects derived their authority and their value in several ways, as I discussed in Chapter 1. Putting a painting in an art museum, for example, took it out of a real and dynamic economic market and placed it outside the boundaries of that market. Anthropological objects not only stood in for the cultures that produced them but also represented notions of exoticism and dominion, and they implied exploration, adventure, and all that came with that. Some natural history specimens carried those associations, especially the large mammals arranged in dramatic dioramas. But the vast bulk of museum specimens in natural history museums, for which there was little economic value, served to illustrate larger concepts about the organization of the natural world and, in turn, to help refine ideas about the natural world.

Where, then, did commercial objects draw their significance? As I suggested earlier, they did not ultimately succeed in constituting a taxonomy of commerce in the way that butterflies or clam shells did in the world of natural history. While some of the objects themselves might have struck visitors as strange or exotic, their purpose in the Commercial Museum was precisely the opposite. The museum hoped to normalize these objects and put all this material into the mainstream of economic activity. In so doing it hoped to shrink the distance between the United States and the rest of the world by turning every place into a potential market, governed by rules that the museum could help teach. Finally, unlike a work of art whose value comes in large measure because of its uniqueness, the particular objects on display at the Commercial Museum, while themselves not for sale, would be of value to American businessmen only if those objects were absolutely identical to things that they could buy and sell. In short, because of the commercial purpose of the Commercial Museum, its objects could not establish an effective and enduring museum identity.

As a place where, in the words of another visitor, "science is allied to commerce," the Commercial Museum strained the boundaries that were supposed to separate the educational from the money making, the public from the private.[44] The museum might foster a scientific study and understanding of commerce, but commerce itself, as so many protested, had no place in a museum.

That boundary was becoming harder to maintain by the time the ice cream makers arrived to hold their convention at the Philadelphia Commercial Museum. In the period after Wilson's death, those who took charge of the museum had decided that the best way to foster commerce was to foster commerce directly. The Commercial Museum may well stand as the first museum in the United States to confront what happens to its public mission when it becomes commercialized. The first, perhaps, but certainly not the last. One of the major stories of the twentieth-century museum is the extent to which it became a place of commerce—directly and indirectly. More and more museums today find themselves faced with difficult choices between their public responsibilities and their financial exigencies, between public good and private gain. The Philadelphia Commercial Museum did not survive this confrontation.

When, then, is a commercial museum not a commercial museum? The traces left by the Philadelphia Commercial Museum suggest that the answer is when the objects cease to provide coherence to the ideas behind their collection and display, when the ideas themselves fail to coalesce into a coherent body of knowledge, and when other institutions position themselves better as producers and providers of information. Which is not to say that the objects assembled around the turn of the twentieth century and housed at the Commercial Museum couldn't have been used to constitute some other kind of museum—of world's fairs, of economic history perhaps—but rather that these objects within these frameworks failed to do so.

In this too, while the Philadelphia Commercial Museum may have been among the first institutions to die for these reasons, it will probably not be the last. Beyond the basic requirements that all institutions need to operate, museums need ideas that continue to compel and inspire and around which their objects can be organized and displayed. Without them, museums risk becoming little more than "musty collections."

Figure 31. The sad state of the Commercial Museum, shortly before demolition. Photo: Steven Conn.

Coda

Even as I approach the end of this chapter I am left with more unanswered questions than answered ones. Or rather, I am left with questions that are probably unanswerable. I am certainly not the first historian to be faced with a paucity of sources or stymied by archival dead ends. It may well be that the absence of a paper trail for the Commercial Museum from the 1920s through its official end in the 1990s must simply be chalked up to the fickle nature of historical luck. But without making too much of the point, perhaps we can read something else into it as well. Institutions tend to be more assiduous record keepers than most individuals, and those records help form an institution's identity and memory. Perhaps the very absence of such a record from the Commercial Museum is the final evidence of a loss of institutional identity and the recognition that no one wanted to maintain its memory. Unmoored from its past, the museum drifted, directionless, across much of the twentieth century. Perhaps no one wanted to keep a record of that drift.

Chapter 6
Museums, Public Space, and Civic Identity

On November 11, 2006, the art world woke up to the shocking news that Thomas Jefferson University, a venerable and distinguished medical school and research center in Philadelphia, planned to sell *The Gross Clinic* by Thomas Eakins. It would have been a stunning announcement under any circumstance, but the price—$68 million—and the buyer, a strange and never thoroughly explained partnership between the National Gallery and a Wal-Mart heiress—sent many people in the cultural world reeling.

On the face of it, this was a story of irresponsible cultural stewardship, naked greed, and shameless opportunism. Alice Walton was building her own art museum in Crystal Bridges, Arkansas, and needed a collection to go with it. She had been quietly trolling the nation for art objects, and for her, money was clearly no object. At the same time, while many hospitals around the country were in dire financial straights, victims themselves of the nation's broken health-care system, Thomas Jefferson University wasn't one of them.[1] Rather, it saw a chance to cash out on an easily salable asset. Never mind that the painting had been a gift to the university a century ago from a group of alumni.

To its credit, when Jefferson announced the news, it also announced that cultural institutions in the city had roughly six weeks, until December 26, to match the Wal-Mart–National Gallery offer. Six weeks. Sixty-eight million dollars. Happy holidays.

The howls of protest that greeted this proposed transaction from art historians, museum people, and Jefferson's own staff and alumni—many of whom threatened not to donate money to the institution as a consequence—were perfectly predictable. What took many by surprise, however, was the much wider outrage the news generated among artists, students, state and local politicians, and ordinary Philadelphians of many stripes. At one point, Philadelphia mayor John Street threatened to tie up the sale in court for months by having the painting declared a historical landmark. During those six weeks, walking through downtown Philadelphia, you very well might have been accosted by petitioners, button sellers, and people handing out leaflets all in support of keeping *The Gross Clinic* in the city. Toward the end of November I was invited to be a guest on the local right-wing talk radio show—during drive time no less!—and was taken aback to find not only the host but the callers hopping mad about the sale of the painting.

On that show I predicted, with my usual acumen, that there was no way to raise $68 million in time to save the painting, not in Philadelphia, which has historically failed to rise to philanthropic challenges and which has seen some of its finest cultural assets sold off to other places because of this.

I was wrong.

Galvanized by the widespread public outcry, the Philadelphia Museum of Art and the Pennsylvania Academy of the Fine Arts joined together to spearhead a fund-raising campaign that included local banks, foundations, politicians, and dozens of individual contributors big and small. It worked. The painting stayed in Philadelphia.[2]

The Gross Clinic, painted by Eakins in 1875, is a truly great painting. It is arguably among the two or three great masterpieces of nineteenth-century American art, whatever such assertions are worth. But virtually no one ever saw it. Jefferson built a special exhibition space for the painting some years ago and then kept it locked and inaccessible much of the time. Indeed, part of Jefferson's justification for the sale in the first place was that the painting had been so well hidden that fewer than one thousand people a year ever came to visit it. (This was utterly disingenuous. Jefferson never advertised the painting or put up any directional signage. Even many of the guards at Jefferson had never heard of the painting or had any idea where it was). So, how to explain the outcry over a painting that had effectively been put in cold storage?

Let me offer this: Whatever one wants to say about the art historical importance of *The Gross Clinic*, it is unarguably a Philadelphia painting. Eakins himself spent his entire career in the city and painting its people. He trained at the Pennsylvania Academy and then taught there, until he was fired, infamously, for insisting that female students be allowed to draw male nudes. Dr. Samuel Gross, the subject of the painting, came from modest circumstances, grew up not far away from Philadelphia (in Easton, Pennsylvania), and rose to the very top of his profession as a professor and practitioner at Philadelphia's Jefferson Medical College. Eakins, painting the seventy-year-old Gross, shows him still at the peak of his powers and still an innovator in the surgical world. The operation Gross is directing, while he lectures to an amphitheater full of students, is being performed with chloroform anesthetic—a recent and miraculous breakthrough. Eakins, commissioned to do this portrait by several of Dr. Gross's former students, glorifies him not as rich or powerful but as simply the best at what he does. We watch Gross perform this surgery, but by extension we get his history. A Philadelphia story as told through a Philadelphia doctor in a Philadelphia hospital painted by a Philadelphia painter.

And as Philadelphians learned about all this, a great credit to the educational blitz that the Philadelphia Museum of Art and others carried out, I think they got offended as Philadelphians. Without exaggerating it too much, my sense is that response to the threatened sale of *The Gross Clinic* grew from a shared sense of civic identity, a sense that as Philadelphians they needed to rally and save this important piece of their shared cultural history.

And without extrapolating too much from these events, I do think that *l'affaire* Gross underscores the role that museums and the objects in their collections have played and can play still in helping to create a civic identity, an identity rooted in belonging to a place rather than one rooted in the accidents of biology—race, gender, sexual orientation, and so on. A civic identity, I believe, needs a public sphere and public spaces, and in this chapter I explore the relationship between museums, public spaces, and this sense of civic identity.

To do this, I first discuss what I see as the relationship between the museum and the public sphere, both of which are necessarily urban phenomena. Then I look at the relationship between museums and three different publics: the first, a Progressive-era public, which emerged in the nation's rapidly growing cities and which was composed of a significant number of immigrants; the second, a midcentury public, shaped in important ways by the New Deal; and finally, a post-1960s public, fragmented not only by competing ideas of "identity" but also by the overall drift into the private realm that the nation has experienced since that time. Each of these publics brought different expectations to the museum, and each made different demands on it.

Museums, as I hope this chapter will demonstrate, tried to keep up with these shifting publics across the twentieth century. One consequence of those efforts was to change the relationship between visitors and objects. The Progressive-era public, as I discussed in Chapter 1, was greeted with an overabundance of objects and little else; by the mid-twentieth century fewer objects were on display, and museums had begun to offer a variety of educational programming to supplement the exhibits. More recently, the categorical organization of some objects has become increasingly contested, the single, authoritative voice with which the museum spoke to the public has been challenged, and some museums have decided that objects are not necessary for their didactic purposes.

Three museum publics and three relationships to museum objects. Yet while I chart the way these relationships to objects changed over the course of the twentieth century, I also suggest that the museum itself, and its role as a public space, has been and continues to be an important part of how we fashion a sense of civic identity.

Museums and the Urban Public

Let me begin by making a set of perfectly straightforward observations about museums and civic life in the United States. As I have mentioned already, while we can identify several important examples of museum building in the early national and antebellum periods—in Philadelphia; Charleston, South Carolina; Salem, Massachusetts; New York; and Washington, D.C., to name five—not until the post–Civil War era did Americans get serious about building museums. To quickly run down the list of museums founded and built between the Civil War and the Great Depression is to be astonished both by their sheer number and by their remarkable ambition: The Metropolitan Museum of Art, the Boston Museum of Fine Arts, the Philadelphia Museum of Art, the Detroit Institute of Arts, the Cleveland Museum of Art, the Art Institute of Chicago, the American Museum of Natural History, the Field Museum, the Carnegie in Pittsburgh, and the University of Pennsylvania Museum—all these and many more were founded in the last quarter of the nineteenth century or the first quarter of the twentieth. Indeed, by one count, more than two thousand museums of science and art were established during these years.[3]

Second, this "golden age" of museum building corresponded with the arrival of what I might call the nation's "urban moment." The nation urbanized rapidly across the entire nineteenth century, but the post–Civil War, pre-Depression years saw big American cities grow truly big. At the outbreak of the war, Philadelphia and New York, the two largest American cities, were each home to roughly 500,000 souls; by 1930 four American cities had populations of a million or more, and several more stood on that threshold. When Chicago was incorporated in 1837, 4,170 people resided on the marshy banks of Lake Michigan. By the 1920s nearly three million people called the city home. In the late nineteenth and early twentieth centuries, immigrants drove the growth of these cities. Simply put, by the 1920s American cities were immigrant cities.

Beyond their size and the rate at which they grew, cities became during these years the inescapable fact of the American imagination. In literature, Stephen Crane, Theodore Dreiser, and all the writers who descended from them made the city, or rather the City, a central character in their fiction. The group of painters known as the Eight rejected the genteel tradition of American painting in favor of a more "social realism" in which city scenes figured prominently. The skyscraper, born in Chicago and grown to first maturity in New York, emerged as the iconic American building form, never mind how Henry James and others might complain about it. By the 1920s, from the Harlem Renaissance to the Chicago poets to Kansas City jazz, American culture was overwhelmingly an urban culture and that which wasn't—the southern Agrarians, or the vogue for folklore, for example—existed largely in reaction to urban America.

Third, whatever it is we mean when we talk about the public sphere or the public realm, it was also an urban phenomenon. Most scholars date the emergence of the public sphere to the seventeenth and eighteenth centuries, and whether they say so explicitly, they mean the seventeenth- and eighteenth-century city. We can certainly look to other, smaller communal experiments—the New England town meeting, for example—as having contributed important democratic experiences to our history, but these tended to be built more formatively around notions of exclusion as well as inclusion. Only in the city did the full range of "the public" develop as we understand it now. As Richard Sennett has described it, "The city has served as a focus for active social life, for the conflict and play of interests, for the experience of human possibility, during most of the history of civilized man."[4]

Finally, the so-called museum movement of these years was an entirely urban phenomenon and was not simply coincident with, but was central to, America's urban moment. Again, at the risk of stating the obvious, while many of the nation's finest colleges were founded in small towns or rural areas in the eighteenth and nineteenth centuries, the nation's important museums were built in the city. At one level, the equation here is easy to explain: the growth of industrial capitalism drove the growth of American cities, and industrial capitalists, in turn, drove the growth of American museums. At another level, however, we should see museums as part of a larger movement to build an urban cultural infrastructure in these burgeoning and often chaotic cities. In this sense, museums joined public parks, public libraries, and the new research-focused universities, among other things, on a cultural landscape intended to provide the urban public with education and recreation. This urban cultural infrastructure was designed to turn what was simply and crudely urban into something urbane.

There has been a scholarly perception that this urban public and this urban public infrastructure were mismatched at the turn of the twentieth century. Or rather that these instruments of "culture" only served the interests of those who built them, and they did not in any meaningful way respond to the needs and desires of the public for whom they were ostensibly intended. The Smithsonian's Stephen Weil, a distinguished writer on museum matters, implied a profound disjunction between the public and public museums at the turn of the twentieth century in several of his essays. Further, he argued, museums are only now catching up to the demands made by the public. He sees museums as changing almost entirely in their relationship to the public when he writes, "At the museum's birth . . . its position vis-à-vis the public was one of superiority. . . . At some point . . . the relative positions of the museum and the public will have revolved a full 180 degrees. In their emerging new relationship . . . it will be the public, not the museum, that occupies the superior position. The museum's role will have been transformed from one of mastery to one of service." Weil went on to ask, "Is not that precise shift of focus, subordinating a concentration on the museum's expectations of the public to a concentration on the public's expectation of the museum, at the very center of the revolution under consideration? I would submit that it is."[5]

Weil's sentiments are, I suspect, widely shared by many in the museum world. But his assertion rests on the assumption that the public has been static, that the public of the late nineteenth century had the same interests and expectations as the public of the late twentieth. Weil and others thus do not acknowledge changes in the way the public thinks of itself and how museums have shaped, in addition to being shaped by, that definition.

American museums, therefore, emerged at a moment when American cities had arrived on the center stage of American life, and when the growth of those cities was driven by the arrival of a vast number of new kinds of Americans. Put another way, in the late nineteenth and early twentieth centuries, the urban and social contexts—the spaces and the peoples—that constituted an American "public" changed dramatically.

Architecture and the Museum Public

The language of architecture functions to create expectations and meanings for those who see it and live with it. As this urban public realm took shape in the United States across the nineteenth century, Americans settled on several vocabularies to give visual definition to certain spheres: state capitol buildings, for example, often borrowed from Greece and Rome—or some strange hybrid of the two—thus producing an architectural consistency to the look of government; likewise, churches routinely turned to the Gothic past for architectural inspiration. Museums, on the other hand, searched longer for an architectural vocabulary to express their sense of purpose and mission. Until late in the century, museum architecture ran to the eclectic—variations of Gothic, Grecian, and the less easily identifiable, such as Frank Furness's wild, exuberant design for the Pennsylvania Academy of the Fine Arts in 1876. In 1893 Chicago's Art Institute opened in a Renaissance palazzo whose pale limestone façade was restrained and barely ornamented, and it proved enormously influential. Spare neoclassicism became the architectural form for most major—and many minor—museums that followed. These buildings may well have issued the stern warning to visitors, as Jay Cantor has nicely put it, that "culture was taking place" inside, but their architectural uniformity from museum to museum and from city to city reflected a widely shared set of assumptions and a uniformity of purpose.[6]

That sense of uniformity, the idea that the public could expect all museums to provide largely the same experience for them, was reinforced even more strongly once visitors came inside. Whatever the various architectural sources that might have inspired the façades of these buildings, their interior spaces resembled each other to a remarkable degree. As early as 1819, Frenchman Jean-Nicolas-Louis Durand drew what he called an "Ideal Design for a museum plan" and envisioned a symmetrical, geometrically perfect building with corridors of galleries laid out around four interior courtyard spaces with a dome in the center.

The plan responds to several things, not the least of which is the building technologies available in the early nineteenth century and the needs of both ventilation and lighting in a premechanical age. Many in the nineteenth century saw museum construction as primarily an engineering problem rather than an aesthetic one: how to bring light in; how to keep dust and dirt out; how to accommodate storage, preparation, and exhibition functions. But the plan also responds to the implicit assumption that a building designed specifically as a museum—as opposed to buildings recycled as such—should be built around the collections of objects and for their proper display. In this sense, while Durand's specific building was never built, to my knowledge, his plan—or rather the assumptions behind it—also proved remarkably influential. Compare it, to take one example, with the 1916 plan for the Cleveland Museum of Art: neoclassical symmetry with galleries organized around a central rotunda and two flanking courtyards. There is a small gathering space behind the portico—a concession to the realities of tickets and coat checks. Most museums built in the United States between 1870 and 1930 organized their interior spaces as variations on this theme.

First and foremost, then, galleries were designed as places to display objects and collections of objects. Indeed, when Richard Morris Hunt

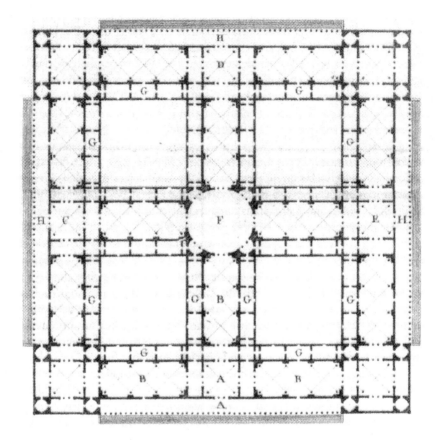

Figure 32. A museum built as a home for objects. Jean-Nicholas-Louis Durand's conception of an "ideal museum," from his 1817–19 publication *Précis des leçons de l'architecture données à l'Ecole royal polytechnique.*

was engaged to design the Fifth Avenue home of the Metropolitan Museum of Art, he created spaces with specific collections in mind.[7] So too did Fiske Kimball design the interior of the Philadelphia Museum of Art around individual architectural pieces he knew would be installed in the building. Only secondarily did these museum designs consider or accommodate the visitors who came to look at those objects.

Implicit in these designs were assumptions about where people belonged in the museum and what they were supposed to do there. What strikes us now about these earlier floor plans is that they amount to long corridors designed to be walked through, not necessarily to be gathered in. More than that, as often as not, they were designed to be

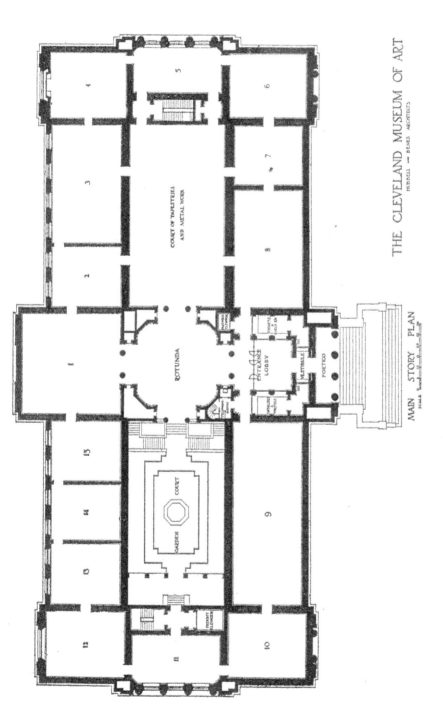

THE CLEVELAND MUSEUM OF ART
HUBBELL AND BENES ARCHITECTS

MAIN STORY PLAN
SCALE

Figure 33. When the Cleveland Museum of Art opened in 1916, it resembled Durand's ideal that museums should be built around the objects on display. From *Catalogue of the Inaugural Exhibition of the Cleveland Museum of Art*.

walked through in a single direction or along a designated course. In Cleveland the galleries were numbered sequentially in a way that suggests an order through which they are to be toured: Through the rotunda to number 1, turn right, and off you go. The Philadelphia Museum of Art's new building, designed in the 1920s as a great Greek temple perched atop an acropolis, was arranged, as we have seen already, to form a "main street" of art.

The interior organization of these museums reflects how their builders expected them to function for the public and, in turn, how they expected the public to function in the museum. Following the corridors, visitors were supposed to study the objects on display in them, carefully and in sequence. That emphasis on engaging visually with objects was equally as strong in natural history museums as it was in art museums. For late Victorian museum builders, objects were a source of knowledge, and that knowledge could be gleaned through careful observation—that faith in an "object-based epistemology" I mentioned in the introduction.[8]

Taken together, the objects in these galleries told stories, and only by following their arrangement in the proper order could visitors hope to read those stories. The narrative unfolded as one moved from one gallery to the next. Usually the narrative charted a historical or evolutionary progress: from lowest to highest, from simplest to most complex, from oldest to most recent. This, then, was the education that museums offered the American public, the visual explanation and reaffirmation of the most important Victorian verities. Space inside the museum reinforced its educational aspirations. This organization of the space also reveals how museums perceived the visiting public. They imagined that the galleries would be occupied by attentive observers who came to the museum for education and enlightened entertainment.

Unity of architectural form implied a unity of knowledge. Museums at the turn of the last century confidently displayed knowledge, whether about art, anthropology, or the natural world, as a coherent whole. The museum aspired to represent the world in microcosm. Implicit in that goal for encyclopedic wholeness was an assumption that the museum audience too was, for the most part, singular. Which is not to say that museum builders weren't perfectly aware of the different classes and ethnicities that came to the museum but rather that, once inside, those visitors were understood as a unity.

National Identity or Local Identity

Some scholars have found in this conception of the public and of the public role of museums a more insidious drive to conformity and con-

trol. Museums, in this view, stand as simply one more piece of an apparatus of bourgeois hegemony. In one direction, this view comes from the
drift in the "social history" of the 1960s and 1970s that cast a suspicious,
antiauthoritarian eye on all institutions, from schools to hospitals to
public parks. From another direction has come a more Foucauldian
analysis, with its stress on "discourses" of power. Tony Bennett, for
example, sees museums as "spaces of emulation" where visitors went to
learn as much about how to behave as they learned about art or science.
As places where these codes of proper deportment were themselves on
display, museums became instruments through which "the crowd comes
. . . to regulate itself." Museum galleries thus functioned "for the self-
display of bourgeois-democratic" values.[9]

There can be no question, I think, that museums in the late Victorian
world helped to underscore many of the rules and to reinforce many of
the boundaries that governed that society. Indeed, it would be genuinely
surprising if institutions sponsored either by the state or by groups of
wealthy plutocrats had any other agenda. And yet I think such an analysis misses a great deal about the public function of the museum. For
starters, Bennett and others have written largely about European museums (for whatever reason, scholarship on European museums has been
more extensive and more lively than scholarship about American ones).
At the risk of sounding too much like an American exceptionalist, I do
believe that the relationship between institutions, the state, and the public here is a bit different from that in Europe. In order to understand
how American museums defined their public and how the public utilized museums, we need to acknowledge those differences. As Francis
Henry Taylor chided in 1945, "The American Museum is, after all, neither an abandoned European palace, nor a solution for storing and classifying the accumulated national wealth of the past. It is an American
phenomenon."[10]

A first difference lies exactly in the relationship between museums
and the notion of national identity. Many scholars, again particularly in
the European context, have commented that museums played an important role in the creation of national identities, especially in the nineteenth century. As Flora Kaplan has written, this process often involved
the assertion of a general national identity over more various and more
specific ethnic or regional identities. The relationship between great
museums and the emergence of European nationalism in the nineteenth century seems straightforward. Major national art museums built
in the dominant capital cities—London, Paris, Berlin—burnished
national prestige and power with culture, while large-scale natural history museums collected and displayed the fruits of empire.

Americans, however, chose quite deliberately not to build a European-style capital city, a place simultaneously the center of politics, money, and culture. Briefly, Philadelphia functioned like that at the end of the eighteenth century, and Peale's museum had those nationalizing aspirations. Peale's museum exhibited the specimens sent back by the Lewis and Clark expedition, evidence of the nation's natural resources and its expansionist goals. But as I mentioned previously, Peale's did not last long, and the national capital moved to Washington, D.C. While the Smithsonian Institution was founded in the 1840s, Washington itself remained an inconsequential place until the early years of the twentieth century. No "national" museum there could really compete with bigger, better-funded museums located in bigger, more important cities. The natural history and anthropology collections amassed by the Smithsonian were certainly of the first importance, but the National Gallery, the nation's art collection, didn't open until the 1940s.

Instead, the growth of American museums in the late nineteenth and early twentieth centuries was linked to the decentralized growth of its urban centers: Boston, New York, Philadelphia, Detroit, Chicago, and so on. On top of that, the major museums of this era were founded privately by local groups of the wealthy and prominent, and while they received widely varying degrees of support from local governments, they did not get their money or their governance from Washington. Without a doubt, museums in all these places shared a certain set of assumptions about culture and national identity. The art museums in all these cities, for example, promoted the idea that the United States was heir to the cultural traditions of Western Europe.

At the same time, however, museum building in any given city was also driven by a booster's competition with other cities: Philadelphia with Boston, Chicago with New York, Pittsburgh with Cleveland.[11] This competition manifested itself in all kinds of ways, big and small. When Frederick Ward Putnam came to Chicago to oversee exhibits at the 1893 World's Columbian Exposition, he goaded Chicagoans to build a permanent natural history museum with the example of New York: "Surely," he told the wealthy and influential members of Chicago's Commercial Club in 1891, "this opportunity [to build a museum] must not be lost." After all, he reminded them, a grand museum of natural history was necessary for the city's "culture and fame." In his role as cultural emissary from the East Coast, Putnam knew how to tweak members of Chicago's business elite.

Even New York was not immune to this civic anxiety. While New York claimed to be the first to propose building a great museum of science and technology, Chicago beat it to the punch. Upon learning the news of Chicago's museum, the *New York Times* lamented, "Still we of New York continue saying the things. While we in New York are still saying it,

Chicago has risen to it." The *Times* hastened to assure its readers that Chicago's project "will not lessen the need of a like museum here—even a greater one."[12] When Chicago's "Rosenwald Museum of Industry" changed its name a few years later to the "Museum of Science and Industry," New York's version of the same institution immediately did the same thing. Fifteen years later, the plagiarism still stung, and it prompted the Chicago museum's Russell Anderson to write a bitter letter to the editors of *Science,* complaining, "When we changed our name . . . they changed to 'The New York Museum of Science and Industry.' At the time we protested the close copy of our name, but they declined to change." Anderson impatiently requested that *Science* only use "museum of science and industry" when referring to Chicago. In fact, whatever its name, New York's science and industry museum never really left the launch pad. When the *New York Times* urged the city to create this "missing museum" in 1959, it pointed out that "other cities have such museums, of great usefulness, among them Chicago, Philadelphia and Boston."[13]

More modestly, as the Cleveland Museum of Art assembled works of art in preparation for its opening in 1916, it knew that it might be able to compete with Boston's Museum of Fine Arts in the collection of Asian material. Announcing the acquisition of a Chinese Buddhist sculpture, the museum's bulletin took the opportunity for a comparison: "This little stone figure . . . reminds us of the large statue of Kwanyin acquired lately by the Museum of Fine Arts, Boston."[14] Edward Morse even thought that this sense of civic pride through museums ought to extend to smaller towns. In 1893 he had predicted, "A wholesome spirit of rivalry might naturally arise, and each town having its museum would excel in certain departments, in the same way that each town can pride itself on certain special features, such as a fine park, spacious town hall, public library, or superior high-school building."[15] Notice the litany of public good translated into public spaces: park, town hall, library, school, and, of course, museum.

So it went, and so it still goes, as cities try to establish their claim to cultural legitimacy against one another through building museums. When the Broad Museum of Art opened as part of the Los Angeles County Museum of Art in February 2008, *New York Times* architecture critic Nicolai Ouroussoff began his review of the building with the almost insufferably condescending remark: "This city is growing up." No surprise, really, that Ouroussoff went on to pan Renzo Piano's architecture, but Ouroussoff didn't miss the opportunity to reach back and take a New Yorker's swipe at the original LACMA building, opened in 1965 as "an imitation of Lincoln Center." Recognizing the civic competition involved, Ouroussoff wrote, "As a monument to the civic aspira-

tions of Los Angeles, Mr. Piano's design is remarkably uninspired."
Across the page, Roberta Smith was equally dismissive of the art on display in this uninspired Los Angeles building. Her headline read,
"Rounding Up the Usual Suspects." While Smith wrote that the Broad
Museum "represents a healthy shift in the balance of power between
Los Angeles and New York," she reminded us that this power balance is
really what is at issue. Furthermore, she simply brushed off the art: "It
[the Broad] should be embarrassed by the dominance of New York artists (21 out of 30) at a point when Los Angeles has one of the liveliest
art scenes on the planet."[16] Translation: See, even Los Angelenos understand that New York artists are the best and most important.

At the turn of the twentieth century, as Robert Wiebe demonstrated
in his now-classic book *The Search for Order*, most Americans did not conceive of their identity in national terms but rather in local terms. A Chi-
cagoan first, a Bostonian first, but an American second perhaps, and the
museums built during that era grew in the soil of urban aspiration. We
can also assume that in an age before easy tourism, museums were built
primarily for the locals. In this sense, while Chicagoans might point to
their museums as evidence that they were the equal of New York, those
museums served to foster feelings of local pride and of civic identity
rooted in the city itself.

A Democratic Public?

When Charles Willson Peale opened his museum in Philadelphia, he was
explicit about the democratic aspirations he had for it. He described the
utility of the museum in quite specific terms: he imagined that the
knowledge on display in his museum, filled as it was with natural history
specimens, ethnographic material, and portraits painted by himself and
his children, would be important to the merchant, the mechanic, and
the farmer. As he put it famously in the introduction to his public lectures, "The farmer ought to know that snakes feed on field mice and
moles, which would otherwise destroy whole fields of corn. . . . To the
merchant, the study of nature is scarcely less interesting, whose traffic
lies altogether in material either raw from the stores of nature or *wrought*
by the hand of ingenious art. . . . The mechanic ought to possess an
accurate knowledge of many of the qualities of those materials with
which his art is connected."[17] Farmer, merchant, mechanic—as good a
typology of the "middling sorts" of the early Republic as any, and Peale
designed his museum to appeal to each of them and their needs.

Three-quarters of a century later, the founders of New York's Metropolitan Museum of Art imagined their mission in somewhat vaguer but
no less inclusive terms. The museum would be dedicated "to our whole

people" and would provide "free and ample access for innocent and refined enjoyment, and also supplying the best facilities for practical instruction and the cultivation of pure taste in all matters connected with the arts." In 1927 Richard Bach of the Metropolitan Museum of Art wrote that "there are adults of various types . . . such as the designer, the homemaker, the advanced student, the cultivated layman, the manufacturer, the salesperson, the business man, the artisan. And there is the whole range of childhood and youth." In the face of this variety, Bach insisted that the museum must "satisfy the demands of all." A quarter century later, the American Museum of Natural History updated Peale's typology for the mid-twentieth century: "The Museum should be all things to all men. It should meet the needs of the housewife, the farmer, the industrialist, the teacher, the college student, the child. Each must find . . . an answer to his questions."[18]

It is easy certainly to dismiss these kinds of claims—and all museums made and continue to make them—of democratic inclusivity as being nothing more than self-congratulatory pronouncements by and for wealthy robber barons justifying the institutional palaces they built for themselves and their friends. But to do so would be too easy and would miss too much. We ought to examine more seriously the claims made for the public function of these museums a century ago, and the way in which these institutions responded to—rather than simply coerced—the public's sense of itself.

First, we ought to remember that the majority of museums founded in the United States during this period displayed science, in one form or another, not fine art. Whatever might be said about the art museum as a place for taste-training and for the display of collections assembled by a wealthy few does not as easily apply to the natural history museum whose cases were filled with perfectly quotidian specimens gathered by museum scientists, academics, and ordinary people.[19] A few natural history museums—the American Museum of Natural History and the Field Museum, for example—amassed collections truly international in scope, but most collected locally or regionally. To visit these more modest places was to see one's own world collected, organized, and put on display, not the high cultural heritage of aristocrats.

Second, as I mentioned earlier, American museums constituted only one part of a larger project to build a "public sphere," at least in urban America. Since its "discovery" by intrepid historical explorers over the last generation, the public sphere has proved a slippery place to map. German philosopher Jürgen Habermas, whose delineation of the public sphere has been particularly influential, stresses the importance of a set of public institutions in shaping that realm, particularly the press and print culture. But his analysis, I think, tends to be somewhat disembodied and placeless.[20] Echoing Habermas, for example, Philip Ethington, in his study of San Francisco, draws a sharp distinction between the public sphere and public space and believes that the public sphere "resides in communication." Habermas is concerned chiefly with the way the public sphere generates public discussion that serves as a check on the power of the state.

The stress of the centrality of communication for a public sphere stretches at least as far back as John Dewey's 1927 book *The Public and Its Problems.* Though he did not tack on the word *sphere,* his concerns about the public were largely the same. He wrote in his characteristically muddy prose, "We have the physical tools of communication as never before. The thoughts and aspirations congruous with them are not communicated, and hence are not common. Without such communication the public will remain shadowy and formless. . . . Communication can alone create a great community."[21] But at the same time, while the public sphere may encompass something larger than public space—many scholars stress the function of the press—it is hard to imagine a fully constituted public existing purely in the world of communication. A public requires spaces in which to communicate, act, be seen, and so forth. Further, museums were (and are) spaces of communication, if not precisely of debate, and so in this sense I do think that they ought to be viewed as part of that urban public sphere.

Certainly, many saw museums as an essential part of what defined the public good. Writing in 1893 in the pages of the *Atlantic,* Edward S. Morse asked readers, "If Public Libraries, Why Not Public Museums?" and went on to argue that every town that had built a public library ought to build a public museum as well.[22] We also ought to remember that all the infrastructure that helped form the urban public sphere served huge numbers of people. We cannot know in any great or specific detail just how many—keeping annual attendance figures didn't become a routine museum practice until the middle decades of the twentieth century, as far as I can determine—but the anecdotes suggest that parks, libraries, and, yes, museums were crowded much of the time.

Admiring his work in Central Park, Frederick Law Olmsted wrote in 1870 of seeing "a hundred thousand" New Yorkers gathered in the park, "all classes largely represented, with a common purpose. . . . You may thus often see vast numbers of persons brought closely together, poor and rich, young and old, Jew and Gentile."[23] At the museum, it would have been quite easy to limit the crowds by charging admission, but the majority of them did not (at least not initially), and that was clearly a deliberate choice on the part of those who ran these places. At the cornerstone-laying ceremony for the American Museum of Natural History in 1874, New York City Parks commissioner H. G. Stebbins believed that the museum would become "a school where the children of the rich and poor alike can come to study the wonders of nature . . . here to be gathered together, and freely exposed for the common benefit of all." That well might have overstated the case, but when the *Philadelphia Inquirer* reported in 1897 on a city appropriation to fund a new museum of art, the new Philadelphia Commercial Museum, and a new main branch of the Free Library, the headline read, "Great Museum Free to the People."[24]

Nor can we know with any specificity just who utilized this infrastructure, but again the anecdotal evidence compels us to think more broadly about who came to these museums. We can start with the now-famous fights at the Metropolitan, which had taken a beating in the New York press for being snooty and exclusive, thus hypocritically betraying the democratic rhetoric of its own founding statement. In 1879 the *Evening Post* sneered, "Could any prospect be more uninviting than that presented at present to a skilled workman in search of knowledge, when he has to set foot within the precincts of our Museum of Art?" Through the 1880s the press fought a running battle with Met trustees over the question of whether the museum would open on Sundays, the only day working people might be able to attend. "Let the Poor View the Art Treasures," demanded the *New York Herald* in 1891, and the Met finally capitulated. Smarting from that defeat, the guardians of art voted in 1897 to ban the wearing of overalls in the Met's galleries. When a plumber, resplendent in his overalls, entered the building, he was unceremoniously tossed out. The press went to town. The *New York Journal's* sarcastic headline read: "Overalls in Museum? Never! Workmen in Workmens' Garb Not Fit to Gaze on Art."

This all made for good reading and probably for good paper sales, but without overemphasizing the significance of these episodes I think we can draw several conclusions about the relationship between the public and these museums. They reveal that while the museum's trustees might not have really taken those mission statements about public education seriously, the broader public did. The fight over Sabbath day opening—a fight that took place in many places and that the guardians of the Sabbath always lost—suggests that on the one day when working people might venture out to the museum many chose to do so, or at least demanded that they have that option. Even the editors of the *Christian Union*, in an 1890 editorial, announced their conviction that museums (and libraries as well) ought to be open on Sundays. "We who have homes of our own," the editors wrote, "do not lock up our books, nor cover our pictures nor drape our statues." "Why," the paper went on to ask, "should we lock up the books, and pictures and statues of the people who have none in their homes and many of whom have no other day to read a book or look at a picture except the Lord's Day?" Pointing specifically to the examples of St. Louis and Boston, the paper proudly reported that "workingmen and their families" made great use of the libraries and museums in those cities on Sundays. Nearly twenty years later, in 1909, Benjamin Ives Gilman of Boston's Museum of Fine Arts wrote in an almost triumphant tone: "The Sunday visitors especially represent the American public at its best. All sorts and conditions of men contribute their quota to the well-behaved, interested, almost reverent throng."[25]

Finally, we know about these conflicts over who could enter the museum and under what circumstances because the press thought they were important enough to cover, and interestingly, they took the side of the plumbers. In these cases, two of the institutions that helped constitute the public sphere—the newspaper and the museum—clashed over the definition of who belonged in that sphere, and the press, speaking on behalf of the plumbers, won. After all, as the *Christian Union* reminded its readers, the objects on display in museums, treasures though they might be, belonged to "the people." Looking back from the 1920s, writer Dorothy Canfield Fisher claimed that in 1910, "There were in this country . . . seventy six active well-supported intelligently conducted museums. . . . Every one of them . . . is the center of enthusiastic appreciation of the people about it. Every one of them is supported *by the public.*"[26]

In 1929, the Pennsylvania Museum of Art (not yet renamed the Philadelphia Museum of Art) attempted more systematically to quantify this public. The museum had opened its new building in 1928 and in its first year counted 1 million visitors. No doubt many had come simply for the novelty of the new, monumental building, but the museum took the opportunity to survey 1,000 of those visitors with an extensive questionnaire in what must surely be among the earliest examples of the kind of practice that would become common in later generations. Though the museum freely admitted that "the figures cannot be considered absolutely accurate," the "reasonable approximations" made from this survey underscore that the art museum was not merely the domain of a local elite.

The survey broke visitors first into male and female (slightly more women came than men) and, extrapolating from the 1,000 responses, discovered that "housewives" constituted far and away the largest group of visitors (260,000). Next came students (roughly 140,000) and businessmen (60,000), but the museum estimated 50,000 "artists and craftsmen" and 40,000 factory workers as well. Further, the museum asked these visitors for criticism and suggestions. Many (no number given) suggested public lectures, trained guides to lead them through the galleries, and better signs. Without making too much of them, these responses do suggest that this cross section of the population wanted exactly the kind of directed educational programming museums would provide, and they felt justified in asking for them. Given this data, crude though it may have been, the museum felt it reasonable to conclude that its "service is not restricted to a limited section of the public. Its exhibits appeal to all groups."[27]

Museums and a "Transnational" Public

In thinking about the public role in which museums functioned a century ago, and more specifically the educational task they assigned themselves, we would do well to remember the importance of visual information—as opposed to verbal or linguistic information—in the turn-of-the-century city. We all know that a staggering percentage of city residents did not speak English as a first language, quite apart from whatever number of them could or could not read English. Images of all sorts thus became a shared form of communication—from shopkeeper's signs and advertising billboards to photographs and movies. Chicago poet Vachel Lindsay, writing specifically about motion pictures in 1916, recognized that what he called "photoplay" "cuts deeper into some stratifications of society than the newspaper or the book have ever gone." The pervasiveness of images in American culture created what historian Warren Susman, borrowing from Lindsay, called "a hieroglyphic civilization."[28] Even as sharp a critic of traditional museums as John Cotton Dana, who found much to dislike about the museums of the late nineteenth century, believed in the "formal and informal training through the eye."[29]

Knowledge conveyed visually was what museums had to offer and thus, in contrast to libraries, which catered necessarily to the literate, were more accessible to people who could not read, or at least could not read in English. Yale professor Maurice Davie believed that museums constituted an "essential part of public life" because they provided "free, general, visual education."[30] Moreover, the orderliness of visual information as museums displayed it may well have come as a kind of relief to city dwellers who otherwise had to contend every day with a visual cacophony.

As I mentioned earlier, we can't know with any certainty the extent to which immigrants visited these museums. Even when museums did begin recording the number of visitors, they certainly did not break up the data by ethnicity. Given this, it is worth considering the observations of Alfred Goldsborough Mayer. Mayer was a curator at the Brooklyn Institute of Arts and Sciences and in 1903 reminded readers of the *North*

American Review that in considering the public function of the urban museum, "we have overlooked the fact that the vast foreign immigration of the past few years has brought among us a population accustomed to museums, and who seek the amusement and instruction which these institutions afford with much keener appreciation, respect and interest than is manifested by native-born Americans." And he continued this implicit indictment: "Museums, Zoological and Botanical Gardens, Aquaria and Public Parks are all appreciated more thoroughly and visited more frequently by foreigners than by our native-born."[31]

That seems a remarkable and unlikely claim, and we should probably not take it at face value. It is hard to imagine that many of those immigrants from the villages of Italy or the shtetls of Eastern Europe had been to too many museums. And yet Mayer was in a position to know, and his assertion should make us examine more carefully our assumptions about who did and did not come to museums at the turn of the twentieth century. As late as 1930, the education department at the American Museum of Natural History could report that "the most interesting feature" of its adult education programming was "the contact with the foreign-born through a series of illustrated lectures by staff members."[32] Perhaps we should see early twentieth-century museums as one of the important public places where the extraordinary heterogeneity of American cities gathered on Sabbath day afternoons.

Moreover, by the late nineteenth century, those in the professionalizing world of education believed that visual information had an untapped power to teach. Edward Morse complained that "lessons from books, and not from nature, have been the tiresome lot of school children. Questions and answers, cut and dried, have tended to deaden the inquiring spirit," and he offered museums as the antidote. Ten years later, in 1903, Mayer suggested that the situation had not improved much, complaining that "the development of museums within the United States during the past thirty years has been insignificant in comparison with the enormous growth of libraries and universities." It is worth noting that Mayer's comparison put museums exactly in the same group as libraries and universities as comprising a triumvirate of educational institutions. And of the three, museums stood as inadequate: "It is apparent that our museums are only beginning to make themselves felt as factors in our system of education."[33]

Put more simply, the urban public at the turn of the twentieth century used the public institutions available to it and expected these institutions to be a part of their lives. In 1890 the Pennsylvania Museum of Art counted 312,000 visitors, a figure equal to about 30 percent of the city's entire population. Clearly, those visitors weren't only the small handful of the city's wealthy coming over and over and over again. Half a century later, James Truslow Adams cited a study that counted 50 million annual visitors to the nation's museums. Observing the crowds at Chicago's Museum of Science and Industry in 1947, Harland Manchester wrote, "You see kids of all colors, races and home backgrounds merging happily in popeyed exuberance."[34] If the claims made by these museums to openness, public service, and inclusivity ring disingenuously to us today, that may reflect our own condition of living in an eroded public sphere and our distrust of any claim made now for the public good. Those suspicions may not do justice to the way these museums functioned to constitute the urban public sphere of the late nineteenth and early twentieth centuries. In other words, the historical consensus about museums and the public reveals as much about our current moment as it does about the past.

With all this in mind, let's return to the critique of the museum as a place where the late Victorian bourgeoisie went to get disciplined and punished and turn its somewhat sinister implications on their head. Rather than see museums as places that imposed a particular ethos from above on a public that did not want it, we might see them as shaped by a set of more widely shared expectations about what constituted the public good and about how public institutions ought to foster it. According to Richard Sennett, "As in behavior, so in belief, the citizens of the 18th Century capitals attempted to define both what public life was and what it was not. The line drawn between public and private was essentially one on which the claims of civility—epitomized by cosmopolitan, public behavior—were balanced against the claims of nature—epitomized by the family. . . . Behaving with strangers in an emotionally satisfying way and yet remaining aloof from them was seen by the mid-18th Century as the means by which the human animal was transformed into a social being."[35]

Sennett sees this separation between public life and private life as crucial to democratic societies, and his book *The Fall of Public Man* laments the loss of public life in favor of private life. In this sense, museums were indeed places that helped in the crucial task of defining what the public was. Carol Duncan and Alan Wallach, writing about the universal survey museum, observed that "in this type of museum, the visitor moves through a programmed experience that casts him in the role of an ideal citizen—a member of an idealized 'public' and heir to an ideal, civilized past."[36] And while this may be what museum builders aspired to create, we ought to acknowledge that this may have also been precisely what some number of museumgoers wanted. Bringing a set of expectations about what would go on inside and about how it would go on, the hundreds of thousands of American city dwellers who visited museums each year exhibited exactly Sennett's "cosmopolitan, public behavior." Museums became yet another place in the turn-of-the-century city where an individual was "transformed into a social being." Absolutely, then, museums functioned as places of emulation, where urban people learned how to conduct themselves, not merely in public but as a public. As Sennett reminds us, without that kind of education, we cannot have a public in any meaningful sense at all.

From Confidence to Confusion: The Midcentury Museum

Museums in the first half of the twentieth century certainly stood as universalizing institutions. Whether focusing on the natural world or the cultural world, museums made large, generalized claims. The exterior architecture and the arrangement of interior spaces said as much, underscoring, as I have discussed earlier, the progressive narratives museums told. Behind the columns and pediments, the stories visitors saw unfold in these museums, though illustrated with different specific objects, had a basic uniformity. By the mid-twentieth century that universalist impulse had broadened in American life, though it coexisted with a variety of parochialisms as well. Ideologies of world socialism, of international labor, or even of pan-Africanism hit their zenith in the midcentury. Culturally, one only has to think of some of the other iconic productions of the midcentury—from Alfred Kinsey's *Sexual Behavior in the Human Male* (1948) to Edward Steichen's *Family of Man* (1955)—to recognize the powerful reach of this universalism.[37] All participated in a phenomenon that substituted "we" for "I."

Some in the museum world in the 1930s and 1940s cast their work in these largest, almost epochal terms. Albert Parr, taking over as director of the American Museum of Natural History in 1942, just as the United States entered World War II, believed that in addition to helping "man understand his relation to his environment," natural history museums "can play an important part in helping man understand himself in relation to the other people of the world." As he stated in a 1953 address, "Through the medium of the natural sciences, we can show the great diversity of conditions under which people are forced to conduct the struggle for existence. We can penetrate below these superficial differences imposed by the natural environment and show that man's problems and efforts everywhere are basically the same. In this way, we can create a feeling of companionship in the triumphs and vicissitudes of the universal struggle."[38] The natural history museum could put that family of man in its proper scientific context.

Likewise, writing in 1937, as the fascist nightmare descended fully on Europe, T. R. Adam believed that museums, through their educational role, were positioned crucially to preserve "the democratic ideal of equal cultural opportunities for all citizens." He added this warning: "When groups possessing social or economic power fail to fulfill their educational responsibilities to the common man, democracy is betrayed to the extent of their neglect." The fight in 1937 was starkly between democracy and tyranny, and museums sat on the front lines of cultural freedom. Eight years later, surveying the wreckage of the war and staring at a future filled with anxiety, Francis Henry Taylor thought that museums could help pick up the pieces. "More than ever before," he wrote, "the American museum will be called upon to fulfill a social function. The museum must become the free and informal liberal arts college for a whole generation of men and women who are now, and for some time to come will be, devoting themselves to the arts of destruction." The wartime generation, Taylor believed, deserved museums and were entitled to them, and American society owed them these places: "When they come home, too old for the classroom, we must be prepared to give them, in a form they can comprehend and enjoy, the fruits of a civilization for which they have risked their lives."[39]

We can notice several subtle, though no less important, shifts in the conception of the museum, from the turn of the century to the middle of it, in the writings of these two authors. First and foremost, the somewhat abstract notion of a public education provided by the Progressive Era museum had, by the 1930s, been translated more specifically and programmatically into work with schoolchildren and adult education. Herman Bumpus, of the American Museum of Natural History, writing in 1906, could describe the education in museums as "silent teaching" whose "period of instruction is limited only by the desire of the visitor."[40] By the 1930s, that "silent teaching" was no longer seen as adequate. Museums, the big ones at any rate, added both space and trained personnel devoted specifically to education during these years. In his large 1932 book on the "problems of city life," Professor Davie discussed museums as an integral part of adult education and believed that those who ran museums were finally "letting the public in . . . and adapting the museum to the needs of the masses." In 1938, Grace Ramsey, of the American Museum of Natural History, published an entire manual on museum education running to nearly three hundred pages with chapters covering everything from museum field trips to how museums and radio stations might interact. At the same moment, the AMNH established a division of adult education.[41] Gone now was the easy, uncomplicated sense that museum exhibits could convey their educational lessons more or less transparently—and visually—and without translation or mediation. Gone too were many of the objects. Galleries once filled with hundreds of items were gradually replaced with exhibits that tried to do more with less.

In this sense, museums continued to occupy a public space akin to the public library and the college. But Taylor's use of the "liberal arts college" analogy was telling. With the slowly expanding world of institutional higher education came a growing divide between those who went to college and those who did not. Museums could be the campus for those "too old for the classroom." Indeed, T. R. Adam worried that the museum needed to develop different kinds of educational strategies because "a danger now exists of museums adopting educational programs that tend to duplicate the work of universities and extension courses."[42] Museums of the earlier generation had been central to what was implicitly understood as "adult education"; by the 1930s, they had considerable competition for that role from the expansion of other institutions.

At the same time, by the 1930s the spread of popular entertainment and mass culture—especially movies, radio, and recorded music—served to draw the distinction between highbrow and lowbrow, between the avant-garde and kitsch, ever more sharply. (Clement Greenberg's hugely influential essay of that latter title appeared in 1939.)[43] "Two cultural nations exist side by side in America," Adam worried. Museums at the turn of the twentieth century had served, at least for some and at some level, as a form of popular entertainment. At the very least, in a world before movies and spectator sports, the museum had less competition. Now, Adam was concerned that there was that "narrow world of fine scholarship and trained aesthetic taste; and beneath it and all around it the popular arena of semiskilled sports and hobbies, flamboyant movies, radio drama, and sensational literature."[44] In such a divided cultural world, where would museums reside?

Adam, of course, wrote just as the new museums of science and technology in Chicago and Philadelphia arrived on the scene. As we discussed in Chapter 4, they replaced objects with interaction, the visual with the physical. And more to the point, they advertised themselves as fun places that had removed the forbidding "Do Not Touch" signs. In the milieu of the midcentury public, no wonder they succeeded so spectacularly.

Mass culture, of course, requires the masses. While those in the Progressive Era referred generally to "visitors" or "the people," those writing in the midst of Roosevelt's New Deal thought of the public in terms of "the common man" and "the masses." This signals a shift in how the public defined itself, or was defined, by the 1930s and 1940s. Adam, for one, saw this quite clearly. Previously, as Adam saw it, "social pressure" made "some form of cultural participation almost obligatory for ambitious people." Now, he noted, social pressure "appears to have changed its direction toward the petty fields of sport and entertainment. The Linnaean societies and pre-Raphaelite groups of our grandfathers have been replaced by our country clubs and bridge parties." And he insisted to his readers that "the general public looks to the museum as the only trustworthy authority accessible to the ordinary man."[45]

Certainly, this shift was generational, from cities filled with immigrants to cities filled with their children. But it was also related to an expansion and transformation of public spaces during those years brought about in no small part by the government. We still live with the achievements of the Public Works Administration (PWA) and Works Progress Administration (WPA) and other such agencies, but it is worth remembering the sheer scale of them. The WPA alone built 40,000 new buildings and improved 85,000 additional ones, including schools, libraries, auditoriums, and recreational centers. It created 1,700 parks covering 75,000 acres. As we fret—and not much more—about climate change, we ought to remember that the Civilian Conservation Corps (CCC) planted more than 3 billion trees.[46]

Beyond the vast scope of all this public infrastructure, however, was a significant expansion in the notion of what the public was and what it needed. As historian Daniel Rodgers has provocatively pointed out, the reforms of the Progressive Era took the city as the central problem in American life and equated the solution of urban problems with the solution of national ones. "A century ago," as Rodgers states, "the city stood at the vital center of transatlantic progressive imaginations. . . . If the nation was to be reformed, it would be by first seizing the social possibilities of the cities."[47]

In this sense, then, we might see the New Deal public works projects as a continuation of Progressive reforms through an expansion of the urban public sphere into corners of the nation that had never quite had one before in an effort to achieve a vision of cultural democracy. City residents since the second half of the nineteenth century, for example, had enjoyed recreational parks; before the New Deal many states had no state parks at all. Likewise, the WPA built fifty-two county fairgrounds and rodeo grounds, presumably all a long way from New York and Chicago. In particular, as Jane De Hart Mathews has noted, new community arts centers stood as the "physical symbols of the New Deal effort to decentralize the nation's cultural resources."[48] No mere coincidence that Holger Cahill, who had been an assistant at John Cotton Dana's pioneering Newark Museum, was appointed to run the Federal Arts Program. What had been a part of urban life now became part of national life, and the availability and use of public spaces became an expectation of the American public for the first time.

In this way, the expansion of the public realm in the 1930s and 1940s helped achieve, as Robert Leighninger has argued, a broader integration of the American populace. Without waxing too rhapsodic about it, and without ignoring the obvious and blatant exclusions in American life, we can say that New Deal public spaces brought together an ethnically diverse nation and gave it shared experiences, usually for free. We shouldn't dismiss Roosevelt's speech at the opening of Glacier National Park as mere bloviation: "The country belongs to the people; that what it is and what it is in the process of making is for the enrichment of the lives of all of us."[49]

In the midst of this general enthusiasm for expanding the public realm, many of those in museums seem to have felt uneasy. Both Francis Henry Taylor and T. R. Adam—and others as well—expressed a certain frustration that the whole enterprise of museum-based education was not working or was in some way inadequate. "The public are no longer impressed and are frankly bored with museums and their inability to render adequate service," opined Taylor, and his view was widely shared.[50] Some of this critique may have been generated by the politics of the decade. New Dealers, those further to the left, and many others during the 1930s objected broadly to anything that might carry a whiff of elitism; fine art and the museums in which the fine arts were entombed were no exception. Rather than being vital, accessible institutions, as Thomas Parker put it late in the decade, museums and the objects they displayed had became "fragments of the past." The Brooklyn Museum's Philip Youtz, writing in 1933, agreed that the problem for museums was largely one of technique. "I am convinced," he wrote, "that if the public indifference and antipathy could be analyzed and measured it would be found to rest . . . on our outmoded methods of showing objects." Taylor, the director of the Metropolitan Museum of Art, fretted that museums need to deploy "our resources in the light of their potential usefulness to society, and by reconciling the layman and the scholar—therein lies our only hope for survival in the modern world."[51]

Whether attitudes like these reflected the feeling of the public who came to visit museums in the 1930s or whether these sorts of comments reflected the ideological posturing of their speakers scarcely matters. The confidence with which museums announced themselves and their purpose at the turn of the twentieth century had diminished. John Cotton Dana, perceptively writing in 1927, charged, "We can go further and say that in spite of the efforts made by museums to hold some of the slight power to attract, which they once enjoyed, their influence wanes."[52] Dana's comments suggest first that the museums of the late nineteenth century did indeed enjoy public influence, and they hint that the nature of the urban public was changing by the late 1920s.

If Dana was right, and if the museums themselves hadn't changed much, then clearly the public—its expectations, demands, and sense of itself—had, and that unease may have stemmed from precisely this shift in what the public expected its public sphere to be. With some notable exceptions, most of the major museums in the country continued to be run by what we might call now the nonprofit sector—private boards of trustees not directly accountable to the public. The New Deal turned public space into a matter of national and local politics, and museums may have struggled to keep up with these changes. Put another way, by the 1930s the public sphere was seen to be a part of the democratic process, subject at least in an airy way to the will of the people.

The confidence with which museums had been built in the Progressive Era had clearly eroded by the second quarter of the twentieth century, and the critique of the museum as being elitist and out of touch with the public dates, I think, to writers from this period. It is a critique that, as I mentioned earlier, has largely stuck. My suggestion here is that the Progressive Era museum may have suited its public to an extent we have not acknowledged, but by the 1930s that "public" had changed. The challenge museums struggled with was to refashion themselves to meet the new and different demands made of them by a public with new expectations of what "public" meant.

Museums and a Declining Public

In this section let me return briefly to some of those earlier observations I made and make a set of equally straightforward ones in order to look at what has happened to the relationship between the museum and the public in the more recent past. First, America's urban moment did not last long. Officially, the nation's population ceased to be urban in 1980 according to the census, and by that time nearly two-thirds of all American manufacturing had relocated to suburban or exurban areas. By the end of the 1960s, most major American cities experienced tragic episodes of racial violence, though the causes of those explosions had roots deep in the social and economic changes that had taken place in the 1950s. Perhaps no moment captured the urban crisis of the mid-twentieth century better than the headline the *New York Daily News* ran in 1975 when the city asked the federal government to help it out of its financial collapse: "Ford to City: Drop Dead." We might quibble over where to date the end of America's urban moment, but it clearly happened sometime in the third quarter of the twentieth century.

Second, during that same period, the nation lost its commitment to almost all things public. Americans in the first half of the century built the infrastructure of the public; in the second half we watched it crumble. John Kenneth Galbraith's famous 1958 summation of the nation as "private affluence and public squalor" was more prophetic than he could have ever known.[53] Public housing, public transportation, public education, public health, public welfare—now these are all under-funded, de-funded, privatized, or ignored altogether. At a political level, a number of historians have charted the decline of New Deal liberalism, dating it back in some cases to the New Deal itself.[54] Much of this schol-arship considers the New Deal and its descendants as a set of policy goals and political strategies. We should also recognize the extent to which those policies and strategies transformed the physical shape of the nation and in so doing helped recast the way Americans thought of and experienced the "public" and the "private."

Take the question of housing as an obvious example: On the one hand, the New Deal and its subsequent variants created public housing on a large (if never adequate) scale. On the other hand, the federal gov-ernment, through the Federal Housing Agency, subsidized tens of thou-sands of mortgages, which enabled hundreds of thousands of Americans to move into private homes in the suburbs. Thus space itself, in this case domestic space, became the way Americans encountered New Deal liber-alism on a daily basis.

In turn, space served as a kind of referendum on the success or failure of liberalism and helped people choose sides in the debate between the public and the private. Spaces served both to shape people's actual expe-riences and to symbolize the larger notion of liberalism. As the heady and hopeful years of the 1950s and 1960s slouched into the bitter and cynical 1970s and 1980s, the crumbling public housing projects, the antiquated and inefficient public transit networks, dangerous public parks, and a failing public education system stood metaphorically and literally for the collapsing public sphere. The denigration of our public infrastructure was both a consequence and a cause of the broader decline of liberalism.

Simultaneously, the universalizing conception of the public—that "family of man"—also began to erode. John Higham sees the disintegra-tion of universalism beginning in midcentury, but it surely accelerated in the 1960s and 1970s, and it came from two directions. From one side, as some Americans asserted specific racial, ethnic, or gender identities in opposition to that universalizing impulse, the "unum" was replaced with the "pluribus." As Higham describes it, "The tendency of cultural pluralists to emphasize the separateness of ethnic cultures in this coun-try [took] on a darker, anti-American meaning. Now any claim for cen-teredness, any affirmation of a unifying national culture, became *ipso facto* oppressive."[55] From the other, the attack on that New Deal liberal-ism, and on its public and urban aspects, replaced a notion of public good with a valorization of private pursuits. That substitution has contributed crucially to the growth and success of the New Right in American politics.

So by the end of the twentieth century, the institutions and spaces that constituted the public sphere had diminished considerably, and at the same time the public who utilized and shaped that infrastructure no longer saw itself as singular but rather as plural, if it saw itself as part of a larger whole at all. Americans, many of them at least, stopped dreaming common dreams.[56]

These three developments are related in all kinds of ways that have yet to be fully explored by historians. Before Habermas became required reading in American graduate seminars, Richard Sennett, as I have noted already, located the entire notion of the public sphere, and all its discontents, squarely in the city. Space, for Sennett, was a critical component of public life, and he complained, "Dead public space is one reason, the most concrete one, that people will seek out on intimate terrain what is denied them on more alien ground." More specifically, he thought urban public space was essential for public life and that only in an urban context could we really achieve that life. Writing in 1977, just two years after Ford told New York City to "drop dead," Sennett worried, "The extent to which people can learn to pursue aggressively their interests in society is the extent to which they learn to act impersonally." Sennett believed that "the city ought to be the teacher of that action, the forum in which it becomes meaningful to join with other persons without the compulsion to know them as persons. . . . But just that civilized possibility is today dormant."[57]

Museums—again, overwhelmingly urban institutions—participated in and responded to these shifts in several ways. Most directly, museum building has come to mirror the multiple constituencies that began to demand attention in the 1960s. We have already discussed in Chapter 1 the new museums founded around ethnic or racial specificity—Jewish museums, African American museums, and more recently the National Museum of the American Indian, which opened on the Mall in 2004; the Arab American National Museum, which opened in Dearborn, Michigan, in 2006; and the Italian American Museum in New York, which opened in 2008. At the same time, larger, well-established museums, especially those with increasingly contested collections of anthropological material, have strained to achieve a new social relevance. We might date the beginning of those efforts to 1967 when the Smithsonian sponsored the creation of the Anacostia Museum and located it in that economically struggling black section of the city, and to 1969 when Thomas Hoving mounted the huge and hugely controversial exhibit "Harlem on My Mind" at the Metropolitan.

In that same year, across the river in Brooklyn, a number of museums, community groups, and others came together for a three-day seminar on neighborhood museums. The transcripts of that seminar read now as almost quaint in their period anger, a reminder that even the records of the attempts to be relevant, to say nothing of the attempts themselves, run the risk of growing outdated very quickly. At one particularly preposterous moment, Jon Hendricks of the Guerilla Art Action Group interrupted the proceedings to denounce the assembled museum administrators, cultural workers, and community activists: "This gathering has all the smell of a Pentagon military strategy meeting, plotting for a Bay of Pigs invasion." As audience members, and not a few speakers, simultaneously denounced the museum and demanded more from it, Richard Grove of the John D. Rockefeller III Fund found himself puzzled: "The definition of a museum ordinarily means a place with a collection. In some cases I think we're talking about an activity center. My question is, which thing are we talking about?"[58] Which thing indeed?

Yet all this anger directed at the museum—this symposium in Brooklyn can serve as a three-day encapsulation of a much larger phenomenon swirling in the later 1960s and early 1970s—and all the denunciations that museums were not relevant to pressing social issues of the day only underscore just how important museums continued to be for people. The demands here were for inclusion, broadening, and a greater attention to a greater number of constituencies. If museums really were as hopeless as some of the overwrought rhetoric would have it, why bother getting so worked up in the first place? Instead, as symposium organizer Emily Dennis Harvey observed, people reached for "an entirely new way of thinking about museums and the public they served."[59] And museums have moved increasingly in these directions in the decades since. In the forty years since "Harlem on My Mind," efforts at relevance have produced exhibits that range from challenging and thought-provoking to pedantic and ham-handed. Whatever the result, the guiding principles have been largely the same. As Neil Harris put it in an address given in 1986, "The museum's voice is no longer seen as transcendent. Rather it is implicated in the distribution of wealth, power, knowledge, and taste shaped by the larger social order," and I suspect most museums would now fully agree. Echoing those assembled in Brooklyn in 1969, albeit in quieter tones, Richard Sandell, to take one example, believes that "museums and galleries of all kinds have both the potential to contribute towards the combating of social inequality and a responsibility to do so."[60]

While this concern for relevance, inclusion, and social responsibility began as a response to the politics of the 1960s, it also winds up tracking the Reaganite retreat from the public sphere we discussed earlier. To read the table of contents of Sandell's 2002 collection is to be presented with a social agenda. It includes essays about gay rights, the rights of indigenous people, overcoming trauma, public health, and racism. But to insist that museums take responsibility for social inequality is to acknowledge that these fights have largely left the political realm and are being fought instead on cultural terrain, at museums, universities, film festivals, and the like. By the turn of the twenty-first century, this confusion or elision of cultural politics with real politics had become endemic to both museums and universities, and while museums may have come a long way in confronting questions of "the distribution of wealth, power, knowledge and taste," real politics, the exercise of power on the public, has gone in exactly the opposite, vicious direction.

Museums have also responded to the changing conception the public has of itself as increasingly private, privatized, and suburbanized. Whereas once museums drew a line to separate their public obligations from the world of private commerce and profit, in the last quarter of the twentieth century museums began to erase that line. Corporate sponsorship of exhibits—especially "blockbuster" exhibits—grew during the 1980s, mirroring a kind of Reaganite ethos of that decade. Again the Metropolitan stood as exemplary, and particularly the exhibitions mounted by Diana Vreeland, but the phenomenon has been by no means limited to Fifth Avenue, nor to the world of art museums.[61] In the 1990s, as I've mentioned, the Field Museum entered into a sponsorship agreement with McDonald's to purchase Sue, the world's largest *Tyrannosaurus rex* skeleton.

More permanently, museums have devoted more and more of their interior space to commercial purposes—restaurants, cafés, bookstores, gift shops, and the like. When one can now buy reproductions of what one has just seen—"museum quality," after all—a trip through a museum today makes the worlds of art and commerce appear seamless. In this, as Neil Harris has astutely pointed out, museums help track a fundamental shift in the American political economy from producer to consumer. While Americans began to develop "consumer habits" in the 1920s, and museums began to recognize this changed nature of the American public in the 1930s, not until the 1960s did they begin to act on that recognition. According to Harris, "Thirty years after the Depression . . . museum professionals seemed stuck in a time warp. Few experiments had been tried or completed." That changed when museums began to apply the methods of social science opinion polling to the museum experience. Visitors now might find themselves filling out forms, answering questions, being asked to comment before, during, and after their stroll through the galleries. Thus museums entered, in Harris's apt phrase, the "age of populist deference," in which, after "many decades of indifference, ignorance, or neglect, carefully constructed sample surveys were created, with redefined mission statements and rhetorical commitments to change."[62]

Harris is largely right, but I would amend his observations slightly. Public opinion polling does not simply enable museums—or politicians or marketers, for that matter—to figure out what people really think or want. As Sarah Igo has demonstrated, asking Americans for their opinions about all sorts of things contributes to a changed way the public sees itself.[63] These opinion polls did not merely record that Americans saw themselves more and more as consumers—and less and less as citizens—in the second half of the twentieth century. More, it helped foster that process. Thus museum visitors now see themselves as consumers of whatever culture or entertainment museums have on offer in part because, by treating them more and more like consumers, museums in turn create those consumerist expectations. In other words, individuals feel that the museum should not respond to some sense of "us" but should cater to "me."

This reorientation of the museum's relationship with the public has been expressed architecturally, as various flavors of modernism replaced neoclassicism as the architectural vocabulary. Richard Bach had complained in 1927 that "to make [the museum] palatial, pompous or grand is to build up a kind of psychological barrier to its greatest use," and when the National Gallery of Art opened on the National Mall in 1941, it represented a last gasp of that older classicism.[64] When the East Wing of the National Gallery was built in 1978, I doubt the building committee spent much time thinking about columns and capitals. And certainly neoclassical idioms all but disappeared from museum architecture after the Second World War.

Without reading too much into the changing nature of these façades, we might see the arrival of modernist (and then postmodernist) architecture as part of that loss of universalism I mentioned earlier. If all turn-of-the-twentieth-century museums looked approximately the same, then that sameness signaled at some level that what went on inside them was approximately the same as well. At the turn of the twenty-first century, museums reach for an architectural particularity. This new generation of museums continues to exhibit objects, but now a certain distinctiveness rather than a kind of uniformity is the goal.

The Guggenheim presaged perhaps better than any other postwar institution the changing nature of the museum's relationship with a changing public. From the street, Frank Lloyd Wright's building makes a defiantly, arrogantly antiurban gesture. Wright stands, and I think not coincidentally, as the most celebrated American architect of the twentieth century and as one our most aggressive antiurbanists. His contempt for the American city drips from the pages of any number of his writings, and while some scholars, such as Robert Twombly, have found a characteristically American ambivalence toward the city in Wright's career, it seems unarguable that as he got older contempt replaced ambivalence more and more. "The modern city," Wright announced in 1956, "is a place for banking and prostitution and very little else."[65] The Guggenheim, the last of his buildings built during his lifetime as it turned out, culminated this antiurban career with a poke in the eye to the nation's premier city.

Once inside, visitors found themselves in a space that fundamentally altered their relationship with the objects on display, and thus with a fundamentally different experience than had been the case since the late nineteenth century. The Guggenheim is, simply, a terrible place to look at art and has been regarded as such almost from the moment it opened. The three-quarter-mile-long ramp subordinates the art on display to the building itself. Artist Robert Jay Wolff complained in 1960 that the individual works of art along the ramp "cling like postage stamps to the walls." In the same essay, Wolff made the intriguing suggestion that those postage stamps themselves were chosen for their ability to stand up to the harsh lighting and unrelenting whiteness of the walls. At the Guggenheim, he believed, "only the most aggressive paintings can survive." Of the museum as a whole, Wolff concluded, "The Guggenheim Museum is such an all out, unblushing revelation of the neurotic ego-mania behind current art patronage that all other museums, by comparison, can claim a pure and selfless dedication to the work of art."[66] We have moved from museum buildings built around collections to collections built around buildings.

I don't mean to browbeat the Guggenheim too much, but I do think it represents the first example of the museum building's replacing the museum collection as the focus of our attention. Nor do I think it purely coincidental that the Guggenheim has been an institution that has reconceived of the relationship between institution and public, locating itself on the cutting edge of where the museum meets commerce. It has pioneered the franchise museum; it has crossed the boundary between corporate sponsorship and corporate promotion with its special exhibit of Harley Davidson motorcycles, for example; and it has brought "high" art to Las Vegas. Former Guggenheim director Thomas Krens, explaining this last move, quipped, "You go where the heathens are," but in fact he is taking the Guggenheim where the money is, and where the consumption is most shamelessly conspicuous.

Krens is also responsible for the most naked, but perhaps most honest, definition of a successful museum in the twenty-first-century consumer age. He reduced the formula for success to these elements: "great collections, great architecture, a great special exhibition, a great second

Figure 34. Interior of the Solomon R. Guggenheim Museum, New York, a museum built to display the visitors. When the Guggenheim opened, it broke dramatically from the architecture that had governed museums for nearly three-quarters of a century. Photograph by Robert E. Mates, © The Solomon R. Guggenheim Foundation, New York.

exhibition, two shopping opportunities, two eating opportunities, a high-tech interface via the Internet, and economies of scale via a global network."[67] Never mind how we might assess "a great special exhibition," we've come a long way from the "public instruction" and "refined enjoyment" of the Progressive Era museum.

However crass Krens might sound, he is right at least at the level of description. Museums insist now on "signature" architecture for their new buildings and rely on that architecture to attract visitors. Indeed, without the commissions from museums and other cultural organizations, many of this generation's best-known architects would probably not have any work at all. Further, museums need the revenue generated from their commercial enterprises to keep up with rising costs and growing demands. Gone too are the days when wealthy museum trustees would simply underwrite the operating costs of museums with personal checks. In a final irony, in a postindustrial economy, cities themselves depend on their cultural institutions to generate significant economic activity. And at that level, regardless of how we might perceive our differences in multicultural America, we are all now consumers.

There is a final role museums now play in and with the public at the beginning of the twenty-first century, and let me come back to Frank Lloyd Wright's Guggenheim ramp for a moment. If you can't see the art very well, we might ask what you can see. The answer is, I think, each other. The sight lines at the Guggenheim, the nature of the spiral, and the vaulted space in the middle all make it far easier and more satisfying to look at the people in the building than at what is ostensibly on display.

This is not insignificant. In an era grown suspicious of the public realm, and with whatever didactic authority museums may once have had, museums continue to be viewed as acceptable, enjoyable, satisfying public space. Museums have fostered this by expanding their functions to include movies, live music, cultural demonstrations, and after-work cocktails. Elaine Heumann Gurian has proposed that the American Association of Museums include in its statement of principles that a core function of any museum is to be "a place of safety," where varieties of people can gather to exchange ideas and to interact with each other.[68] Wright may have been on to something. In an age when we no longer think in public terms or see ourselves as part of a commonweal, museums have become places where we can spend time out in public. They become places where we come to see ourselves, and in a hyperconsumer, postethnic society, while we may go bowling alone, we go to museums to be with other people. In other words, museums have become among the last places where the public can come and behave as a public in Sennett's sense—places where it is still possible to "behav[e] with strangers in an emotionally satisfying way and yet remain . . . aloof from them."

This may provide another explanation for the building boom museums are currently experiencing. In the introduction we discussed the risks and challenges of relying on culture to revitalize the economies of struggling cities. My sense, however, is that museums, whether in Roanoke, Milwaukee, or Chicago, serve as more than economic engines, even if that is usually how they are justified. They reflect and respond to a new interest in the city as well. The urban renaissance of the 1990s has certainly been tentative, has not been experienced equally everywhere, and has not really solved some of the most intractable urban problems.

Yet it is also undeniable that cities have come back. In Chicago, Philadelphia, Boston, and even in Columbus, Ohio, increasing numbers of people have moved into the city, into downtowns and revitalized neighborhoods. They have done so for any number of reasons, no doubt, but among them I am convinced is the desire to live in a place with a sense of place, a desire to develop a sense of civic identity. Museums are part of that equation, fostering as they do a distinctive cultural landscape that belongs to anyone who wants to share it. Their galleries and atriums, exhibits, and social gatherings provide people with the pleasures and possibilities of being out in and among the public.

In other words, museums serve as one of the "cosmopolitan canopies" that sociologist Eli Anderson has described. Those canopies offer public spaces for diverse people to gather. While we may see much of American life as segregated, these urban spaces bring people together, sometimes in ordinary, sometimes in remarkable ways. As I have argued throughout this chapter, museums (and we could add libraries as well) have always functioned in this way, and they continue to do so.[69]

Cities, at their best, are fundamentally public affairs. In a world of privatized space they offer sidewalks and squares; in a nation increasingly segregated by race and income, cities represent the broadest cross-section of American life. And in a nation of alienated individuals, cities offer us the easiest access to a larger civic life. That sense of civic belonging, offering us an identity connected to a place, may be what recommends cities to us more than anything else at the beginning of the twenty-first century. Museums have been and can continue to be part of what shapes that sense of civic identity. In the end, simply bringing us together, whether to marvel at art or explore questions of science, may be more precious than anything we come to see.

Notes

Introduction

1. Special Section, *New York Times*, April 24, 2002.

2. J. Trescott, "Exhibiting a New Enthusiasm across US, Museum Construction, Attendance, Are on the Rise," *Washington Post*, June 21, 1998.

3. See American Association of Museums Web site: www.aam-us.org.

4. Eilean Hooper-Greenhill, *Museums and the Shaping of Knowledge* (London: Routledge, 1992), 3.

5. Art historians Alan Wallach and Carol Duncan were among the very first scholars to bring a critical eye to the art museum, and not simply to the art that hangs on their walls. See Alan Wallach and Carol Duncan, "The Universal Art Museum," *Art History* 3 (1980): 448–69. Duncan later expanded some of the ideas in that essay in her book *Civilizing Rituals*. Among cultural historians, Neil Harris stands as a notable exception to the hagiographers. Harris began writing analytically about museums in the 1960s, placing their history in the larger context of American cultural development. His essays remain essential reading for anyone seeking to understand the history of the American museum and its cultural milieu.

6. Sharon Macdonald, "Expanding Museum Studies: An Introduction," in Sharon Macdonald, ed., *A Companion to Museum Studies* (Malden, Mass.: Blackwell, 2006), 1.

7. Randolph Starn, "A Historian's Brief Guide to New Museums Studies," *American Historical Review*, 110 (2005): 68–98.

8. Tony Bennett, *The Birth of the Museum: History, Theory, Politics* (London: Routledge, 1995), 95.

9. Douglas Crimp, *On the Museum's Ruins* (Cambridge, Mass.: MIT Press, 1993), 287.

10. While this approach "inspired fresh investigation," as Starn puts it, the limitations of Foucauldian analysis have also become quickly apparent. As long ago as 1994 Daniel Sherman and Irit Rogoff could write about a "shared intellectual formation" among museum scholars, but in fact that shared formation has become dogmatic, and as with all dogmas it begins with answers rather than with questions. Regardless of where we look across time or space, the same Foucauldian inputs have too often generated the same Foucauldian outputs. One scarcely has to read past the title of many books or articles to know what the conclusions will be. What's more, much of this scholarship chews more than it has bitten off. The results of the Foucauldian project to "unmask" the alleged disinterested and transparent nature of the museum do not come as a surprise

to anyone who has worked in museums or even to attentive museum-goers. It isn't clear why we need Foucault or Benjamin or Adorno to teach us that museums are large, complicated institutions with vested interests, multiple constituencies, and conflicting agendas. That doesn't mean they can't be many other things as well. Daniel J. Sherman and Irit Rogoff, "Introduction: Frameworks for Critical Analysis," in Daniel J. Sherman and Irit Rogoff, eds., *Museum/Culture: Histories, Discourses, Spectacles* (Minneapolis: University of Minnesota Press, 1994); Ivan Gaskell, review in *Art Bulletin* 77 (1995): 673–75.

11. Timothy W. Luke, *Museum Politics: Power Plays at the Exhibition* (Minneapolis: University of Minnesota Press, 2002), 4.

12. Nick Prior, "Having One's Tate and Eating It," in Andrew McClellan, ed., *Art and Its Publics: Museum Studies at the Millennium* (Malden, Mass.: Blackwell, 2003), 57.

13. Andreas Huyssen, *Twilight Memories: Marking Time in a Culture of Amnesia* (London: Routledge, 1995), 18. Andrea Whitcomb provides a very useful summary of the changing drifts of museum scholarship in chapter 1 of *Re-Imagining the Museum: Beyond the Mausoleum* (London: Routledge, 2003).

14. Michael Ames, "Biculturalism in Exhibitions," *Museum Anthropology* 15: 13.

15. Sally Gregory Kohlstedt, "'Thoughts in Things': Modernity, History and North American Museums," *Isis* 96 (2005): 592–93.

16. In an essay on an entirely different subject, Mark Lilla has wonderfully described the confederation of "critical theory, deconstruction, postmodernism, postcolonial studies, and the like" as a "foggy archipelago." See Mark Lilla, "A New, Political Saint Paul?" *New York Review of Books,* October 23, 2008, 69.

17. See Steven Conn, *Museums and American Intellectual Life, 1876–1926* (Chicago: University of Chicago Press, 1998), esp. chapter 1.

18. Sharon Macdonald, introduction, Sharon Macdonald and Gordon Fyfe, *Theorizing Museums: Representing Identity and Diversity in a Changing World* (Oxford: Blackwell, 1996), 5. Alan Wallach, *Exhibiting Contradictions: Essays on the Art Museum in the United States* (Amherst: University of Massachusetts Press, 1998), 121. See also Patricia Pierce Erikson, "Representing 'The World Boiled Down,'" *American Anthropologist* 106 (2004): 374–79.

19. George Brown Goode, *The Principles of Museum Administration* (York: Coultas and Volans, Exchange Printing Works, 1895), 22. I used Goode's organizational scheme as the basis for my book *Museums and American Intellectual Life, 1876–1926.*

20. Edward Said, "Representing the Colonized: Anthropology's Interlocutors," *Critical Inquiry* 15 (1989): 213.

21. Daniel Sherman, introduction, in Daniel Sherman, ed., *Museums and Difference* (Bloomington: Indiana University Press, 2008), 7–8. Though published after Starn's essay, several of the essays in this volume suffer from exactly the sort of sameness that he pointed out among other studies of museums.

22. I have taken this episode from Neil MacGregor, "A Pentecost in Trafalgar Square," *Antioch Review* 61 (2003): 762–63. Thanks to Bob Fogarty for pointing this out to me.

23. Martin Filler, "Broad-Minded Museum," *New York Review of Books*, March 20, 2008, 15.

24. It is a constant of museum history that those who ran them have fretted about what they were doing. John Cotton Dana, from his post at the Newark Museum, issued the boldest challenges to the function and purpose of the

Beaux-Arts museum in the 1920s and 1930s. Roughly forty years later, in 1972, Brian O'Doherty edited a collection of essay simple titled *Museums in Crisis* (New York: George Braziller). And so it has gone.

25. Sally Kohlstedt, "International Exchange and National Style: A View of Natural History Museums in the United States, 1850–1900," in Nathan Reingold and Marc Rothenberg, eds., *Scientific Colonialism: A Cross Cultural Comparison* (Washington, D.C.: Smithsonian Institution Press, 1987), 169.

26. Quoted in Pamela J. Podger, "With Bold Museum, Virginia City Aims for Visibility," *New York Times*, December 29, 2007.

27. Pierre Nora, "Between Memory and History: Les Lieux de Mémoire," *Representations* 26 (1989): 9, 12.

28. Henry Adams, *The Education of Henry Adams* (Boston: Houghton Mifflin, 1918, 1922), 382, 496–97.

29. This comes from Judt's book *Reappraisals: Reflections on the Forgotten Twentieth Century*. I have quoted it from Jonathan Freedland, "A Case of Intellectual Independence," *New York Review of Books*, October 9, 2008, 34.

30. Paul Ricoeur, *Memory, History, Forgetting* (Chicago: University of Chicago Press, 2004), 413.

Chapter 1

A version of this chapter was presented at the Ethnohistory Workshop at the University of Pennsylvania in January 2007. I would like to thank Greg Urban and Nancy Farriss for inviting me to what proved to be a wonderful and lively conversation, and Robert Preucel and Crystal Biruk for their sharp critiques. Another version was presented at the University of Michigan Museum Studies Program. Thanks to Ray Silverman and Hannah Smotrich for bringing me to Ann Arbor. And thanks to Bruce Grant, who, with his usual generosity of spirit, cut to the chase with this chapter and showed me how to improve it.

1. Stephan Bann, "The Return to Curiosity: Shifting Paradigms in Contemporary Museum Display," in McClellan, ed., *Art and Its Publics: Museum Studies at the Millennium*, 118.

2. Cited in Igor Kopytoff, "The Cultural Biography of Things," in Arjun Appadurai, ed., *The Social Life of Things: Commodities in Cultural Perspective* (Cambridge University Press, 1986), 90.

3. Goode, *Principles of Museum Administration*, 22.

4. Stephen Weil, "From Being *about* Something to Being *for* Somebody: The Ongoing Transformation of the American Museum," in *Making Museums Matter* (Washington, D.C.: Smithsonian Institutions Press, 2002), 28–29.

5. See, e.g., Sally Gregory Kohlstedt, "Otis Mason's Tour of Europe: Observation, Exchange and Standardization, in Public Museums, 1889," *Museum History Journal* 1 (2008): 181–209.

6. Dorothy Canfield Fisher, *Why Stop Learning?* (New York: Harcourt, Brace and Company, 1927), 250–51.

7. Kopytoff, "Cultural Biography of Things," 82–83.

8. See Walter Benjamin, "The Work of Art in the Age of Mechanical Reproduction," in *Illuminations* (New York: Harcourt Brace and World, 1962), 219–53.

9. Paul Valéry, "The Conquest of Ubiquity," in *Aesthetics*, vol. 13 of *The Collected Works of Paul Valéry*, trans. Ralph Manheim (New York: Bollingen Foundation, 1964), 225.

10. Most important, see George Stocking, ed., *Objects and Others: Essays on*

Museums and Material Culture (Madison: University of Wisconsin Press, 1985). See also Curtis Hinsley, *Savages and Scientists: The Smithsonian Institution and the Development of American Anthropology, 1846–1910* (Washington, D.C.: Smithsonian Institution Press, 1981), and "The Museum Origins of Harvard Anthropology," in *Science at Harvard University: Historical Perspectives* (Bethlehem, Pa.: Lehigh University Press, Associated University Press, 1992). A number of works, especially in the European context, examine the intersection of museums, anthropology, and colonialism. For example, H. Glenn Penny, *Objects of Culture: Ethnology and Ethnographic Museums in Imperial Germany* (Chapel Hill: University of North Carolina Press, 2002), and Tony Bennett, *Pasts beyond Memory: Evolution, Museums, Colonialism* (London: Routledge, 2004).

11. David Hurst Thomas, "Margaret Mead as a Museum Anthropologist," *American Anthropologist* 82, no. 2, In Memoriam Margaret Mead (1901–1978) (June 1980): 354–61.

12. Conn, *Museums and American Intellectual Life*, chapter 3.

13. This episode is described in John Haddad, " 'To Inculcate Respect for the Chinese': Berthold Laufer, Franz Boas, and the Chinese Exhibits at the American Museum of Natural History, 1899–1912," *Anthropos* 101 (2006): 140–41.

14. A. L. Kroeber, "The Place of Anthropology in Universities," *American Anthropologist* 56 (1954): 764.

15. Donald Collier and Harry Tschopik Jr., "The Role of Museums in American Anthropology," *American Anthropologist* 56 (1954): 772–75.

16. Anthony Alan Shelton, "Museums and Anthropologies," in Macdonald, ed., *Companion to Museum Studies*, 71–72.

17. Collier and Tschopik, "Role of Museums," 774.

18. Hudson, quoted in Shelton, "Museums and Anthropologies," 73.

19. William C. Sturtevant, "Does Anthropology Need Museums?" *Proceedings of the Biological Society of Washington, DC* 82 (1969): 619–50.

20. Dell Hymes's edited volume *Reinventing Anthropology* (New York: Vintage Books, 1974) gathered together several important essays assessing this crisis in anthropology and was among the first books to do so.

21. Saloni Mathur, "Redefining the Ethnographic Object: An Anthropology Museum Turns Fifty," *American Anthropologist* 102 (2000): 593. See also David Julian Hodges, "Museums, Anthropology, and Minorities," *Anthropology & Education Quarterly* 9.

22. John Terrell, "Disneyland and the Future of Museum Anthropology," *American Anthropologist* 93 (1991): 149.

23. I should qualify this a little. As far back as 1889, the Cincinnati Museum Association, the organization that built the wonderful Cincinnati Museum of Art, acquired 1,300 African objects from Carl Steckelmann. I do not know much about the Steckelmann collection, nor am I aware of another major art museum in the nineteenth century collecting African material.

24. Arthur Danto, "Defective Affinities: Primitivism in 20th Century Art," *Nation*, December 1, 1984, 590–92. There is an irony, unintended I suspect, in Danto's jibe. At the turn of the twentieth century, department stores aspired to look like museums, and vice versa. The urge toward system and organization in the material world of the late Victorians extended to the home and the store as well as the museum. See, e.g., John Henry Hepp IV, *The Middle-Class City: Transforming Space and Time in Philadelphia, 1876–1926* (Philadelphia: University of Pennsylvania Press, 2003).

25. Ira Jacknis, *The Storage Box of Tradition: Kwakiutl Art, Anthropologists, and Museums, 1881–1981* (Washington, D.C.: Smithsonian Institution, 2002), 261.

26. Steven Conn, "Heritage vs. History at the National Museum of the American Indian," *Public Historian* 28 (2006): 69–73.

27. See Ellen Fitzpatrick, *History's Memory: Writing America's Past, 1880–1980,* (Cambridge, Mass.: Harvard University Press, 2002).

28. Andrew McClellan, "A Brief History of the Art Museum Public," in *Art and Its Publics,* 39.

29. Ralph Appelbaum, "Anthropology, History and the Changing Role of the Museum," in Tsong-yuan Lin, ed., *Proceedings of the International Conference on Anthropology and the Museum* (Taipei: Taiwan Museum, 1995), 252.

30. David Lowenthal, *Possessed by the Past: The Heritage Crusade and the Spoils of History* (New York: Free Press, 1996), 128.

31. I have taken these statements from each museum's Web site.

32. Scelsa, quoted in Carlin Romano, "Italian American Museum Opens in New York's Little Italy," *Philadelphia Inquirer,* October 13, 2008.

33. Emily Dennis Harvey, "Anatomy of Anger," in Emily Dennis Harvey and Bernard Friedberg, eds., *A Museum for the People* (New York: Arno Press, 1971), x. For the most thorough consideration of how the notion of culture was bastardized in the second half of the twentieth century, see David Steigerwald, *Culture's Vanities: The Paradox of Diversity in a Globalized World* (Lanham, Md.: Rowman and Littlefield, 2004).

34. See Edward Rothstein, "Slavery's Harsh History Is Portrayed in Promised Land," *New York Times,* August 18, 2004. Quotes taken from this review.

35. Lois H. Silverman, "The Therapeutic Potential of Museums as Pathways to Inclusion," in Richard Sandell, ed., *Museums, Society, Inequality* (London: Routledge, 2002), 69.

36. See C. Vann Woodward, *American Attitudes toward History* (Oxford: Clarendon Press, 1955), 1–20.

37. Appelbaum in Lin, *Proceedings of the International Conference on Anthropology and the Museum,* 259.

38. Noam Shoval and Elizabeth Strom, "Inscribing Universal Values into the Urban Landscape: New York, Jerusalem and Winnipeg as Case Studies," unpublished paper.

39. American Museum of Natural History, *Guide,* 1972, 127; Sullivan, quoted in Frank Talbot, "Anthropology and the Museum: Cultures in Conflict," in Lin, *Proceedings of the International Conference on Anthropology and the Museum,* 4.

40. Stephan F. de Borhegyi, "A New Role for Anthropology in the Natural History Museum," *Current Anthropology* 10, no. 4 (October 1969): 368.

41. Ibid.

42. Edward Rothstein, "Museums That Tell What to Think," *New York Times,* April 20, 1997.

43. I take this figure from Robert Kohler, *All Creatures: Naturalists, Collectors, and Biodiversity, 1850–1950* (Princeton, N.J.: Princeton University Press, 2006), 113.

44. John Pickstone, *Ways of Knowing: A New History of Science, Technology and Medicine* (Manchester, UK: Manchester University Press, 2000), 73.

45. Albert Parr, review, *Progressive Architecture,* July 1966, found in AMNH Archives, Parr Mss., Call No. P372.

46. Flowers, quoted in "Museums and Their Purposes," *The Museum News* 1 (March 1906): 110.

47. David Murray, *Museums: Their History and Their Use* (Glasgow: James MacLehose and Sons, 1904), 187–88, 285.

48. Albert Parr, "A Plea for Abundance," *Curator* (1959), reprint without page numbers, in AMNH Archives, Parr Collection, Call No. P373.

49. Pickstone, *Ways of Knowing*, 75.

50. Leonard Krishtalka and Philip Humphrey, "Can Natural History Museums Capture the Future?" *BioScience* 50 (2000): 611–17. See also Peter Davis, *Museums and the Natural Environment: The Role of Natural History Museums in Biological Conservation* (London: Leicester University Press, 1996).

51. Oskar von Miller, "German Museum in Munich," *American Society of Civil Engineers, Proceedings* 52 (1926): 13.

52. I thank Robert Anderson for showing me the notebook he found detailing this long march through the Deutsches Museum.

53. Quoted in Donald A. Shelley, "Henry Ford and the Museum," *Antiques at the Henry Ford Museum* (New York: 1958), 4–6.

54. Bernard Finn, "The Science Museum Today," *Technology and Culture* 6 (1965): 78.

55. See Samuel J. M. M. Alberti, "Objects and the Museum," *Isis* 96 (2005): 559.

56. Finn, "Science Museum Today," 77.

57. Quoted in Susan Stewart, *On Longing: Narratives of the Miniature, the Gigantic, the Souvenir, the Collection* (Baltimore: Johns Hopkins University Press, 1984), 162.

58. Thanks to Crystal Biruk and Sally Kohlstedt for helping me clarify my thoughts about this.

Chapter 2

1. Barbara Gallatin Anderson, "Adaptive Aspects of Culture Shock," *American Anthropologist* 73 (1971): 1121.

2. Mark Leone, Parker Potter, and Paul Shackel, "Toward a Critical Archaeology," *Current Anthropology* 28 (1987): 284.

3. James C. Faris, "'ART/Artifact': On the Museum and Anthropology," *Current Anthropology* 29 (1988): 771n8.

4. See, e.g., Cressida Fforde, Jane Hubert, and Paul Turnbull, eds., *The Dead and Their Possessions: Repatriation in Principle, Policy and Practice* (London: Routledge, 2002); Tamara Bray, ed., *The Future of the Past: Archaeologist, Native Americans and Repatriation* (New York: Garland Books, 2001); Joe Edward Watkins, *Sacred Sites and Repatriation* (Philadelphia: Chelsea House, 2006); Kathleen Dare, *Grave Injustice: The American Indian Repatriation Movement and NAGPRA* (Lincoln: University of Nebraska Press, 2002). For an important consideration of repatriation and antiquities, see James Cuno, *Who Owns Antiquity: Museums and the Battle over Our Ancient Heritage* (Princeton, N.J.: Princeton University Press, 2008).

5. I largely agree with Marshall Sahlins, who quipped that for academics resistance has come to mean "translating the apparently trivial into the fatefully political." For a terrific critique of resistance, at least in the context of contemporary anthropology, see Michael Brown, "On Resisting Resistance," *American Anthropologist* 98 (1996): 729–35.

6. *New York Times Magazine,* June 24, 2007.

7. Jack F. Trope and Walter R. Echo-Hawk, "The Native American Graves

Protection and Repatriation Act Background and Legislative History," in Devon A. Mihesuah, ed., *Repatriation Reader: Who Owns American Indian Remains* (Lincoln: University of Nebraska Press, 2000), 123.

8. I am indebted to my colleague Lucy Murphy for bringing this to my attention.

9. See John Henry Merryman, "Two Ways of Thinking about Cultural Property," *American Journal of International Law* 80 (1986): 831–53.

10. Ibid., 845, 846.

11. Edward Sapir, "Culture, Genuine and Spurious," *American Journal of Sociology* 29 (1924): 404–5.

12. Thanks again to Lucy Murphy for supplying this information.

13. James Riding In, "Repatriation: A Pawnee's Perspective," in Devon A. Mihesuah, ed., *Repatriation Reader: Who Owns American Indian Remains*, 115. Riding In, despite his deep misgivings about Western institutions, is a faculty member at Arizona State University. While the title of the essay promises "a Pawnee's perspective," there is nothing in it that is in any way unique to the Pawnee, at least as far as I can discern.

14. Rick Hill, "Repatriation Must Heal Old Wounds," in Tamara L. Bray and Thomas W. Killion, eds., *Reckoning with the Dead: The Larsen Bay Repatriation and the Smithsonian Institution* (Washington, D.C.: Smithsonian Institution, 1994), 185.

15. In December 2007 Romney said, "Religion is seen as merely a private affair with no place in public life. It is as if they are intent on establishing a new religion in America—the religion of secularism. They are wrong."

16. Vine Deloria Jr., "Secularism, Civil Religion, and Religious Freedom," in Devon A. Mihesuah, ed., *Repatriation Reader: Who Owns American Indian Remains*, 169–79. Deloria claims that abortion is the only issue into which right-wing religion has successfully injected itself. One could argue that that issue was important enough on its own to recommit us to the thorough separation of church and state. But Deloria does not acknowledge the other ways in which religion has infected the public realm. The neocreationists, for example, have scored some successes in either including creationism in the science class or forcing curricula to misrepresent Darwinian evolution as "only a theory," but they have been much more successful in intimidating teachers into not teaching anything about the origins of life on the planet at all. (Similarly, they have intimidated doctors to such an extent that more and more do not perform abortions, fearing their own personal safety.) Overwhelming majorities of my students report that their high school science teachers skipped the topic entirely for fear of offending the local Christian mafiosi. Deloria's own investment here may have been particularly personal because his grandfather was an Episcopal priest and his father an Episcopal archdeacon. Deloria himself received a degree in theology from the Lutheran School of Theology. Thanks to David Watt for pointing this out to me.

17. Hill, "Repatriation Must Heal Old Wounds," 185; Russell Thornton, "Repatriation as Healing the Wounds of the Trauma of History," in Cressida Fforde, Jane Hubert, and Paul Turnbull, eds., *The Dead and Their Possessions: Repatriation in Principle, Policy and Practice*, 23.

18. John Higham, "Multiculturalism and Universalism: A History and Critique," *American Quarterly* 45 (1993): 211.

19. Adam Kuper, "Culture, Identity and the Project of a Cosmopolitan Anthropology," *Man*, n.s., 29 (1994): 538.

20. Hill, "Repatriation Must Heal Old Wounds," 186.

21. Jonathan Friedman, for one, sees an academic corollary. He attributes the "spate of articles and collections on ethnicity in the past few years" written by academics as a reaction "to the tidal wave of ethnicity and roots that has engulfed their identityless, if not alienated, existences." See Jonathan Friedman, "The Past in the Future: History and the Politics of Identity," *American Anthropologist* 94 (1992): 849.

22. I get these numbers from Robert Preucel of the University of Pennsylvania Museum. Many thanks.

23. See Kwame Anthony Appiah, *Cosmopolitanism: Ethics in a World of Strangers* (New York: W. W. Norton and Company, 2006); Michael F. Brown, *Who Owns Culture* (Cambridge, Mass.: Harvard University Press, 2003); and Michael F. Brown, "Can Culture Be Copyrighted?" *Current Anthropology* 39 (1998): 193–222.

24. Appiah, *Cosmopolitanism*, 130.

25. Ibid., 124.

26. Michael F. Brown, *Who Owns Native Culture?* (Cambridge, Mass.: Harvard University Press, 2003), 243.

27. Kwame Anthony Appiah, "Whose Culture Is It?" *New York Review of Books*, February 9, 2006.

28. Ibid. Appiah's ideas are further elaborated in his book, *Cosmopolitanism*.

29. Steigerwald, *Culture's Vanities*, 196. See particularly chapters 5 and 6.

30. I sketch this out in my book *History's Shadow: Native Americans and Historical Consciousness in the Nineteenth Century* (Chicago: University of Chicago Press, 2004).

31. Dell Hymes, "The Use of Anthropology: Critical, Political, Personal," in Hymes, ed., *Reinventing Anthropology*, 3.

32. The highest profile repatriation controversy involves the remains of Kennewick Man.

33. Ruth Benedict, *Patterns of Culture* (Boston: Houghton Mifflin, 1934), xi.

34. Redfield, quoted in Patty Jo Watson, "Archaeology, Anthropology, and the Culture Concept," *American Anthropologist* 97 (1995): 683.

35. Ibid., 685.

36. Alfred Kroeber and Clyde Kluckhohn, *Culture: A Critical Review of Concepts and Definitions* (New York: Vintage Books, 1952), 3.

37. Ibid., 357, 365.

38. Ibid., 272–73.

39. James Clifford, "On Collecting Art and Culture," in Simon During, ed., *The Cultural Studies Reader* (London: Routledge, 1993), 61, Mead quoted on 60.

40. Jacknis, *Storage Box of Tradition*, 209; Anna Laura Jones, "Exploding Canons: The Anthropology of Museums," *Annual Review of Anthropology* 22 (1993): 202.

41. Ian Hodder, "Post-modernism, Post-structuralism and Post-processual Archaeology," in Ian Hodder, ed., *The Meaning of Things: Material Culture and Symbolic Expression* (London: Unwin Hyman, 1989), 72–73.

42. Jonathan Haas, "Power, Objects, and a Voice for Anthropology," *Current Anthropology* 37 (1996): S 1.

43. Wolf, quoted in Watson, "Archaeology, Anthropology, and the Culture Concept," 684.

44. NAGPRA, Section 1D. The National Park Service maintains a terrific NAGPRA Web site where the text of the legislation can be found: http://www.nps.gov/history/nagpra/MANDATES/INDEX.HTM.

45. Many thanks to Wendy White, Office of General Counsel, University of Pennsylvania, for clarifying this for me.

46. See Johannes Fabian, *Time and the Other: How Anthropology Makes Its Object* (New York: 1983); and most famously Edward Said, *Orientalism* (New York: Pantheon Books, 1979), quote from 325.

47. Kuper, "Culture, Identity and the Project of a Cosmopolitan Anthropology," 542.

48. See, e.g., several of the essays in Mary Bouquet, ed., *Academic Anthropology and the Museum: Back to the Future* (New York: Berghahn Books, 2001).

49. Kuper, "Culture, Identity and the Project of a Cosmopolitan Anthropology," 545.

50. I am grateful to my colleague Angela Brintlinger for suggesting the analogy between Bakhtin's chronotope and the issue of repatriation.

51. Lowenthal, *Possessed by the Past*, 128.

52. Brown, *Who Owns Native Culture?* 4.

53. Friedman, "The Past in the Future," 853–54.

54. Clifford, "On Collecting Art and Culture," 51–52.

55. See Kopytoff, "Cultural Biography of Things." Samuel J. M. M. Alberti has written nicely about this idea in the context of objects in museums in his essay "Objects and the Museum," 559–71.

56. Laurier Turgeon, "The Tale of the Kettle: Odyssey of an Intercultural Object," *Ethnohistory* 44 (1997): 17.

57. Ibid., 21.

58. For a complete account of the Raven Cape, see Adria H. Katz, "The Raven Cape: A Tahitian Breastplate Collected by Louis Shotridge," in Susan A. Kaplan and Kristin J. Barness, eds., *Raven's Journey: The World of Alaska's Native People* (Philadelphia: University Museum, University of Pennsylvania, 1986), pp. 79–82. Quotes taken from this essay. I thank my two children, Olivia and Zachary Brintlinger-Conn, for bringing this object to my attention.

59. Appiah, *Cosmopolitanism*, 126.

Chapter 3

Parts of this chapter appeared in Steven Conn, "Where Is the East? Asian Objects in American Museums from Nathan Dunn to Charles Frees," *Winterthur Portfolio* 35 (2000): 157–73. The author thanks Avital and Hannah Smotrich-Barr, Anne Theisen, Lui Haiping of Nanjing University, Ankeny Weitz, Barbara Groseclose, Judy Wu, Peter Conn, Chris Reed, and Colleen Hennesey of the Freer Library and Archives, and Angela Brintlinger for their help. Other parts are greatly expanded from a paper I delivered at a symposium examining the display of Asian art in Western museums; the symposium was held at King's College, Cambridge, in 2004. I am indebted to the participants for their enthusiasm for this paper and for their good ideas.

1. Van Wyck Brooks, *New England: Indian Summer* (New York: Dutton, 1940), 367–68.

2. I use the term *Asia* when in fact I largely mean China and Japan. I do so because of my sense that people at the time had little interest in, or cognizance of, Southeast Asia or the Korean peninsula. The Indian subcontinent presents another case altogether, but I will not touch on it here.

3. Throughout this chapter I use the words *objects, material*, and *artifacts* more or less interchangeably. I do so precisely because they are vague terms and

underscore the confusion concerning how to categorize Asian cultural production. Benjamin March, *China and Japan in Our Museums* (Chicago: University of Chicago Press, 1929), 2.

4. Ibid., 34, 50, 87.

5. Craig Clunas, "Oriental Antiquities/Far Eastern Art," in Tani E. Barlow, ed., *Formations of Colonial Modernity in East Asia* (Durham, N.C.: Duke University Press, 1997), 418.

6. Stewart, *On Longing*; James Clifford, *The Predicament of Culture: Twentieth Century Ethnography, Literature, and Art* (Cambridge, Mass.: Harvard University Press, 1988).

7. For an account of Dunn's museum, its origins, and its fate, see John Haddad, "The Romantic Collector in China: Nathan Dunn's Ten Thousand Chinese Things," *Journal of American Culture* 21, no. 1 (Spring 1998): 7–26; Warren Cohen, *East Asian Art and American Culture: A Study in International Relations* (New York: Columbia University Press, 1992).

8. Hubert Howe Bancroft, *The Book of the Fair* (Chicago: Bancroft Company, 1893), 760.

9. Cohen, *East Asian Art,* 35.

10. Ibid., 87.

11. E. C. Wines, *A Peep at China in Mr. Dunn's Chinese Collection* (Philadelphia: Nathan Dunn, 1839), 10.

12. Buckingham, quoted in John Haddad, *The Romance of China: Excursions to China in U.S. Culture, 1776–1876* (New York: Columbia University Press, 2006), chapter 4, p. 14, formerly located at www.egutenberg-e.org. For more on the East Asia Marine Society, see Haddad, "Romantic Collector in China," 17–18.

13. Benjamin Silliman, "Nathan Dunn's Chinese Collection at Philadelphia," *American Journal of Science and Arts* 35 (1839): 391.

14. For descriptions of the museum, see Wines, *Peep at China*: Silliman, "Nathan Dunn's Chinese Collection at Philadelphia," 391–400; Nathan Dunn, *"Ten Thousand Chinese Things": A Descriptive Catalogue of the Chinese Collection in Philadelphia* (Philadelphia: Printed for the proprietor, 1839); and Haddad, "Romantic Collector in China"; "Review of William Langdon's 'Ten Thousand Things,'" *Chinese Repository* 12, no. 11 (November 1843): 563.

15. There are important connections between American and European museum practices; on Asian art in British museums, see Clunas, "Oriental Antiquities/Far Eastern Art." The debate between art and anthropology also seems to have taken place in England in the nineteenth century. "Review of E. C. Wines, *A Peep at China,*" *Chinese Repository* 8, no. 11 (March 1840): 583–84; Dunn, *"Ten Thousand Chinese Things,"* title page.

16. Wines, *Peep at China,* 12–14; Philadelphia *Public Ledger*, December 28, 1838; "Chinese Collection," *Philadelphia Saturday Courier,* December 22, 1838.

17. Robert Nicholas Fowler, *A Visit to Japan, China and India* (London: Sampson Low, Marston, Searle and Rivington, 1877), 79–80.

18. *North American Review* 47, no. 101 (October 1838): 404; *North American Review* 67, no. 404 (October 1848): 269.

19. *North American Review* (1838): 404.

20. Wines, *Peep at China,* 96; *North American Review* (1848): 270.

21. Wines, *Peep at China,* 90, 96; Silliman, "Nathan Dunn's Chinese Collection at Philadelphia," 395.

22. Hone and Langdon are both quoted in Cohen, *East Asian Art,* ii. Lawrence Levine, *Highbrow/Lowbrow: The Emergence of Cultural Hierarchy in America*

(Cambridge, Mass.: Harvard University Press, 1988); *North American Review* (1848): 270.

23. On the question of Orientalism, see Said, *Orientalism*; Edward Graham, "The 'Imaginative Geography' of China," in Warren Cohen, ed., *Reflections of Orientalism* (East Lansing: Michigan State University Press, 1983). On the relevance of Said to China scholarship, see Gail Hershetter, "The Subaltern Talks Back: Reflections on Subaltern Theory and Chinese History," *positions* 1 (1993): 103–30. For the most recent in a long series of books that have exposed the conceptual and evidentiary limits of Said's hugely influential book, see Daniel Martin Varisco, *Reading Orientalism: Said and the Unsaid* (Seattle: University of Washington, 2007); Ibn Warraq, *Defending the West: A Critique of Edward Said's Orientalism* (Amherst, N.Y.: Prometheus, 2007); and Robert Irwin, *Dangerous Knowledge: Orientalism and Its Discontents* (Woodstock, N.Y.: Overlook, 2006).

24. *North American Review* (1838): 404.

25. For more on Peters, see Haddad, *Romance of China*, chapter 7.

26. On Dunn's London experience, see Haddad, "Romantic Collector in China." For a description of the Boston museum, see "The Chinese Museum in Boston," *The Merchant's Magazine and Commercial Review* 14, no. 4 (April 1846): 347–49; on Peter's Museum and Barnum's display, see John Kuo Wei Tchen, *New York before Chinatown: Orientalism and the Shaping of American Culture, 1776–1883* (Baltimore: Johns Hopkins University Press, 1999), esp. 113–23.

27. Frank Leslie, *Frank Leslie's Historical Register of the Centennial Exposition, 1876* (New York: Frank Leslie, 1877), 244, 248.

28. Haddad, *Romance of China*, esp. chapter 1.

29. "Fogyism and Progress," *Cincinnati Daily Gazette*, May 24, 1876.

30. *The Empire of Japan: A Brief Sketch of the Geography, History, and Constitution* (Philadelphia: William F. Kildare, 1876); James McCabe, *The Illustrated History* of the Centennial Exhibition (Philadelphia: National Publishing, 1876), 415–17. On the Japanese exhibits in 1876, see Sylvia Yount, " 'Give the People What They Want': The American Aesthetic Movement, Art Worlds, and Consumer Culture, 1876–1890" (Ph.D. diss., University of Pennsylvania, 1995), 72–85; Neil Harris, "All the World a Melting Pot? Japan at American Fairs, 1876–1904," in Akira Iriye, ed., *Mutual Images: Essays in American-Japanese Relations* (Cambridge, Mass.: Harvard University Press, 1975), 46.

31. William R. Johnston, *William and Henry Walters, The Reticent Collectors* (Baltimore: Johns Hopkins University Press in association with the Walters Art Gallery, 1999), 73, 189–90.

32. McCabe, *Illustrated History*, 418–19.

33. Frank Leslie, *Masterpieces of the Centennial International Exhibition* (Philadelphia: Gebbie and Barrie, 1876), 249–50. In a similar vein, Thomas Eakins's 1875 masterpiece, *The Gross Clinic*, was relegated to the medical exhibits.

34. Rand, McNally, and Co.'s *Handbook of the World's Columbian Exposition* (Chicago: Rand, McNally, and Co., 1893), 156. The quote from Uncle Jeremiah appears in Robert Rydell, *All the World's a Fair: Visions of Empire at American International Expositions, 1876–1916* (Chicago: University of Chicago Press, 1984), 50.

35. Emilie V. Jacobs, *Asia in Topical Outline* (Philadelphia: Christopher Sower, 1913), 12, 48. Japan's virtues also impressed Harvard philosopher Josiah Royce, who made frequent reference to Japanese society, especially in his lectures on "loyalty." See Josiah Royce, *The Philosophy of Loyalty* (New York: Macmillan Company, 1924).

36. For a discussion of the Japanese and Chinese participation in the fair,

and for a larger discussion of the racial dimensions of anthropology at the fair, see Rydell, *All the World's a Fair,* esp. 48–52; "Empire in Catalepsy," *Spectator* 80 (April 9, 1898): 501, 502; "Vivisection of China," *Atlantic* 82, no. 49 (September 1898): 329–38; "Three Rotten Cultures: Roman, Chinese and Indian," *Spectator* 82 (March 18, 1899): 375–76.

37. Mason, quoted in Rydell, *All the World's a Fair,* 55–58.

38. Ernest Fenollosa, "Chinese and Japanese Traits," *Atlantic* 69, no. 416 (June 1892): 769–74.

39. Haddad, " 'To Inculcate Respect for the Chinese,' " 124.

40. Boas quoted in ibid., 131.

41. Boas quoted in Haddad, " 'To Inculcate Respect for the Chinese,' " 134.

42. Clark Wissler, quoted in Haddad, " 'To Inculcate Respect for the Chinese,' " 141.

43. *Bulletin of the Free Museum of Science and Art* (June 1899): 71. See University of Pennsylvania Alumni Register (January 1900): 4, 5, 7, for another description of the original layout of the museum.

44. "Eastern Art and Western Critics," *Edinburgh Review* 212, no. 434 (October 1910): 456.

45. Silliman, "Nathan Dunn's Chinese Collection," 391.

46. *Bulletin of the Cleveland Museum of Art,* November 1915, 3.

47. Foreword by Worcester Reed Warner in *Selections from Oriental Objects of Art Collected by Worcester Reed Warner* (Tarrytown, N.Y., for the Cleveland Museum of Art 1921).

48. Catalogue of the Inaugural Exhibition of the Cleveland Museum of Art (Cleveland, Ohio: Cleveland Museum of Art, 1916), 139.

49. Laurence Binyon, "The Art of Asia," *Atlantic Monthly* 6, no. 3 (September 1915): 348; Grace Dunham Guest, "Collection of American and Oriental Art Exhibited at the Freer Gallery in Washington," *United States Daily,* July 8, 1927.

50. Agnes Meyer, "The Charles L. Freer Collection," *The Arts* 12, no. 2 (August 1927): 76–78. On the creation of the museum and negotiations with Samuel Pierpont Langley of the Smithsonian, see Charles Lang Freer to Samuel Pierpont Langley, January 18, 1904, correspondence file, "Gift to Nation, 1902, 1904, 1905," Charles Lang Freer Papers, Freer Gallery of Art Archives, Washington, D.C. (hereafter cited as Freer Archives); Charles Moore to Theodore Roosevelt, November 1, 1905, correspondence file, "Gift to Nation, 1902, 1904, 1905," Charles Lang Freer Papers, Freer Archives.

51. Mary Warner Blanchard, *Oscar Wilde's America: Counterculture in the Gilded Age* (New Haven, Conn.: Yale University Press, 1998). On Whistler and Japanese motifs, see Clay Lancaster, *The Japanese Influence in America* (New York: Walton H. Rawls, 1963), 34. Jeffrey Nunokawa, "Oscar Wilde in Japan: Aestheticism, Orientalism, and the Derealization of the Homosexual," *positions* 2 (1994): 51. For a discussion of Freer's enthusiasm for aestheticism, see Thomas Lawton and Linda Merrill, *Freer: A Legacy of Art* (Washington, D.C.: Smithsonian Institution Press, 1993). For a larger discussion of the movement and its relation to consumer culture, see Yount, "Give the People What They Want," 170.

52. Catalogue of the Inaugural Exhibition of the Cleveland Museum of Art, 165.

53. Binyon, "Art of Asia," 359, 357; "New Books Reviewed," *North American Review* 197, no. 689 (April 1913): 567.

54. Julia Meech, "Collecting Japanese Art in America," in Julia Meech and Gabriel Weisberg, *Japonisme Comes to America: The Japanese Impact on Graphic Arts, 1876–1925* (New York: Harry N. Abrams, 1990), 47.

55. Van Wyck Brooks, "Ernest Fenollosa and Japan," *Proceedings of the American Philosophical Society* 106 (1962): 107–10.

56. Meyer, "Charles L. Freer Collection," 69, 81–82.

57. *Washington Intelligencer,* October 26, 1919; *Boston Evening Transcript,* May 5, 1923; Meyer, "Charles L. Freer Collection," 67; Linda Merrill, ed., *With Kindest Regards: The Correspondence of Charles Lang Freer and James McNeil Whistler, 1890–1903* (Washington, D.C.: Smithsonian Institution Press, 1995), 42.

58. Freer to Langley, January 18, 1904, Freer Archives; Binyon, "Art of Asia," 354.

59. Freer to Langley, December 27, 1904, Freer Archives.

60. Ernest Fenollosa, "The Collection of Mr. Charles L. Freer," *Pacific Era* 1, no. 2 (November 1907): 57–66.

61. As long ago as 1954, the Wenner-Gren Foundation sponsored a conference at the University of Pennsylvania Museum to consider the place of museums in the history and future of American anthropology. See Collier and Tschopik, "Role of Museums in American Anthropology," *American Anthropologist* 56 (October 1954): 768–79. For more on the relationship between anthropology and museums, see Hinsley, "Museum Origins of Harvard Anthropology," 521; George Stocking, "Philanthropoids and Vanishing Cultures: Rockefeller Funding and the End of the Museum Era in Anglo-American Anthropology," in Stocking, ed., *Objects and Others;* Conn, *Museums and American Intellectual Life,* chapter 3. On Boas's museum career, see Ira Jacknis, "Franz Boas and Exhibits: On the Limitations of the Museum Method of Anthropology," in Stocking, ed., *Objects and Others,* 75–111.

62. Clunas, "Oriental Antiquities/Far Eastern Art," 419; *Handbook, Section of Oriental Art* (Philadelphia: University of Pennsylvania Museum, 1917), 3.

63. Carter, quoted in March, *China and Japan,* v–vi.

64. John C. Huntington and Dina Bangdel, *The Circle of Bliss: Buddhist Meditational Art* (Chicago: Serindia Publications for the Columbus Museum of Art, 2003), 19. In fairness, some of the massive catalogue, at more than five hundred pages and weighing in at probably seven pounds, does address these Western art historical concerns. I haven't had the heart to tell my friend, however, that Hinduism is given pretty short shrift in this huge book.

65. Stewart, *On Longing,* 151.

66. Huntington and Bangdel, *The Circle of Bliss,* 19.

67. For more on the founding of the museum, see my book *Museums and American Intellectual Life, 1876–1926,* esp. chapter 3.

68. Harry Dillon Jones, "God, Gems, and Mascots: The Life-Work of Maxwell Sommerville," *Booklovers Magazine* 4 (July 1904): 59.

69. Ibid., 59. Sommerville published an account of his travels in Thailand in 1897 as *Siam on the Meinam from the Gulf to Ayuthia* (London: Sampson, Low Marston and Co.), a book described by Michael Smithies as "banal." See Smithies, ed., *Descriptions of Old Siam* (Oxford: Oxford University Press, 1995), 238.

70. Stewart Culin, "The Professor of Glyptology," unpublished, undated ms in the Culin Collection, Brooklyn Museum of Art. The word isn't in the dictionary anymore, at least not in the *Oxford English Dictionary* I consulted. Sommerville's gem collection was widely known and admired, at least for a time. The Metropolitan Museum of Art wanted the gems badly and even had display cases custom built for them—at no small expense—in the hope of enticing Sommerville to donate them. See letter from Director di Cesnola, April 18, 1891, in the Sommerville Correspondence File, archives, University of Pennsylvania Museum.

71. *Evening Telegraph,* May 3, 1899; letter from Sommerville to Pepper, December 3, 1895, Sommerville Correspondence File, archives, University of Pennsylvania Museum.

72. *Philadelphia Times,* May 4, 1899; *Philadelphia Press,* May 4, 1899. Both clippings can be found in the Maxwell Sommerville biography file in the archives of the University of Pennsylvania Museum.

73. Maxwell Sommerville, *Monograph of the Buddhist Temple in the Free Museum of Science and Art* (Philadelphia: Sherman and Co. Press, 1900), 3.

74. Ibid., 3.

75. Ibid., 7.

76. Jones, "God, Gems, and Mascots," 59.

77. Somerville, 3; *Philadelphia Times,* May 4, 1899; *Evening Telegraph,* May 3, 1899.

78. "Oriental Loath to Leave Buddha," *Philadelphia Inquirer,* April 1, 1903.

79. Jones, "God, Gems, and Mascots," 61.

80. Culin, "Professor of Glyptology."

81. March, *China and Japan,* 50.

82. For more on Cushing and his role in the formation of ideas about "culture," see Brad Evans, "Cushing's Zuni Sketchbooks: Literature, Anthropology, and American Notions of Culture," *American Quarterly* 49 (1997): 717–45. The essay cites most of the important work on Cushing.

83. T. J. Jackson Lears, *No Place of Grace: Antimodernism and the Transformation of American Culture, 1880–1920* (New York: Pantheon, 1981), xiii.

84. Brooks, *New England,* 367–68.

85. Lears and Chanler, both quoted in Lears, *No Place of Grace,* 228.

86. Sommerville, *Monograph of the Buddhist Temple,* 19.

87. Ralph Adams Cram, *Impressions of Japanese Architecture and the Allied Arts* (New York: Baker and Taylor, 1905).

88. Lears, *No Place of Grace,* 187.

89. For a description of the early exhibits at the East India Marine Society museum, see Walter Muir Whitehill, *The East India Marine Society and the Peabody Museum of Salem: A Sesquicentennial History* (Salem, Mass.: Peabody Museum, 1949).

90. Brooks, "Ernest Fenollosa and Japan," 106.

91. The best biography of Fenollosa remains Lawrence Chisolm, *Fenollosa: The Far East and American Culture* (New Haven, Conn.: Yale University Press, 1963), though the book is a bit too hagiographical for my taste.

92. Adams to Hay, July 9 and 27, 1886, in Worthington Chauncy Ford, *Letters of Henry Adams, 1858–1891* (Boston: Houghton Mifflin, 1930), 366–69, 372.

93. See Chisolm, *Fenollosa,* esp. 243; and Robert Kern, *Orientalism, Modernism, and the American Poem* (Cambridge: Cambridge University Press, 1996), chapter 5.

94. For more on the relationship between Cram, Wright, and modernism, see Peter Conn, *The Divided Mind: Ideology and Imagination in America, 1898–1917* (Cambridge: Cambridge University Press, 1983).

95. *Evening Telegraph,* May 3, 1899.

96. Brooks, "On Creating a Usable Past," *Dial* 64 (1918): 337–41.

97. Ibid., 340.

98. Van Wyck Brooks, *Fenollosa and His Circle; with Other Essays in Biography* (New York: Dutton, 1962).

99. Quoted in Thomas Donaldson, *The George Catlin Indian Gallery in the U.S.*

National Museum (Washington, D.C.: Government Printing Office, 1887), 719. For a fuller discussion of Catlin and his project, see my book *History's Shadow: Native Americans and Historical Consciousness in the Nineteenth Century,* chapter 2.

100. Randolph Bourne, "Trans-National America," *Atlantic Monthly* 118 (1916): 86–97.

101. Arif Dirlik, "Chinese History and the Question of Orientalism," *History and Theory* 35 (1996): 102, 112, 113.

102. Chisolm, *Fenollosa,* 97.

103. *Philadelphia Inquirer,* September 6, 1897.

104. "Chinamen Appeal," *Philadelphia Inquirer,* March 8, 1895.

105. Culin, "Professor of Glyptology."

106. Chisolm certainly believes this was behind Fenollosa's work.

107. Brooks, "On Creating a Usable Past," 338.

108. See Chisolm, *Fenollosa,* 48; Adams to Hay, August 22, 1886, in Ford, *Letters of Henry Adams,* 374–76.

109. Stewart, *On Longing, 139.*

110. See Conn, *Museums and American Intellectual Life, 1876–1926,* esp. chapter 1.

111. Quoted in Chisolm, *Fenollosa,* 7.

112. "Doubtful Treasures," *New York Tribune,* January 1, 1906.

113. For a thorough description of Dunn's museum, see Haddad, *Romance of China,* chapter 4.

114. Culin, "Professor of Glyptology."

115. Eighteenth-century English painter Sir Joshua Reynolds, to take just one example, famously drew this line between fact and truth when talking about history painting.

116. I generalize here. On the one hand, many small art museums consist largely of single collections, reflecting the taste and idiosyncrasies of the collector. On the other hand, the Metropolitan coalesced as a collection of collections. "Philadelphia's Great Art Museum," *Philadelphia Inquirer,* November 29, 1927; "New Museum Plan Is Pageant of Art," *Philadelphia Inquirer,* December 11, 1927; Fiske Kimball, "Museum Values," *American Magazine of Art* 19, no. 9 (September 1928): 480–82; Kimball Collection, PMA Archives. The completion of Kimball's "main street" had to wait until the 1990s. For a variety of reasons, legal and otherwise, it was only then that the PMA could undertake a major reinstallation of its holdings and complete the walk.

117. In the art museum in Shanghai, which I had the opportunity to visit shortly after it opened in 1997, objects are arranged so that medium is privileged over chronology or geography. The major galleries are organized by ceramics, jade, lacquer, painting, and so on.

Chapter 4

I want to thank Sally Kohlstedt for reading—and improving—this chapter.

1. Watson, quoted in Alan Riding, "Napoleon's Toothbrush Finally Has a Home," *New York Times,* June 21, 2007.

2. Figures cited in Franklin Institute *Annual Report,* 1999, 1.

3. Natalie Angier, *The Canon: A Whirligig Tour of the Beautiful Basics of Science* (Boston: Houghton Mifflin, 2007), 1–2.

4. "President's Message," American Museum of Natural History, *Annual*

Report, 1945, 4; "President's Message," American Museum of Natural History, *Annual Report*, 1947–48, n.p.

5. I have taken this from a letter Osborn wrote to R. C. Andrews, June 9, 1927, American Museum of Natural History archives. I suspect he used it elsewhere as well.

6. American Museum of Natural History, *Annual Report*, 1874, 46.

7. Albert Parr, American Museum of Natural History, *Annual Report*, 1945, 11; Minutes of the Plan and Scope Committee, March 9, 1942, American Museum of Natural History Archives.

8. Albert Parr, American Museum of Natural History, *Annual Report*, 1942, 17; Unidentified manuscript, American Museum of Natural History archives, Parr Mss P373.

9. Ann Reynolds has examined Warburg Hall in relation to Parr's ideas about education. See Ann Reynolds, "Visual Stories," in Lynne Cooke and Peter Wollen, eds., *Visual Display: Culture Beyond Appearances* (Seattle, Wash.: Bay Press for the Dia Center for the Arts, 1995), 82–109.

10. American Museum of Natural History, *Annual Report*, 1952–53, 10; Department of Education, *Annual Report*, 1952–53, 8.

11. Albert Parr, "Confidential Report," 1944, American Museum of Natural History Archives, Parr Mss, P371, 1.

12. Quoted in Reynolds, "Visual Stories," 90.

13. "President's Message," American Museum of Natural History, *Annual Report*, 1942, 1 and 3.

14. Alfred Parr, "Towards New Horizons," American Museum of Natural History, *Annual Report*, 1946–47, 9–10.

15. "President's Message," AMNH, 1945, 3.

16. Parr, "Confidential Report," 1944, 6–7.

17. Ronald Rainger, *Agenda for Antiquity: Henry Fairfield Osborn and Vertebrate Paleontology at the American Museum of Natural History, 1890–1935* (Tuscaloosa: University of Alabama Press, 1991), see 3–23.

18. Parr, "Confidential Report," 6–7.

19. Albert Parr, "Thoughts on Museum Policy in Regard to Research," undated pamphlet, American Museum of Natural History Archives, Parr Mss, P372.

20. *Buffalo Courier-Express,* June 18, 1953.

21. AMNH, *Annual Report*, 1874, 42.

22. "Report of the President," American Museum of Natural History, *Annual Report*, 1923, 1; and "The American Museum and Education," *Annual Report*, 1924, 5.

23. American Museum of Natural History, *The American Museum of Natural History: An Interpretation* (New York: published for the American Museum of Natural History, 1931), 43.

24. In certain respects, the AMNH was catching up with other natural history museums. Lecturers had been used in the Boston Museum of Natural History since the turn of the century, and several museums had created special children's rooms. Thanks to Sally Kohlstedt for bringing this to my attention.

25. Henry Fairfield Osborn, "The American Museum and Education," *Annual Report*, 1924, 5.

26. AMNH, *American Museum of Natural History: An Interpretation*, 49.

27. American Museum of Natural History, *Annual Report*, 1945, 1947–48, 1949–50, 13, 1, and n.p.

28. Figure cited in American Museum of Natural History, *Annual Report*, 1971–72, 2.

29. American Museum of Natural History, *Annual Report*, 1949–50, 1965–66, n.p., 11.

30. AMNH, *Annual Report*, 1971–72, 8.

31. John Michael Kennedy, "Philanthropy and Science in New York City: The American Museum of Natural History, 1868–1968" (Ph.D. diss., Yale University, 1968), Jesup quoted on 92 and 60.

32. Ibid., see 149, 213–14.

33. Cited in Mary Anne Andrei, "Nature's Mirror: The Taxidermists Who Shaped America's Natural History Museums and Saved Our Endangered Species" (unpublished ms), 257.

34. AMNH, *Annual Report*, 1965–66, 11.

35. Much of the material from the Centennial did go to Washington, D.C., to fill the new Arts and Industries building next to the Smithsonian's "Castle," where some of it can still be seen today.

36. Charles Richards, *The Industrial Museum* (New York: Macmillan, 1925), 48. Thanks to Ben Gross for bringing this book to my attention.

37. Bruce Sinclair, *Philadelphia's Philosopher Mechanics: A History of the Franklin Institute, 1824–1865* (Baltimore: Johns Hopkins University Press, 1974). Recently Princeton graduate student Ben Gross has begun serious research on some of the institute's twentieth-century history. I have relied on Sinclair and on Gross's unpublished essay "The Antithesis of the Attic" (2007) for this early history of the institute.

38. Walter A. R. Pertuch, "Reminiscences," *Journal of the Franklin Institute* 259 (1955): 1. The building still stands, now the home of the Atwater Kent Museum.

39. Maurice R. Davie, *Problems of City Life: A Study in Urban Sociology* (New York: John Wiley and Sons, 1932), 509. Davie noted that both museums were modeled on the Deutsches Museum in Munich, which he called "the most remarkable institution of its kind in the world."

40. Waldemar Kaempffert, "The Great Museum of the Machine Age," *New York Times*, October 26, 1930.

41. Herman Kogan, *A Continuing Marvel: The Story of the Museum of Science and Industry* (Garden City, N.Y.: Doubleday and Company, 1973), 51–52.

42. "Oomph for Science," *Time*, September 2, 1940, 42.

43. Mike Wallace, "Progress Talk: Museums of Science, Technology and Industry," in *Mickey Mouse History and Other Essays on American Memory* (Philadelphia: Temple University Press, 1996), 81.

44. F. C. Brown, "Building a Museum to Human Specification," *Scientific Monthly* (1928): 193–94.

45. Ibid., 195–96, 201.

46. Harland Manchester, "Museums Don't Have to Be Stuffy," *Saturday Evening Post*, January 15, 1949, 90.

47. See Robert P. Multhauf, "European Science Museums," *Science* 128 (1958): 512–19.

48. Robert P. Shaw, "Scientific Exhibits and Their Planning," *Scientific Monthly* 35 (1932): 372.

49. Howard McClenahan, "Present and Proposed Activities of the Franklin Institute," *Journal of the Franklin Institute* 206 (1928): 747–48.

50. Ibid., 747–48.

51. Shaw, "Scientific Exhibits and Their Planning," 370; Kaempffert's ideas are recounted in Kogan, *Continuing Marvel,* 61–62.

52. Manchester, "Museums Don't Have to Be Stuffy," 90–93.

53. McClenahan, "Present and Proposed Activities of the Franklin Institute," 748, 750.

54. David G. Wittels, "Where Every Man's an Einstein," *Saturday Evening Post,* August 29, 1942, 16+; Manchester, "Museums Don't Have to Be Stuffy," 32.

55. Wittels, "Where Every Man's an Einstein," 17; Manchester, "Museums Don't Have to Be Stuffy," 32.

56. Herbert Nichols, "Where Doing Is Believing," *Christian Science Monitor,* January 4, 1941, 8.

57. Parr, "Plea for Abundance," n.p.

58. Figures from Manchester, "Museums Don't Have to Be Stuffy," 94.

59. Ibid.

60. See Franklin Institute, *Annual Report,* 1960, n.p.; undated, unidentified Fact Sheet, Franklin Institute Archives; Michelle Tucker, "A Partnership for Public Education: Reinventing the Franklin Institute, 1925–1934," *Penn History Review* 8 (2000): 10.

61. Benjamin C. Gruenberg, *Science and the Public Mind* (New York: McGraw-Hill, 1935), 117; Robert H. Morey, "Education in Science Museum," *Science,* June 30, 1944, 535–36; *The Institute News,* May 1936, n.p.

62. See Kogan, *Continuing Marvel,* 83–84.

63. Ibid., 42.

64. For a quick history of the Committee on Science and the Arts, see A. Michael McMahon, "The Committee on Science and the Arts of the Franklin Institute, 1824–1900" (Wilmington, Del.: Scholarly Resources, n.d.), xiii–xxxiv.

65. Thomas Coulson, "The First Hundred Years of Research at the Franklin Institute," *Journal of the Franklin Institute* 256 (1953): 24. I have quoted Bartol from this essay as well.

66. A. Michael McMahon, " 'Bright Science' and the Mechanic Arts: The Franklin Institute and Science in Industrial America, 1824–1976," *Pennsylvania History* 46 (1980): 366–68.

67. See "An Unplanned Legacy: The Story of the Franklin Institute," unidentified ms, Franklin Institute Archives, 3; Franklin Institute, *Annual Report,* 1983, 1, 10.

68. Franklin Institute, *Annual Report,* 1989, n.p. Interestingly, the Deutsches Museum, which served as the initial inspiration for the Franklin Institute Science Museum, continues to maintain its research and academic activities. They occupy a large section of this sprawling museum complex.

69. Paul Goldberger, "A Born-Again Franklin Institute Banishes Stodginess," *New York Times,* June 10, 1990.

70. Franklin Institute, *Annual Report,* 1960, n.p.

71. "Everyman's Learning Laboratory: A Plan for the Franklin Institute Science Museum's 150th Anniversary" (Philadelphia: Franklin Institute Research Labs, 1969), 9.

72. Albert Parr, "The Museum Meets the Public," *Natural History,* May 1943, 161.

Chapter 5

I presented an initial version of this essay at the Powerhouse Museum in Sydney, Australia, in 2005 as part of the museum's anniversary celebration. Thanks to Roy Macleod for his kind invitation.

1. There were at least a few other "commercial" museums founded at roughly the same moment, including one in Germany and the museum now called the Powerhouse in Sydney.

2. Andrew Carnegie, "Value of World's Fairs to the American People," *The Engineering Magazine* 6 (January 1894): 417.

3. *The Philadelphia Museums: Dedication of the Museums by President McKinley, Report of the Annual Meeting of the International Advisory Board* (Philadelphia: n.p., 1897), 52.

4. Unidentified newspaper clipping, Saturday, May 14, 1927.

5. W. E. Hoyle, "The Philadelphia Commercial Museum," *The Museums Journal* 1 (1901–2): 107.

6. Morris Jastrow to Pepper, May 3, 1897, Pepper Papers, Department of Special Collections, Van Pelt Library, University of Pennsylvania, vol. 8, 1571.

7. Paul Cherington, "The Philadelphia Commercial Museum," *World Today*, May 14, 1908.

8. See Conn, *Museums and American Intellectual Life, 1876–1926*, esp. chapter 1.

9. Field Museum Archive, Director's Correspondence, William P. Wilson to Edward Ayer, July 16, 1894.

10. W. P. Wilson, "The National Export Exposition," *Lippincott's Magazine* 64 (1899): 465.

11. I have taken the phrase from Joel Williamson's *A Rage for Order: Black-White Relations in the American South since Emancipation* (New York: Oxford University Press, 1986). That book covers a very different subject but much the same period. The phrase itself has a much earlier history in American scholarship, including in Austin Warren's 1948 book on literary criticism.

12. Hepp, *Middle-Class City*, 4–7.

13. See Hepp, *Middle-Class City*; Stephen Kern, *The Culture of Time and Space, 1880–1913* (Cambridge, Mass.: Harvard University Press, 1983).

14. See, e.g., William Leach, *Land of Desire: Merchants, Power, and the Rise of a New American Culture* (New York: Pantheon Books, 1993); Hepp, *Middle-Class City*, chapter 6; and Susan Porter Benson, *Counter Cultures: Saleswomen, Managers and Customers in American Department Stores, 1890–1940* (Urbana: University of Illinois Press, 1986).

15. John Wanamaker, "The Evolution of the Mercantile Business," *Annals of the American Academy of Political and Social Science* 15 (1900): 123–35.

16. William Pepper, *Proceedings of the 1st Annual Meeting of the Advisory Board*, June 3 and 4, 1896, 12.

17. *The Philadelphia Commercial Museum* (Philadelphia: Commercial Museum, 1909), n.p.

18. *Philadelphia Museums*, 75.

19. William Harvey, "A School for American Businessmen," *Appleton's Magazine* 11 (February 1908): 216–26.

20. Wilson, "National Export Exposition," 465.

21. John S. Lopez, "First Aid for the Exporter," *Harper's Weekly*, April 24, 1912, 9–10.

22. See *Philadelphia Museums*, 87.

23. Unidentified clipping, May 24, 1945. In fact, the postwar era was a pivotal time in the history of women's stockings. See Susan Smulyan, *Popular Ideologies: Mass Culture at Mid-Century* (Philadelphia: University of Pennsylvania Press, 2007). Thanks to Michael Kammen for pointing this out to me.

24. Unidentified newspaper clipping, May 12, 1956.

25. Unidentified newspaper clipping, March 18, 1960.

26. See Conn, *Museums and American Intellectual Life, 1876–1926*, chapter 7.

27. T. R. Adam, *The Museum and Popular Culture* (New York: American Association for Adult Education, 1939), 133.

28. Ibid.

29. Joseph Jackson, *Encyclopedia of Philadelphia*, vol. 2 (Harrisburg, Pa.: National Historical Association, 1931), 508–9.

30. *Elementary School Journal* (September 1921): 12.

31. William Wilson, "The Philadelphia Commercial Museum," *Forum* 28 (September 1899): 116.

32. W. M. Davis, "The Progress of Geography in the United States," *Annals of the Association of American Geographers* 14 (1924): 201.

33. Dorothy Frafly, "Art from the Congo Is on Display," *Philadelphia Evening Bulletin*, August 3, 1958.

34. I have taken these quotes from Steven Sass, *The Pragmatic Imagination: A History of the Wharton School, 1881–1981* (Philadelphia: University of Pennsylvania Press, 1982), 21–23.

35. Unidentified newspaper clipping, May 14, 1927.

36. See Wharton files, University of Pennsylvania Archives.

37. Wilson, "National Export Exposition," 466.

38. George Bruce Cortelyou, "Some Agencies for the Extension of Our Domestic and Foreign Trade," *Annals of the American Academy of Social and Political Science* 24 (1904): 2.

39. B. M. Headicar, "Industrial and Commercial Libraries of the Future," *Economica* 3 (October 1921): 261.

40. Oliver Farrington, "The Museum as an Educational Institution," *Education* 17 (1897): 482.

41. Pepper, *Proceedings of the 1st Annual Meeting of the Advisory Board*, June 3 and 4, 1896, 12.

42. Harvey, "School for American Businessmen," 219; Wilson, "National Export Exposition," 469.

43. Davie, *Problems of City Life*, 508.

44. J. A. Stewart, "Where Science Is Allied to Commerce," *Chautauquan* 38 (1903): 264–66.

Chapter 6

I presented an early version of this chapter at the Humanities Institute at Temple University. Many thanks to Susanna Gold and Richard Immerman for the invitation. Parts of it were also presented to a splendid panel at the American Studies Association meeting in October 2007.

1. I should confess that I have had my own small history with Thomas Jefferson University. Some years ago I was involved in a public conflict over the pro-

posed construction of a new parking garage that required more than a dozen zoning variances for approval. Those of us who opposed this parking garage were accused by Jefferson's lawyer in a public hearing of "holding up a cure for cancer." The behemoth garage was eventually built, occupying an entire city block, but as of this writing Jefferson has not announced a cure for cancer.

2. The victory was not without its costs. The Pennsylvania Academy sold *The Cello Player,* another wonderful Eakins painting, to raise cash.

3. Francis Henry Taylor, *Babel's Tower: The Dilemma of the Modern Museum* (New York: Columbia University Press, 1945), 31.

4. Richard Sennett, *The Fall of Public Man* (New York: Alfred A. Knopf, 1977), 340.

5. Stephen E. Weil, "The Museum and the Public," in *Making Museums Matter* (Washington, D.C.: Smithsonian Institution Press, 2002), 195–96, 213.

6. Jay Cantor, "Temples of the Arts: Museum Architecture in Nineteenth-Century America," *The Metropolitan Museum of Art Bulletin,* n.s., 28 (April 1970): 350.

7. Ibid., 353.

8. See Conn, *Museums and American Intellectual Life, 1876–1926,* esp. chapter 1.

9. Bennett, *Birth of the Museum,* 95, 98.

10. Taylor, *Babel's Tower: The Dilemma of the Modern Museum,* 21.

11. Sophie Forgan points out that this was true even in Europe, stressing that it is important to consider the urban as well as the national context of museums in the major metropolises. See "Building the Museum: Knowledge, Conflict, and the Power of Place," *Isis* 96 (2005): 580.

12. "Chicago Doing It First," *New York Times,* August 19, 1926.

13. Russell Anderson, Letter to the Editor, *Science* 103 (1946): 342; "The City's Missing Museum," *New York Times,* November 23, 1959.

14. *Bulletin of the Cleveland Museum of Art,* November 1915, 3.

15. Edward S. Morse, "If Public Libraries, Why Not Public Museums?" *Atlantic* 72 (1893): 119.

16. Nicolai Ouroussoff, "Art Museum Mixes Pomp and Hint of Pop," and Roberta Smith, "Rounding Up the Usual Suspects," *New York Times,* February 15, 2008.

17. Peale, quoted in David Brigham, *Public Culture in the Early Republic* (Washington, D.C.: Smithsonian Institution Press, 1995), 5. Of course, many farmers probably already understood the relationship of snakes to moles.

18. Richard Bach, "The Fogg Museum of Art," *Architectural Record* 61 (1927): 466. American Museum of Natural History, *General Guide, 1953* (New York: American Museum of Natural History), 8.

19. See Kohler, *All Creatures.* Kohler's is the first major study I have found of the process behind amassing the collections of American natural history museums.

20. See Jurgen Habermas, *The Structural Transformation of the Public Sphere* (Cambridge, Mass.: MIT Press, 1989).

21. Philip Ethington, *The Public City: The Political Construction of Urban Life in San Francisco, 1850–1900* (Cambridge: Cambridge University Press, 1994), 15; John Dewey, *The Public and Its Problems* (New York: Henry Holt and Company, 1927, 1946), 142.

22. Morse, "If Public Libraries, Why Not Public Museums," 112–19.

23. Frederick Law Olmsted, "Public Parks and the Enlargement of Towns,"

in Frederick Law Olmsted, *Civilizing American Cities: Writings on City Landscapes*, ed. S. B. Sutton, (New York: De Capo Press, 1997), 75.

24. See AMNH, *Annual Report*, 1874, 42; *Philadelphia Inquirer*, November 27, 1897.

25. "Sunday Opening of Museums," *Christian Union*, June 19, 1890; Gilman, quoted in McClellan, "Brief History of the Art Museum Public," 19.

26. Fisher, *Why Stop Learning?* 241–42.

27. "Report of a Survey of Visitors," *Pennsylvania Museum Bulletin* 25 (1929): 2–11.

28. Warren Susman, *Culture as History: The Transformation of American Society in the Twentieth Century* (New York: Pantheon Books, 1984), 54. In fact, I think the original phrase may be Lindsay's, though at this writing I cannot find his use of it.

29. Vachel Lindsay, *The Art of the Moving Picture* (New York: Macmillan Company, 1916); Susman, *Culture as History*, xvii; John Cotton Dana, *The New Museum* (Woodstock, Vt.: Elm Tree Press, 1917), 15.

30. Davie, *Problems of City Life*, 506.

31. Alfred Goldsborough Mayer, "Educational Efficiency of Our Museums," *North American Review* 177 (1903): 565.

32. American Museum of Natural History Archives, Administrative Records, Education Department Annual Report, 1930, 2.

33. Mayer, "Educational Efficiency of Our Museums," 564.

34. James Truslow Adams, *Frontiers of American Culture: A Study of Adult Education*, (New York: Charles Scribner's Sons, 1944), 234. Adams quotes the figure but does not provide the source. Manchester, "Museums Don't Have to Be Stuffy," 94.

35. Sennett, *Fall of Public Man*, 18.

36. Wallach and Duncan, "Universal Art Museum," 451–52.

37. For the best treatment of this phenomenon, see David A. Hollinger's essay "How Wide the Circle of the 'We?': American Intellectuals and the Problem of the Ethnos since World War II," *American Historical Review* 98 (1993): 317–37.

38. American Museum of Natural History Archives, Unidentified mss, Parr Mss, Call No. P372.

39. T. R. Adam, *The Civic Value of Museums* (New York: American Association for Adult Education, 1937), viii; Taylor, *Babel's Tower*, 50.

40. Herman Bumpus, "The Museum as a Factor in Education," *Independent* 61 (1906): 269.

41. Davie, *Problems of City Life*, 509; Grace Fisher Ramsey, *Educational Work in Museums of the United States: Development, Methods and Trends* (New York: H. W. Wilson, 1938). For the AMNH adult education division, see Adam, *Civic Value of Museums*, 88. It is certainly true that other museums, notably in Boston, had established education departments well before the 1930s. Thanks to Sally Kohlstedt for bringing this to my attention.

42. Adam, *Civic Value of Museums*, 98.

43. Clement Greenberg, "Avant-Garde and Kitsch," *Partisan Review* (1939): 34–49.

44. Adam, *Civic Value of Museums*, 103.

45. Ibid., 7, 57.

46. For a recent assessment of this achievement, see Nick Taylor, *American Made: The Enduring Legacy of the WPA* (New York: Random House, 2008).

47. Daniel Rodgers, *Atlantic Crossings: Social Politics in a Progressive Age* (Cambridge, Mass.: Belknap Press of Harvard University Press, 1998), 112.

48. Jane De Hart Mathews, "Arts and the People: The New Deal Quest for Cultural Democracy," *Journal of American History* 62 (1975): 323.

49. See Robert D. Leighninger Jr., "Cultural Infrastructure: The Legacy of New Deal Public Space," *Journal of Architectural Education* 49 (1995–96): 226–36.

50. Taylor, *Babel's Tower*, 23; Francis Henry Taylor, "Museums in a Changing World," *Atlantic Monthly* 164 (1939): 792.

51. De Hart Mathews, "Arts and the People," 320; Youtz, quoted in Neil Harris, "Polling for Opinions," *Museum News* 69 (1990): 49.

52. John Cotton Dana, "Should Museums Be Useful?" in William A. Peniston, ed., *The New Museum: Selected Writings by John Cotton Dana* (Newark, N.J.: Newark Museum and the American Association of Museums, 1999), 136.

53. The phrase comes from his book *The Affluent Society* (Boston: Houghton Mifflin, 1958).

54. See Alan Brinkley, *The End of Reform: New Deal Liberalism in Recession and War* (New York: Alfred A. Knopf, 1995); and Steve Fraser and Gary Gerstle, eds., *The Rise and Fall of the New Deal Order, 1930–1980* (Princeton, N.J.: Princeton University Press, 1989).

55. Higham, "Multiculturalism and Universalism," 206.

56. I have taken this phrase from the title of Todd Gitlin's book *Twilight of Common Dreams* (New York: Metropolitan Books, 1995).

57. Sennett, *Fall of Public Man*, 15, 340.

58. Harvey and Friedberg, eds., *Museum for the People*, 53, 71.

59. Harvey, "Anatomy of Anger," ix.

60. Richard Sandell, "Museums and the Combating of Social Inequality: Roles, Responsibilities, Resistance," in Sandell, ed., *Museums, Society, Inequality*, 3.

61. See Debora Silverman, *Selling Culture: Bloomingdale's, Diana Vreeland, and the New Aristocracy of Taste in Reagan's America* (New York: Pantheon Books, 1986).

62. Harris, "Polling for Opinion," 49, 51.

63. See Sarah Igo, *The Averaged American: Surveys, Citizens and the Making of a Mass Public* (Cambridge, Mass.: Harvard University Press, 2007).

64. Bach, "Fogg Museum of Art," 476.

65. See Robert C. Twombly, "Undoing the City: Frank Lloyd Wright's Planned Communities," *American Quarterly* 24 (1972): 538–49. Wright quoted on 538–39.

66. Robert Jay Wolff, "The Great White Way," *Art Journal* 20 (1960): 25.

67. Krens, quoted in James Cuno, "Against the Discursive Museum," in Peter Noever, ed., *The Discursive Museum* (Ostfildern-Ruit, Germany: Hatje Cantz, 2001), 45.

68. Quoted in Weil, "Museum and the Public," 207. Michael Kimmelman wrote a wonderful essay in the *New York Times* about visiting the Metropolitan Museum of Art shortly after the attacks of September 11, 2001, and finding peace and solace there.

69. Elijah Anderson, "Cosmopolitan Canopies," *Annals of the American Academy of Political and Social Science* 595 (2004): 14–31.

Index

Academy of Natural Sciences (Philadelphia), 139–40, 151
Adams, Henry, 18, 124, 127–28, 132, 157, 160
adult education. *See* museums
African objects and exhibits, 35, 37–38, 60, 110, 190
Agassiz, Louis, 48
American Association of Museums (AAM), 2, 9, 153, 231
American Museum of Natural History (AMNH), 1, 13, 29, 31, 34, 46–50, 103–4, 140–52, 200, 211, 212, 216, 218, 219; and Henry Fairfield Osborn, 140–41, 143, 145, 146–47; and Albert Parr, 141–46, 148–52
American Swedish Museum (Philadelphia), 41–42
anthropology,13, 31–33, 40, 59, 60, 72–73, 77, 78–79, 101, 145; and art, 35–38, 74; and Asia, 87–88, 103–6, 109, 111, 113–14, 135; and "culture," 59, 74–75; and museums, 5, 9, 29–34, 40, 46–48, 73, 76, 79, 86, 102, 134, 145, 157, 175, 177, 206, 208; and objects, 29–38, 75–76, 77, 112; and World's Columbian Exposition, 102–3, 113
Appadurai, Arjun, 76
Appiah, Kwame Anthony, 70–71, 85
Arab American National Museum (Dearborn, Mich.), 42, 43, 225
"ART/artifact," 37, 60
Art Institute of Chicago, 96, 200, 203
Asian Art Museum of San Francisco, 136–37
Atwater Kent Museum (Philadelphia), 190

Bakhtin, Mikhail, 80
Bamiyan Buddhas, 72

Baudrillard, Jean, 4
The Beatles, 172
Benjamin, Walter, 26–27, 37
Bennett, Tony, 3, 207
Bigelow, William Sturgis, 101, 103, 125, 127, 132–33
"Bilbao effect," 1
Boas, Franz, 29, 31, 64, 74, 104, 112, 145
Bourne, Randolph, 129–32
Broad Museum (Los Angeles), 11, 209–10
Brooks, Van Wyck, 86, 109, 125, 127, 129, 130, 132, 135; and *Fenollosa and His Circle*, 130; and *The Flowering of New England*, 86, 135; and "On Creating a Usable Past," 129, 132
Brown, Michael, 70–71
Buddhist Temple, 117–24, 125, 135. *See also* Sommerville, Maxwell

Cahill, Holger, 221
Calatrava, Santiago, 17
Catlin, George, 129–30
Centennial International Exhibition (1876), 89, 97–100, 117, 131, 153, 176, 185
Century of Progress Exposition (1933), 156
"chronotope." *See* Bakhtin, Mikhail
"Circle of Bliss," 114–16
Civic Center (Philadelphia), 172, 180, 182
Cleveland Museum of Art, 106–7, 108, 134, 200, 203, 209
Clifford, James, 76, 81, 88
Commercial Museum (Philadelphia), 8, 9, 14, 21, 35, 172–96; and Bureau of Information, 187; and *Commercial America*, 184; and William Pepper, 174, 175, 177, 187, 193; and William Wilson, 174–80, 184–87, 191, 192, 194, 195; and World's Fairs, 174–75, 180, 185

Compton, Arthur Holly, 166
"contact zone," 130–31
Cram, Ralph Adams, 124, 126, 128
Creation Museum (Kentucky), 67
Culin, Stewart, 112, 118, 123, 132, 135
Cushing, Frank Hamilton, 124

Dana, John Cotton, 215, 221, 222; and Newark Museum, 221
Danto, Arthur, 37
Deloria, Vine, 66–67
Department of Commerce, 192–93
Detroit Institute of Arts, 87, 124, 200
Deutsches Museum (Munich), 52, 155–56, 161
Dewey, John, 212
Duncan, Carol, 217
Dunn's Museum, 89, 90–97, 99, 106, 117, 134, 173
Durkheim, Emile, 21

East India Marine Society (Salem, Mass.), 91, 126–27, 200
Echo-Hawk, Walter R., 61, 63

Fenollosa, Ernest, 87, 89, 101, 103, 108–9, 111, 126–33, 135
Field Museum (Chicago), 1, 29, 34, 61, 77, 87, 102, 103, 145, 153, 173, 174, 175, 200, 211, 227
"Foucauldian" analysis, 3–4, 207, 217
Foucault, Michel, 3
Franklin Institute (Philadelphia), 13, 52, 53, 55, 140, 153–55, 159–70, 182; and Howard McClenahan, 155, 159–62; in the nineteenth century, 154–55, 169; and scientific research, 166–70
Freer, Charles, 89, 101, 107–11, 113, 127
Freer Gallery (Washington, D.C.), 89, 107, 110–11, 136; and James Abbott McNeil Whistler, 110, 111

Galbraith, John Kenneth, 223–24
Goode, George Brown, 8–9, 21, 30, 38, 52, 117, 153, 175
Greenburg, Clement, 220
Greenfield Village (Dearborn, Mich.), 40
The Gross Clinic (Thomas Eakins), 58, 197–99
Guerilla Art Action Group, 226
Guggenheim Bilbao, 11

Guggenheim Museum (New York), 11, 228–31

Habermas, Jürgen, 211–12, 225
Hague Convention (1954), 62, 63
Harris, Neil, 99, 226, 227–28
Hay, John, 127, 128, 133
Hearst Museum (Berkeley), 30, 31, 73
Henry, Joseph, 141
Higham, John, 68, 224
Hill, Rick, 65–66, 67, 69
Hooper-Greenhill, Eilean, 2, 3
Hymes, Dell, 72

Independence Seaport Museum (Philadelphia), 190
Italian American Museum (New York), 43, 225

Johnson, William, 190
J. Paul Getty Museum (Los Angeles), 58, 71
Judt, Tony, 18

Kaempffert, Waldemar, 155, 156, 161, 166
Kimball, Fiske, 136, 204. *See also* Philadelphia Museum of Art
Kohlstedt, Sally, 5, 15
Kroeber, Alfred, 31, 35, 39, 74–75
Kopytoff, Igor, 26–27, 35, 49, 55, 81
Krens, Thomas, 229–30. *See also* Guggenheim Museum
Kulturgeschichte, 30, 38, 117

La Farge, John, 108, 127, 128
Laufer, Berthold, 104
Lieux de mémoire. See Nora, Pierre
Lindsay, Vachel, 215
Lohr, Lenox, 156, 158–59, 161, 166. *See also* Museum of Science and Industry
Los Angeles County Museum of Art (LACMA), 114, 209. *See also* "Circle of Bliss"
Lowenthal, David, 39, 42, 80, 81

MacDonald, Sharon, 2, 7
Malinowski, Bronislaw, 32
McClenahan, Howard, 155, 159–60, 161–62. *See also* Franklin Institute
Mead, Margaret, 29, 76
Mercer Museum (Doylestown, Pa.), 40, 41
Merryman, John, 62–63

Metropolitan Museum of Art (New York), 1, 11, 35, 58, 71, 96, 101, 200, 204, 210, 211, 213, 222, 225, 227; and Euphronios Krater, 71; and "Harlem on My Mind," 225, 226; and public access, 213; and Rockefeller Wing, 35, 37; and Diana Vreeland, 227

Milwaukee Art Museum, 17

Milwaukee Public Museum, 47

Museum of African American History (Detroit), 48

Museum of Contemporary African Diasporan Art (Brooklyn), 38

Museum of Fine Arts, Boston, 87, 89, 101, 103, 107, 127, 134, 200, 209, 214

Museum of Modern Art (MoMA; New York), 2, 28

Museum of Science and Industry (Chicago), 13, 52, 53, 140, 154–59, 161–66, 167, 170, 209, 217; and Kaempffert, Waldemar, 155, 156, 161, 166; and Lohr, Lennox, 156, 158–59, 161, 166; and Rosenwald, Julius, 52, 155–56, 161, 166, 209

Museum of the Peaceful Arts (New York), 158

museums: and adult education, 2, 164–65, 216, 219–20; and architecture, 202–6, 228–32; and antiquities, 13, 58, 61, 71; and audience, 4, 9, 10–11, 13, 55–56, 139–40, 146, 147–48, 151, 154, 158, 164, 166, 168, 169, 179, 186–87, 193, 197–232; and colleges and universities, 5, 12, 30–32, 38, 48, 50, 51, 64, 73, 74, 82, 87–88, 102–5, 112, 113, 117, 118, 120, 121, 124, 134, 145, 149, 151, 154–55, 165, 169, 190, 200, 201, 216, 220, 227; and "culture wars," 15; and decorative arts, 28; and economic development, 16–17; and ethnicity, 41–43, 225; and identity politics, 15, 42, 66, 67–69, 71, 72, 81, 82, 83; and imperialism, 60, 61, 64, 71, 179; and narrative, 23, 28–29, 30, 33, 40–41, 42, 48, 136, 141, 157–58, 161, 206, 218; and national identity, 20, 42, 63, 69, 207–8; and paleontology, 50–51, 141, 145, 152; and therapy, 45–46, 68–69. *See also* anthropology, and museums; *specific institutions*

museum studies, 2–6

Mustart Museum (Mt. Horeb, Wis.), 22

"naked-eye science," 50, 141, 145, 147, 149

National Gallery (London), 10–11

National Gallery (Washington, D.C.), 107, 197, 208, 228

National Museum of African Art (Washington, D.C.), 38

National Museum of the American Indian (NMAI; Washington, D.C.), 38–39, 45; and Heye Collection, 38–39, 47

National Underground Railroad Freedom Center (Cincinnati, Ohio), 45

National World War I Museum (Kansas City, Mo.), 44

Native American Graves Protection and Repatriation Act (NAGPRA), 58–59, 61–73, 77–82

Newark Museum, 221

New Deal, 199, 220–23, 224

New Right, 225, 227; and religion, 66–67

Nora, Pierre, 17–18

"object-based epistemology," 7, 8, 133, 206

O'Keefe, Georgia, 128

Osborn, Henry Fairfield, 50, 140–41, 143, 145, 146–47

Parr, Albert, 48–50, 141–46, 148–52, 164, 171, 218

Peale, Charles Willson, 91–92, 97, 146, 210, 211

Peale's Museum, 20, 91, 139, 173, 208

Pennsylvania Academy of the Fine Arts (Philadelphia), 198, 203

Pepper, William, 117, 120, 174, 175, 177, 187, 193

Philadelphia Museum of Art, 1, 136, 153, 160, 190, 198, 199, 200, 204, 206, 214, 216

Piano, Renzo, 11, 209

Pound, Ezra, 128

Princeton University, 126, 145, 155, 167

Putnam, Frederick, 112, 208

Radcliffe-Brown, A. R., 32

"Raven Cape," 82–83

Reed, Ishmael, *Mumbo Jumbo*, 35

Richardson, Henry Hobson, 124, 126

Ricoeur, Paul, 18–19

Riding In, James, 64–65

Rodgers, Daniel, 221

"rooted cosmopolitanism," 70

Said, Edward, 9, 78–79, 96, 130
Sapir, Edward, 64
science and daily life (nineteenth century), 176–77
Seattle Asian Art Museum, 136–37
Sennett, Richard, 10, 201, 217–18, 225, 231
Sesquicentennial Exposition (1926), 41, 185
Shotridge, Louis, 82–83
Simmel, Georg, 81
singularity. *See* Kopytoff, Igor
Smithsonian Institution, 8, 21, 23, 37, 39, 53, 61, 73, 89, 101, 111, 117, 153, 175, 202, 208, 225; and Anacostia Museum, 225
Sommerville, Maxwell, 87, 103, 118–24, 125, 128–35
Soviet Union, 3, 7, 85
standard time, 176–77
Starn, Randolph, 2–3, 4
Stewart, Susan, 88, 115, 120, 133
Susman, Warren, 215

Thomas Jefferson University, 58, 197–98. See also *The Gross Clinic*
Trope, Jack F., 61, 63

UNESCO Convention (1970), 62–63
University of Michigan Museum, 88

University of Pennsylvania Museum, 30, 73, 82, 87, 102, 104–5, 113, 117, 190, 200; and Buddhist Temple, 87, 103, 117–24, 125, 135

Valéry, Paul, 27
Victoria and Albert Museum (London), 153
Vogel, Susan, 37

Wallach, Alan, 7–8, 217
Walters, Henry and William, 99–100
Walters Art Museum (Baltimore), 106
Walton, Alice, 197
Wanamaker, John, 177
Watson, James, 138
Weber, Max, 128
Weil, Stephen, 23, 202
Wellcome Collection, 138
Wharton, Joseph, 191
Wharton School (University of Pennsylvania), 191–92
Wiebe, Robert, 210
Wilson, William. *See* Commercial Museum
World Archaeological Conference, 60
World's Columbian Exposition, 29, 89, 100, 101–2, 113, 153, 155, 174, 208; and Andrew Carnegie, 174
Wright, Frank Lloyd, 11, 128, 228–29, 231

Acknowledgments

Buried in the pages of this book is an accumulation of debts owed to many people. Accruing them was a pleasure, and I acknowledge them here with gratitude.

Over the last several years I have had the chance to try out many of the ideas presented in this book to audiences and colleagues from Cambridge University to Sydney, Australia, and at the University of Michigan, Temple University, and the University of Pennsylvania. I have thanked the people who made those visits possible specifically in individual chapters. Parts of Chapter 3 appeared as an article in *Winterthur Portfolio* 35 (2000).

I have been helped immensely by staff at several institutions, including Ancil George at the Van Pelt Library of the University of Pennsylvania, the staff in the University Museum archives, Virginia Ward and Erin Johnson at the Franklin Institute Museum of Science, Ritch Kerns and Scott Sanders at the Antioch library, Barbara Mathe at the American Museum of Natural History, Sean O'Connor at the Museum of Science and Industry, and Nina Cummings at the Field Museum. Wendy White deserves a special mention for helping me sort through some questions of law. Ben Gross shared his own work with me when he discovered that some of our research overlapped.

As I wrote these chapters, I imposed on many friends and colleagues to read them or to discuss them with me. Some were already friends; others I simply contacted out of the blue, and they responded with remarkable generosity. All of them made this book better. In the former category I want to thank Alice Conklin, Bruce Grant, Sharon Macdonald, Lucy Murphy, Jennifer Rosengarten, Susan Schulten and David Steigerwald. In the latter, I am grateful to Sally Kohlstedt, Michael Brown, John Pickstone, and Ray Silverman.

Finally, there are several people who labored much more intensively to get this book into shape. Bob Lockhart at the University of Pennsylvania Press never lost his patience with me, and Casey Blake read the manuscript thoroughly and asked a whole set of difficult questions. My father, Peter Conn, continues to be a close intellectual companion and even closer friend. My children Olivia and Zachary remain my best museum companions. My wife, Angela, to whom this book is dedicated, has endured the book and its author the longest. That she has never lost her beautiful smile in the midst of our wonderfully hectic life together is a testament to what a remarkable woman she is.

CPSIA information can be obtained
at www.ICGtesting.com
Printed in the USA
BVOW09s0330260717
490260BV00001B/39/P